THE CRITIC AS ANTI-PHILOSOPHER

THE CRITIC AS
ANTI-PHILOSOPHER

Essays & Papers
by F. R. LEAVIS
Edited by G. Singh

THE UNIVERSITY OF GEORGIA PRESS

ATHENS

Photoset, printed and bound in Great Britain.

Published in 1983 in the United States
of America by the University of Georgia Press,
Athens, Georgia 30602.

ISBN 0–8203–0656–8

CONTENTS

SOURCES

AND

ACKNOWLEDGEMENTS

'Justifying One's Valuation of Blake' – a lecture given at Bristol University in 1971 – was published in *The Human World*, 7 May, 1972, and later included in *William Blake: Essays in Honour of Sir Geoffrey Keynes*, ed. by Morton D. Paley and Michael Phillips, Clarendon Press, Oxford. 'Wordsworth: The Creative Conditions' was also given at Bristol University in 1970 as a Bicentenary Lecture and published in *Twentieth Century Literature in Retrospect*, Harvard English Studies 2, ed. by Reuben A. Brower, Harvard University Press, 1971. 'Coleridge in Criticism' and 'Arnold as Critic' appeared in *Scrutiny* in Volumes 9 and 7 respectively. 'Gwendolen Harleth' was written (but never published) when Leavis was asked by the publishers The Bodley Head to extricate the better part of *Daniel Deronda* as suggested in *The Great Tradition*, so that it could be published separately as *Gwendolen Harleth*. 'Gerard Manley Hopkins – Reflections After Fifty Years' was given as the Second Annual Hopkins Lecture in 1971 and published by the Hopkins Society. 'Hardy the Poet' appeared in the Thomas Hardy Centennial Issue of *The Southern Review*, Summer 1940. 'James as Critic' was published in *Henry James: Selected Literary Criticism*, ed. by Morris Shapira, Heinemann, 1957. 'Joyce and "The Revolution of the Word"' appeared in *Scrutiny* (Volume 2, 1933), and also in Leavis's book *For Continuity* (1933). 'Memories of Wittgenstein' appeared in *The Human World*, No. 10, February 1973. '*Xenia* by Eugenio Montale' was printed in *The Listener*, 16 December 1971 and included in *New Poems* by Eugenio Montale, translated and introduced by G. Singh, New Directions and Chatto and Windus, 1976; the tribute to Montale when he received the Nobel Prize appeared in Leavis's *Reading Out Poetry*, published by Queen's University, Belfast, 1979. 'The "Great Books" and a Liberal Education' appeared in *Commentary*, XVI, No. 3, September 1953. '"Believing in" the University' was printed in *The Human World*, Nos. 15–16, May-August 1974, and 'Mutually Necessary' in *The New Universities Quarterly*, Spring 1976.

For permission to quote copyright material we would like to thank Faber & Faber Ltd and Harcourt Brace Jovanovich Inc., New York, for extracts from 'William Blake' and 'Arnold and Pater' (*Selected Essays*) and from *Ash-Wednesday* and *Four Quartets* (*Collected Poems 1909–1962*), all by T. S. Eliot, and Faber & Faber Ltd and Harvard University Press for extracts from *The Use of Poetry and the Use of Criticism* by the same author.

The essay 'Gwendolen Harleth' is included here by permission of the Bodley Head. Acknowledgements are also due to Heinemann Educational Books for permission to reprint 'James as Critic', which first appeared as the introduction to *Henry James: Selected Literary Criticism*, edited by Morris Shapira, and to New Directions Publishing Corporation, New York, for the essay on *Xenia*, from *New Poems* by Eugenio Montale.

INTRODUCTION

When, a few months before his death, Leavis was suddenly taken ill, he was preparing this volume for publication as the third of a trilogy which had already seen the publication of the first two volumes, *The Living Principle* (1975) and *Thoughts, Words and Creativity* (1976). This volume reflects the continually widening scope, from *Nor Shall My Sword* onwards, of Leavis's interest in the problems and predicaments of contemporary civilization as well as in the nature of thought and art-speech in the non-philosophical sense and how they affect creative writing. Motivating this interest was, as he put it, 'my very painful concern – Lord help me! – ... for the re-establishment of an educated reading public, so that there might again be a living literature continuing what is now "classical", and major creativity might again have some influence on civilization'. It was, of course, by no means a new concern; but during the last years of his life it preoccupied him with an almost obsessive degree of intensity, as he contemplated the changes and developments around him.

Another of Leavis's preoccupations was to define the nature of thought and language which he regarded as inseparable from his concern with the problem of creating a new educated public. 'It is an urgent matter,' he jotted down in his notes, 'to achieve articulate thought about meaning, value and art-speech in a civilization whose philistine commonsense has lost any sense of the difference between life and electricity.' But the nature of this problem and the way he set about resolving it was, as he cogently argued in the essay 'Mutually Necessary', 'most decidedly *not* philosophical'; nor were the criteria that governed his thinking the criteria of a philosopher. What Leavis calls 'my "anti-philosophical" mode of thought' is more or less

ix

operant in all the essays included in this volume – but is more specifically dealt with in the essay 'Mutually Necessary'.

The very title of this volume emerges from Leavis's comments as he was planning it, comments that may be taken as so many headings or aspects under which he was to expound – as in what is included in this volume he does expound – the nature of thought as it interests a literary critic and his own position vis-à-vis that thought: 'Language and Anti-Philosophic Thought', 'Thought and Art-Speech' or 'Art-Speech as Thought', 'Rightness, Precision and Belief: Thought and Impersonality', 'Discrepant Thought-Modes and Dual Word-Values', 'Individuality as Transcendent Thereness of Life'.

In the first books of the trilogy, T. S. Eliot and D. H. Lawrence were the centre of Leavis's critical – and creative – thought; in the last, along with the other authors presented in the present volume, it was to have been Wordsworth on whom Leavis has left behind a substantial body of material in the form of essays, comments and notes which will be published at a later date. The present volume contains the text of the public lectures Leavis gave or the essays he published in the last eight years of his life, as well as some earlier essays which appeared in periodicals now not easily accessible. There are also three essays from *Scrutiny* – one on Coleridge, one on Matthew Arnold and one on Joyce. The first two together with 'James as Critic', join Leavis's other essays on Dr Johnson and Eliot as critics (as in *Anna Karenina and Other Essays*) in constituting a uniquely authoritative appraisal of the great practitioners of English criticism by one who himself indisputably belongs to their ranks. Moreover, what Leavis has to say on other critics indirectly throws valuable light on his own development, approach and ethos as a critic.

The same applies to what Leavis has to say on other authors in this volume. If, for instance, what moved him when he first wrote about Wordsworth in *Revaluation* (1936) moves him still, it does so in an appreciably different manner. Wordsworth, Leavis jotted down in his notes, 'affects us as a creative force of life', as the 'growing tip of life' and as 'robustly individualized as a human being can be'. And even though he is 'of the acclaimed poets the neglected one' he is peculiarly qualified to speak to our 'present sick civilization'. If Eliot demonstrated in this century 'how formidable poetry can be as thought', in the last century it was Wordsworth –

'the poet of genius capable of creating reality' – who did the same.

In his bicentenary lecture on Wordsworth, while discussing the creative conditions which made Wordsworth possible, Leavis sets out to account for the greatness of a poet who was 'in the nineteenth century, and still in my childhood, a very important influence – such an influence as only a great poet could be'. Leavis argues about this greatness through an analytical commentary on 'The Ruined Cottage' which he regards as representative of the major Wordsworth in its 'vital equivocalness' and its 'tense equipoise'.

In the Blake lectures Leavis revalues not only Blake, but also his own commitment to Blake's poetry. 'Blake is for me – has long been – a challenge and a reproach. He is a reproach because the challenge remains still untaken. To take it would mean a very ambitious self-commitment.' When taken, what that challenge and that commitment entail in terms of criticism is impressively exemplified in this lecture.

The essay 'Hardy the Poet', written in 1940 – that is, before Hardy's present reputation as a poet had begun to gain momentum – argues that, although Hardy was not a great poet, he wrote a certain amount of major poetry, and hence derives 'the need for strictly discriminating justice', in the pursuit of which Leavis singles out a very small proportion of Hardy's poetic output – 'Neutral Tones', 'A Broken Appointment', 'The Self-Unseeing', 'The Voice', 'After a Journey', 'During Wind and Rain'.

Leavis's essay on Eugenio Montale's *Xenia*, which in my judgement is the sharpest critique of the poem ever written inside or outside Italy, deals with those qualities in Montale which make his poem 'an English poem' – qualities like 'the use of intelligence … that determined how the actual pondered sense of irrevocable loss can be defined and communicated', the way Montale uses language in order to achieve 'an effect of spontaneous naturalness, going with a great range of varying inflection, tone and distance', and the sophisticated use of wit, irony and humour 'that intensify the effect of profound seriousness characterising his poetry'.

On the other hand in 'Joyce and "The Revolution of the Word"', the earliest essay included in this volume, while examining the very different use of language in *Work in Progress*, Leavis regrets the use to which Joyce put his genius after finishing *Ulysses*. It is not that there is any volte-face in Leavis's attitude to Joyce since his early Cambridge days when, while lecturing on English Prose, he wanted to use *Ulysses* and incurred the disapproval both of the Public Prosecutor and of the Vice-Chancellor in his efforts to import a copy. What Leavis, however, challenges is the claim made on Joyce's behalf that, in his post-*Ulysses* ventures, he was after all doing what Shakespeare had done in his later plays. In rebutting this claim Leavis argues how 'Mr Joyce's liberties with English are essentially unlike Shakespeare's', how 'Shakespeare's were not the product of a desire "to develop his medium to the fullest", but of a pressure of something to be conveyed', and how 'the study of a Shakespeare play must start with the words; but it was not there that Shakespeare – the great Shakespeare – started; the words matter because they lead down to what they came from'. In this essay we can detect the germ of Leavis's ideas and convictions regarding the nature of art-speech and the creative, as opposed to the philosophic or philological use of language, that were to engage him all his life in his dealings with poets and novelists.

In his critique on 'Gwendolen Harleth' Leavis uses the opportunity offered him by a publisher to extricate the better part of *Daniel Deronda* for a drastically critical estimate of the novel as a whole. What makes the novel one of the major classics of the English tradition is precisely that 'very substantial strong part' of the novel which Leavis identifies as 'Gwendolen Harleth', even though he admits that 'it is impossible to purge "Gwendolen Harleth" completely of the voluminous clouds of Zionizing altruism and Victorian nobility that Deronda trails and emits – and for the most part is'.

What 'Memories of Wittgenstein' tells us, in a characteristically Leavisian mode of evoking the past through sharply remembered detail, is in a way as much about Leavis himself as about Wittgenstein. For such traits of Wittgenstein's character and personality as Leavis notes – 'an intensity of a concentration that impressed itself on one as disinterestedness', his being 'a complete human being, subtle, self-critical and un-self-exalting', his 'self-sufficiency, a robust single-mindedness' – were no less characteristic of Leavis's own nature and personality.

'The "Great Books" and a Liberal Education' too has, besides the closely reasoned case he advances concerning the irrelevance of a great number of 'Great Books' in one's liberal education, an autobiographical element, as when Leavis comes to recall his own early education:

I left school with a very good start in French and German. I spent a great deal of time as a schoolboy writing Latin proses, some of which were commended by my headmaster, Mr Ezra Pound's correspondent, Dr Rouse. I could in those days (so soon left behind!) explain in Greek, observing quantity, stress, and tonic accent (the precise value of which Dr Rouse knew), that I was late for school because I had a puncture in my back tyre. With my form I read through semi-dramatically the plays of Shakespeare. I worked enough at history (I remember reading, among other things, Trevelyan's *History of the American Revolution*) to win a University scholarship in that subject.

'Arnold as Critic' appeared in *Scrutiny* in 1938 and had very much Eliot's assessment of Arnold, especially in *The Use of Poetry and the Use of Criticism*, in the background. It is at least partly through his disagreement with Eliot that Leavis makes his point, bringing out Arnold's validity and relevance as a critic and his right to be regarded as a great critic – 'an extraordinarily distinguished mind in complete possession of its purpose and pursuing it with easy mastery'. Whatever Arnold's limitations – of which Leavis is no less conscious than Eliot – he finds Arnold's critical writing, as that of no other English critic's before him, to be 'compellingly alive', and Arnold himself 'more of a critic than the Sainte-Beuve to whom he so deferred'. What even Coleridge, in spite of his possession of 'a rarely gifted mind', has to show by way of 'producible achievement', is, Leavis argues in 'Coleridge in Criticism', disappointingly incommensurate', and 'the literary student who goes to Coleridge in the expectation of bringing away an improved capacity and equipment for dealing critically with works of literature will, if he spends much time on the "philosophy of art", have been sadly misled'.

In Henry James's case, on the other hand, his classical standing as a critic, after his strength and his limitations have been duly recognized, rests on his intelligence as a creative writer, as a practising novelist. The operative manifestation of such an intelligence Leavis finds in the way James deals with Maupassant, Flaubert and Balzac and, in his dealings with them, his being intelligent about the novel is seen as inextricably linked with, and indeed dependent on, his being intelligent about life. For, as Leavis points out, 'there is no eliminating and no escaping the appeal to life, however one may suppose oneself to believe (as Flaubert did) in the ultimateness or self-sufficiency of art'. It is with such a conviction, which Leavis passionately shared with him, that James, for all his admiration for Balzac, sets out to advance 'a drastic limiting or privative judgement' on him. In other words, what he admires in Balzac is 'the antithesis of himself', and this because for all its populousness Balzac's world 'strikes James as dauntingly empty'.

'Mutually Necessary' is the last long piece of Leavis's writing published in his lifetime. A closely argued rejoinder to Michael Tanner's writing published in the special issue of *The New Universities Quarterly* devoted to Leavis and his work on the occasion of his eightieth birthday, it continues Leavis's thinking on the relationship between literary criticism and philosophy which was the subject of his well-known essay in *The Common Pursuit*. The core of the argument is the distinction between literary criticism as such and philosophy – a distinction of which Leavis became all the more conscious in his later criticism. 'The rare real critic,' he observed, 'has a more than average capacity for experience, and a passion at once for sincerity and complete conviction' – a conviction based on and arising from 'the certitude that he has taken possession of the basic major perceptions, intuitions and realizations' which he tries to communicate 'with consummate delicacy to the reader in the mastering of the creative work of a great writer'. 'Mutually Necessary' – and the whole volume it concludes – offer the proof, if proof were needed, that Leavis considered himself to be such a critic. As to the rightness of such a claim, one has to say what Leavis himself has said – namely, that 'it is characteristic of the most important convictions one forms to admit of nothing like proof'.

G. Singh, 1982

JUSTIFYING
ONE'S VALUATION
OF BLAKE

Blake is for me – has long been – a challenge and a reproach. He is a reproach because the challenge remains still untaken. To take it would mean a very ambitious self-commitment. I think one ought to have the courage to plunge, knowing that the upshot could hardly be the kind of success that would, by satisfying it, justify the ambition, which is a strong sense of the need. The compelling power of this motive, then, is inseparable from a realization of the problem it faces one with. In saying these things I am postulating that Blake is a major value, and one of peculiar importance for our time. That conviction, as I hold it, is unaccompanied by doubts, but how is one to enforce it? There you have the problem. To justify and enforce such a conviction would be not only to explain what it means and why one is compelled to hold it, but to show that it is reasonable to believe that Blake might be effectively current as a value of that order.

Everyone knows the kind of difficulty I am thinking of. But that is too easily said. Even when there was an educated public, I mean one capable of supporting an intelligent contemporary performance of the function of criticism, the 'everyone' it comprised was a minority; and it was a minority of a minority that could be looked to as capable of forming, positively and decisively, the kind of conviction now in question. Those considerations don't dispose of the importance of *having* an educated public – an assumption it wouldn't be in place to argue now. What *is* in place is to remind you (this is a university audience) of the context of preoccupations involved in my discussion of Blake – to my sense, necessarily involved; that is, not accidentally or arbitrarily. Think of me, then, as what I am here and there known to be – much concerned for the idea of the university as having for its constitutive function to be a creative centre of an educated public – the educated public society so desperately needs. It is an idea that emphasizes the co-presence of the major studies and disciplines as a necessary condition; emphasizes therefore the distinctive nature of the English School as a liaison-centre that is in an important sense non-specialist – a liaison-centre in the way in which a focus of humane consciousness must be.

The question I have in mind, then, when I speak of Blake as a challenge may be thought of as this: what kind of approach should one make it one's aim to develop in working with students in a university English School? One certainly can't, if at all responsible, say 'Get the Blake in the Oxford Standard Authors and read it through', or 'Dip pertinaciously, sample copiously, and you'll soon begin to find your bearings, and before long have notes for the organized and really repaying study.' There isn't any book one can recommend as a guide, either on Blake in general, or even on *Songs of Innocence and of Experience*. In fact, it is one's responsibility to warn the student against being hopeful of light and profit to be got from the Blake authorities and the Blake literature. More than that, he should be told unequivocally that none of the elaborated prophetic works is a successful work of art.

It is because Blake was a great artist that he matters; the principle that should govern one's dealings with him is implicit in that truism. I use the word 'artist' as it was used by Blake himself, whose genius manifested itself in two arts – the poet's and the artist's in our narrower sense of the word. I shall concern myself only with the poet. It is obviously improbable that anyone studying the work of the poet at all profitably won't develop a decided interest in his visual art, and I see in Blake an opportunity, should there be anyone at hand both informed and intelligent, to foster such an associated interest in a way not normally to be expected in 'English Studies' and hardly likely to stop short at Blake. Associated, and immediately relevant, but an interest in a different art – I find support, or countenance, for this emphasis in a sentence from Eliot's essay on Blake* in which he dwells on the genius as a 'peculiar honesty'. – 'And this honesty never exists without great technical accomplishment.'

* 'Blake', *The Sacred Wood*, London, 1920, pp. 137–43.

'Technique' in an art of language is necessarily so different a kind of thing from technique in any of the visual arts that one doesn't expect a critic who is qualified for intelligent discussion of the engravings and paintings to be very helpfully articulate about the poetry – the inverse of which proposition is equally true. Further, the nature of Blake's genius and of his importance to us favours adequate discussion very much more in terms of the poetry than in terms of line, colour, and visual design.

I had better add at once that 'technique' is not a word I myself, with the point in mind that I had to make, should have chosen to use. What it portends in Eliot's sentence is clear enough because of what one knows of Eliot. In any case, the context makes it plain. The essay, indeed, considered as a whole, offers, for my purpose, which is to convey my notion of the right critical approach to Blake, a rare kind of help – not the less so for also presenting, while it is one in which Eliot's distinction as a critic appears strongly, his distinctive limitations and weaknesses.

He means by the 'honesty' he stresses in Blake that rare capacity to recognize and seize in his art the personal thisness of his experience which is the mark of great creative genius – that thisness in which significance inheres. Such 'honesty', then, entails uncommon percipience, intelligence, and self-knowledge. Throwing incidentally and unconsciously a good deal of light on himself, Eliot says:

> It is important that the artist should be highly educated in his own art, but his education is one that is hindered rather than helped by the ordinary processes of society which constitute education for the ordinary man. For these processes consist largely in the acquisition of impersonal ideas which obscure what we really are and feel, what we really want and what really excites our interest. It is of course not the information acquired, but the conformity which the accumulation of knowledge is apt to impose, that is harmful. Tennyson is a very fair example of a poet almost wholly encrusted with opinion, almost wholly merged into his environment. Blake, on the other hand, knew what interested him, and he therefore presents only the essential, only, in fact, what can be presented and need not be explained. And because he was not distracted, or frightened, or occupied in anything but exact statements, he understood. He was naked, and saw man naked, and from the centre of his crystal.

Defined here, we have the force of 'technique' invoked when Eliot says: 'This honesty never exists without great technical accomplishment.' When we ascribe great technical accomplishment to Tennyson, 'technique' has a different force. People who met him, Henry James, for instance, commented on the surprising contrast between the unsmooth, unemollient, and formidably masculine actual person and the person asking to be divined as the poet of Tennysonian poetry. Tennysonian technique, that is, answered to a specialized poetic sensibility that excluded from creative expression all but a narrow range of conventionally poetic interests, or elements of experience. Since it suffered no surprises, but worked only in the familiar, it could achieve and maintain a kind of perfection. When on the other hand, Eliot says of such honesty as Blake's that it 'never exists without great technical accomplishment' he means what he says but is not always recognized to mean. It is of course obviously true that if the poet hadn't had the skill to communicate the 'peculiar honesty' in his poetry we couldn't have known that it existed. But Eliot means more than that. What he has in mind, he being himself in his paradoxical way a major poet, is that a great creative writer, a truly and significantly *creative* writer, doesn't just think out what he has to say and then develop and refine the procedures for communicating it. It is true that his struggle with technique and the problems in general of procedure is the business of *making communicable*; but that is, at the same time and inseparably, the process of discovering, or arriving at, what communication his profoundest sense of his theme insists that he shall make. Technique, as Eliot uses the work, is heuristic. The point I have made in explaining its use is important in its bearing on Blake's situation and circumstances and the problems they faced him with, and on the nature of his defeats.

In speaking of Blake's struggle with technique I use Eliot's word, which, I have avowed, I would rather have avoided, since it doesn't, for my purpose, point with the needed specificity. That requisite some phrases thrown out by Eliot himself (though not in the same essay) supply. They occur in a place that has a lively general relevance: a later introduction to a limited edition of Johnson's satires. There he says: 'Sensibility alters from age to age in everybody, whether we will or no, but expression is only altered by a man of genius.' The sentence that follows completes the effectiveness of the pointer: 'A great many poets . . . are second-rate just for this reason, that they have not the sensitiveness and consciousness to perceive that they feel differently from the preceding generation, and therefore must *use words* differently.' We have there an implicit account of the 'honesty' that 'never exists without great technical accomplishment'. Eliot avoids the word 'sincerity', no doubt for the obvious reason that, being the first word to hand and the more commonly resorted to, it tends, as 'honesty' in Eliot's dictum hardly does, to pass for self-explanatory and hiding no problems.

Blake was the man of genius who in the eighteenth century 'altered expression' – altered it in a fundamental way. Eliot doesn't say that, but he unmistakably attributes genius to Blake; and the great technical accomplishment he credits him with was a matter of using words. What we have in front of us, in fact, is what, when we come to Wordsworth, who at the end of the century was again faced with 'altering expression' (Blake's work having gone unrecognized), we are taught to discuss as the problem of 'poetic diction'.

Not much profit, I think, has ever, since Wordsworth's 'Preface' provided an academic text for it, come of such discussion, though Wordsworth himself in the 'Preface' is wrestling with real problems. And a major profit of considering the Blakean genius will be a new realization of the vital human issues that, for Wordsworth, were implicit in that curious, enlightening, and certainly not unintelligent document, which deserves a better fate than its conventional status represents. Different as Blake was from Wordsworth, the same issues were involved in Blake's achievement of 'technical' sufficiency.

In Eliot's recognition of the magnitude of the achievement there is something paradoxical and contradictory. Thus he can say of the century in which Blake was born: 'So positive was the culture of that age, that for many years the ablest writers were still naturally in sympathy with it; and it crushed a number of smaller men who felt differently but did not dare to face the fact. . . .' That is a classical statement of the hostility of the Augustan climate to the highest kind of creativity. It was not only that the empiricist ethos evoked by Blake with the names of Newton and Locke prevailed, in its absolutist confidence, as the reigning common sense – asserting itself in the strongly positive stylistic conventions, so that nothing, it was felt, existed for serious expression if not capable of being *stated*, explicitly, rationally, and conventionally. Augustan civilization was also polite, which means that the culture code was, among other things, a code of manners: the assumption conveyed in the conventions was that nothing worthy of literary expression could be at odds with an implicit context – insistently present in tone, gesture, and movement – of overtly social circumstance. But if the truism that man is a social being is to mean this, then the human spirit is doomed to sicken in rebellious inertia. It was Blake's genius to be certain of that with fierce creative intensity, and to live his protest.

The tribute that Shelley, criticizing Wordsworth in 'Peter Bell the Third', paid him as the great liberating creativity of the age applies with equal felicity to Blake:

> Yet his was individual mind,
> And new created all he saw . . .

Mind is necessarily individual mind, and individual minds necessarily imply individual persons who have unique histories and can't be aggregated with others or moulded to standard or generalized. Life is *there* only in individual lives, whence alone the vital creativity can come without which culture, civilization, society, decay. The need for insistence on that truth didn't cease with the 'Romantic' revolution in literature. Eliot's way of registering his sense of Blake's genius – 'He was naked, and saw man naked, and from the centre of his crystal' – shows how he realized the force of that need in the days (around 1920) when he himself achieved a 'technical accomplishment' that involved a major 'alteration of expression'. And yet he can write: 'His philosophy, like his visions, like his insight, like his technique, was his own. And accordingly he was inclined to attach more importance to it than an artist should; this is what makes him eccentric and makes him inclined to formlessness.' What, one is inclined to ask, *could* a Blake's philosophy have been but his own? 'Philosophy', however, is a word that may mean a diversity of things, and, if one had not been familiar with Eliot's own peculiar weakness, his paradoxical and habitual deep-seated self-contradiction, one might, at this point in the essay, have passed the criticism as intellectually respectable. But well before the end of the essay it has become quite impossible not to make a drastic comment on Eliot. After a brief and condescending sentence summarizing in large quasi-cliché terms what he sees as the gifts that give Blake a right to be remembered, he writes: 'Had these been controlled by a respect for impersonal reason, for common sense, for the objectivity of science, it would have been better for him.' That in its gratuitousness is surely just absurd, and tells us more about Eliot than it tells us about Blake. Seeing what respect (which prevailed) for impersonal reason, for common sense, for the objectivity of science meant in the 'positive culture' against which the genius that conceived Urizen had, of its very nature, to wage life-long war, it amounts to saying that it would have been better for Blake (and for us) if he had escaped having genius. Born in the mid-eighteenth century, genius such as Eliot has described had necessarily an intense belief in human creativity, and was dedicated to its vindication.

But Eliot, though himself a major poet, couldn't believe in it; he hadn't the wholeness, with the courage it brings, which *is* belief, and at the best was equivocal. We have the essential paradox in his most sustained and impressive work, *Four Quartets*, where, offering to achieve the assurance he needs by creative means, he reveals his inveterate underlying will to discredit creativity. In that early essay on Blake, continuing his verdict, he goes on: 'What his genius required, and what it sadly lacked, was a framework of accepted and traditional ideas which would have prevented him from indulgence in a philosophy of his own, and concentrated his attention upon the problems of the poet.' What, we ask, *are* the 'problems of the poet'? The problems of a poet that are worth any intensity of study are the problems of a man – one open to being profoundly disturbed by experience, and capable of a troubled soul: Eliot in the 1920s declared his readiness to regard poetry as a 'jeu de quilles'. *Four Quartets* is hardly that, but the writer of this self-contradictory criticism is still there in the religious poet. The question, however, prompted by Eliot in the same place, that really needs answering, and answering with some care, is: what *was* this philosophy of Blake's that Eliot is referring to? Or rather, the prior question is: just what is he thinking of – what kind of thing – when he refers in that ironical way to Blake's 'philosophy'? The care is needed because the answer doesn't readily present itself, as the established tradition of Blake exegesis brings out: Eliot's phrase and his irony call our attention involuntarily to possibilities, even (it is fair to say) probabilities, of confusion in a matter that is of great importance. In fact, these considerations have so much behind them, and so much is at stake, that I don't myself think of attempting to supply an immediate answer. Yet the need to have supplied one will be a dominant and directing presence in my mind through the critical argument that must follow.

7

My use of Eliot is a means of economy; with its rare distinction the context of the prompting phrase I quoted gives the question, as it arises out of his critique, an impelling significance for critical thought it wouldn't otherwise have had. That is not the only reason for bringing in Eliot, our major modern poet, whose difference from Blake enhances the relevance. This observation of mine implies, of course, that I think them both, in what they communicate, highly important to us all who are troubled, as we have reason to be, about the way our civilization is going. I think also that the great importance of Eliot – to my sense of which I have, with some care, more than once testified – is inseparable from the 'no' that must, it seems to me, be one's response to the basic attitude conveyed by his work; and I think the correlative antithesis, the approvable positive, the *x* implicitly postulated in the 'no', is represented by Blake. That is, I think that Blake, who died in 1827, should be a major living force today, and that his attitude to life and civilization has a validity, a salutary and inspiring rightness, that Eliot's hasn't.

The problem, as I've said, is to suggest cogently, within a reasonable compass, how such a conviction can be justified; and to do that would be to intimate with persuasive force how one would proceed to put it, as a conviction the accepted validity of which was grounded in perception and understanding, into effective currency. Eliot himself, with his observations about the significance of Blake's early published work, *Poetical Sketches* (1783), the contents of which were written when Blake was between twelve and twenty, points us to the right and obvious starting-place. His particular remarks, however, I don't find very helpful. He says, after a generalization about boys of real promise: 'So with Blake, his early poems are technically admirable, and their originality is in an occasional rhythm.' Actually the originality strikes me, and should, I think, strike every reader, all the way through, and one might spend with a student group a profitable hour discussing a number of diverse pieces, some of which look at first sight like exercises in contemporary modes, but most of which give proof of an insistent rhythmical preoccupation – one significantly uncontemporary.

I must for the present occasion confine myself to the absolutely essential. I will quote then from Eliot this, which enables me to make the necessary points with economy.

But his affection for certain Elizabethans is not so surprising as his affinity with the best work of his own century. He is very like Collins, he is very eighteenth-century. The poem, 'Whether on Ida's Shady Brow', is eighteenth-century work; the movement, the weight of it, the syntax, the choice of words:

> The languid strings do scarcely move!
> The sound is forc'd, the notes are few!

This is contemporary with Gray and Collins, it is the poetry of a language that has undergone the discipline of prose. Blake up to twenty is decidedly a traditional.

This summing-up seems to me decidedly perverse. It is also very misleading. That 'To the Muses' as a whole answers to the description, 'contemporary with Gray and Collins', is certainly true, though, if there were time, I could say what it is that makes the poem, for me, Blake's, and not by either of the others. As things are, I will merely remark that if 'To the Muses' is placed side by side with the 'song' printed half-a-dozen pages earlier, 'How Sweet I roam'd from Field to Field', the latter, with its subtly transmuted eighteenth-century quality (which is paradoxically personal and unpolite, the transmutation being only brought out by the lapse into 'diction': 'And Phoebus fir'd my vocal rage') is seen to come from the same sensibility, and yet could obviously not have been written by either Gray or Collins – or (I will add) by anyone but Blake. But a good deal more remarkable is that Eliot should have ignored the poem that comes next:

> My silks and fine array,
>   My smiles and languish'd air,
> By love are driv'n away;
>   And mournful lean Despair
> Brings me yew to deck my grave;
> Such end true lovers have.
>
> His face is fair as heav'n
>   When springing buds unfold;
> O why to him was't giv'n
>   Whose heart is wintry cold?
> His breast is love's all-worship'd tomb,
> Where all love's pilgrims come.
>
> Bring me an axe and spade,
>   Bring me a winding sheet;
> When I my grave have made
>   Let winds and tempests beat.

Then down I'll lie as cold as clay:
True love doth pass away!

That also is called 'Song' and is, in its utterly un-eighteenth-century way, unmistakably inspired by the songs in Shakespeare. Eliot perhaps felt that this point was covered by his reference to Blake's 'affection for certain Elizabethans' – 'not so surprising', he says, 'as his affinity with the very best work of his own century'. Surely it is much more surprising and incomparably more significant than the alleged 'affinity' – a word that itself seems to me a misdirection. In any case, the explicit and specific reference to Shakespeare is wholly necessary; for what makes the poem so remarkable is not merely the song-like rising and lapsing flow, but the nature of the relation to *Hamlet*. When we ask what lies behind the effect of poignant pregnancy we find both the tragic Ophelia and the grave-diggers' scene. What is so significant is the spontaneous, uncalculated, inward nature of the relation. For it is the nature and the essential necessity of Blake's liberation from the eighteenth-century *literary* and the eighteenth century in all its modes that we should be studying; and how revealing an index the 'Song' is we realize when, turning the page, we read out (as we have to – if only in imagination) another Shakespearian poem:

Memory hither come
And tune your merry notes...

Again we have that unique Blakean relation to Shakespeare. There are, we know, songs in *As You Like It*, and this, in its movement, is Shakespearian song. But it is not, for all the element of specific reminiscence, mere mimicry in the form of a variation; it is not inspired Shakespearian pastiche. The indebtedness to Shakespeare is a Blakean response to that constituent mood* of the play which we associate with the melancholy Jaques.

I call it the unique Blakean relation to Shakespeare because, if it were a question to be settled by the producible evidence, we could reasonably say that the only man who in the first age of bardolatry could read Shakespeare was Blake; for in general the 'positive culture' acted as a transmuting 'screen'; it stood between the eighteenth century and the revered poet-dramatist. A condition of the advantage Blake enjoyed, or another aspect of it,

---

* See James Smith's essay on *As You Like It*, reprinted in *Selections from Scrutiny*, Vol. 1, Cambridge, 1968.

is to be seen in the very different poem printed immediately before:

> I love the jocund dance,
> The softly-breathing song,
> Where innocent eyes do glance,
> And where lisps the maiden's tongue.

I won't say that this is popular art, for we recognize it as a poem by William Blake. But no one will question that it is related to popular tradition. The movement – a kind that recurs a good deal in Blake – is the movement of children's rhythmic games, or of dance. There is, in fact, in Blake plenty of evidence that a traditional popular culture of a kind that could, and did, affect his poetic use of the English language was strongly alive in the London in which he grew up. It was perverse of Eliot, or (putting it perhaps more justly) an expression of a characteristic basic ignorance in him, to call the young Blake a 'traditional' by reason of an 'affinity' to be discerned in *Poetical Sketches* with Gray and Collins. Actually, we see Blake to be far more deeply rooted than either of those two – a perception that entails a challenge, a dismissive one, to the peculiarly shallow and inadequate conception of the 'traditional' that enfeebles Eliot's thought (both as critic and poet).

Talking with a discussion group, I might – thinking of Eliot's avowal of two starting-points for the development of his own poetic – have said that Blake also had two starting-points: one in traditional popular culture and the other in Shakespeare. These are clearly observable as such in *Poetical Sketches*. Yet, in that, here and here, we have to recognize that they are both *present* but are not altogether distinct from one another, they are not really separable. It was a mark of Blake's genius – a manifestation of his significance in the cultural history that intelligent literary students, repudiating distinctive 'literary values', inevitably find themselves studying – that he successfully, and very early, abrogated for himself the insulation established at the end of the seventeenth century between the recognized culture (now polite) to which literature belonged and cultural tradition as maintained at the popular level. The parallel and contrast between Blake and Wordsworth, who came later and succeeded in becoming an influence, repays study. Blake's own success had no influence – unless, as I have suggested in discussing *Little Dorrit*, it is manifested in Dickens, the last major creative writer who was able to be that and at the same time to draw on a culture that was both traditional and popular (and Dickens too owes an immeasurable debt to Shakespeare).

I turn now to a poem in *Poetical Sketches* that I haven't yet mentioned, and about which it seems to me remarkable that Eliot says nothing: 'Mad Song'. Eliot surely can't have missed seeing its relation to Shakespeare, and its success (to me very impressive) as an intensely Blakean poem makes his omission, in commenting on those early performances in general, to take account of the kind of significance it so clearly has remarkable indeed. 'Mad Song' starts with a hint (recalling 'Poor Tom's a-cold') that it comes from a genuinely mad Edgar, madly inspired; but it gives us too, with the distraught anguished Lear, the human tempest of passion, self-assertion, jealousy, cruelty, and murderous hatred that gets its focal evocation in the scene on the heath:

> The wild winds weep
>   And the night is a-cold;
> Come hither, Sleep,
>   And my griefs infold:
> But lo! the morning peeps
>   Over the eastern steeps,
> And the rustling birds of dawn
> The earth do scorn.
>
> Lo! to the vault
>   Of pavèd heaven,
> With sorrow fraught
>   My notes are driven:
> They strike the ear of night,
>   Make weep the eyes of day;
> They make mad the roaring winds,
>   And with tempests play.
>
> Like a fiend in a cloud,
>   With howling woe
> After night I do croud,
>   And with night will go;
> I turn my back to the east
> From whence comforts have increas'd;
> For light doth seize my brain
> With frantic pain.

The strongly Blakean character of this response to Shakespeare's *Lear* has, for us, an emphasized significance when we read in *Songs of Experience* the two quatrains of 'Infant Sorrow':

> My mother groan'd, my father wept,
> Into the dangerous world I leapt;
> Helpless, naked, piping loud,
> Like a fiend hid in a cloud.
>
> Struggling in my father's hands,
> Striving against my swaddling bands,
> Bound and weary, I thought best
> To sulk upon my mother's breast.

This is pure Blake, with no hint that would have made one say 'Shakespeare!' My 'emphasized' regarded the way in which Blake's profound indebtedness to Shakespeare is made manifest. His sense of the dangerous complexities of life and human nature is his own; but we see that the education of his powers of expression that went with his addiction to Shakespeare was, inseparably, an education of his power to perceive, to recognize, and to imagine – and 'imagine' lays the stress on the heuristic aspect of creative expression; that is, on the perception that is, or that becomes, discovery.

The range and diversity of human life over which Blake's perception and intuition played was immense; hence the incomparable value to him of Shakespeare. Eliot, having remarked that the *Songs of Innocence and of Experience*, and the poems from the Rossetti manuscript, are the poems 'of a man with a profound interest in human emotions and a profound knowledge of them', says: 'The emotions are presented in an extremely simplified abstract form.' That, in the right context (which the reader should supply), is not misleading; both 'simplified' and 'abstract' are words that embrace more than one possibility. Of one obvious kind of simplicity – it represents an attitude that simplifies – he is a master: I am thinking of the 'Introduction' to *Songs of Innocence* and of the poem that follows, 'The Echoing Green'. The touch in these poems is so sure because, while what each communicates is presented as an actuality of human experience that is for Blake a genuine and important value, he has his vivid knowledge of what they exclude, and knows that he has it in him to write 'The Tyger'.

The emotions and intuitions informing that poem belong to 'experience' in inverted commas – to 'experience', then, in a sense that doesn't suggest the reassuring. The unreassuringness is not a mere matter of the power with which the fearful menace of the tiger is evoked; and what we so unmistakably get also is not only the intuition of the cruel potentiality as having an awe-inspiring beauty; these carry with them the unquestioning realization that what the tiger symbolizes is a fact of life, and necessary. The 'necessary' is a recognition that a fact is a fact; it is a recognition that entails a troubled sense of the nature of energy – which life cannot do without. There is no protest. The essential attitude – one neither of protest nor of acceptance, but of constatation – is given in a question that is not so much interrogative as an utterance of profound awe:

Did he who made the Lamb make thee?

'The Tyger', then, though no doubt there is some sense in which it might be called the product of a labour of simplification, exhibits marked complexity. It is complexity of a kind that couldn't have been achieved in a poetry describable with Eliot's intention as 'contemporary with Gray and Collins'. For, to arrive at this 'great technical accomplishment' that Eliot credits him with, Blake had to escape from the 'positive culture'. That is, to become the poet his genius meant him to be, to free his genius, he had to escape from the language that had 'undergone the discipline of prose'. That discipline – about which Eliot shows a paradoxical naïvety when he says: 'To have the virtues of good prose is the first and minimum requirement of good poetry' – makes the map the reality. It implies that, essentially there is only the one mode of literary expression: you have your ideas; you get them clear; you find *les mots justes* to fit them with from among the large words fixed by definition in the dictionary; and you put these words together according to the rules of grammar and logic.

This prescription holds for all purposes that could belong to literature. But the major poet's creativity is heuristic; it is concerned with discovery, or new realization, such as the discipline precludes; with apprehensions and intuitions that of their nature can't be *stated*. That is his importance. I called Eliot's dictum paradoxical because one way of intimating the nature of the originality that gives him importance in history is that he created, and justified, a poetic that makes nonsense of the dictum. That is why in the 1920s Dean Inge, Platonist, scholar and gentleman, called Eliot a 'literary Bolshevik'. What the charge meant was, among other things, that Eliot's poetry didn't make sense – that it didn't lend itself in the ordinary way to paraphrase of the prose sense. It was unintelligible, or offensive, to persons educated in terms of Victorian or Edwardian taste and expectation.

The complexity of 'The Tyger' means that it encourages the idea that it could be paraphrased almost as little as 'Marina' does (I take an obvious but comparatively simple Eliotic example). The poem, of course, is one of those of Blake's which make an immediately compelling imaginative impact. I have said that it conveys no protest; it constates. But what it constates is a fact that is a value, and the problem constituted by the fact that there are other values gets its recognition in the poem itself:

> Did he who made the Lamb make thee?

That might have stood as an epigraph to *Songs of Innocence and of Experience* printed as one creative work – which it is as surely as *Four Quartets* (for all the differences between the modes of Eliot's unity and of Blake's). The problem pointed to in the pregnant epigram of the question is formidably complex; it is presented by the inclusive whole, which insists implicitly that there can be no pointing with epigrammatic neatness to any solution. The constituent 'Songs' vary immensely in kind, convention, and poetic quality, in a way that makes it important not to forget that what they form is more than a pair of parallel aggregations, and that one must not see them or try to see them as merely illustrations of an antithesis or pair of opposing themes.

Some of them, like 'The Tyger', are, standing by themselves, poems of a high order – for instance, 'London', 'The Sick Rose', 'Ah! Sunflower', 'The Echoing Green'. On the other hand (I take my examples from *Experience*, in the arrangement that Blake once prescribed) we have, with the pregnant two-stanza concentration of 'Infant Sorrow' between them as a foil, 'A Little Boy Lost' and 'The Schoolboy'. No one would think of picking either of those six-stanza poems, with their developed explicitness, for an anthology of the Blakean strength. Indeed it is common, I think, to feel some uneasiness, even if in comment this is half-suppressed, at – 'A Little Boy Lost' being in question (to take that) – the implausibility of the utterance ascribed to the child:

> 'Nought loves another as itself,
> Nor venerates another so,
> Nor is it possible to Thought

A greater than itself to know:

'And, Father, how can I love you
Or any of my brothers more?
I love you like the little bird
That picks up crumbs around the door.'

But the tendency to charge Blake with implausibility, banality, too direct and simple explicitness, and sentimentality, can hardly survive the realization, verified and confirmed in the reading and re-reading, that the inclusive work *is* the essential whole that Blake intended. For though, when we revert to the comparison with *Four Quartets*, there isn't a close parallel to be invoked, there *is* an essential analogical bearing. The great diversity of mode, method, and attack is necessary to what is undertaken – and achieved. The poems to which one would not grant anthological status don't stand single, alone, and apart. Nor, it can be added, perhaps not altogether unnecessarily, do those which convey Blake's basic intuitions and reactions, whether of positive certainties or of abhorrence in terms of the creatively evoked, uncommented, and unquestionable immediate. And the diversity is really diversity; it is not reducible to the difference between the poetically strong and the less irresistibly poetic; that is, to the difference between 'The Schoolboy' and 'London', which follows it.

If we look at 'A Little Boy Lost', we see that immediately before comes 'The Garden of Love', one of those simpler poems of 'Experience' which, while they are not bait for the anthologist, we appreciate at once as playing acceptably their part in the thematic build-up. Before 'The Garden of Love' comes the emblematic quatrain called 'The Lily', which follows 'Ah! Sunflower'. And that is one of those miracles of Blakean pregnancy ('The Sick Rose' is another) which need to be discussed. I shall not discuss it now; under these conditions there isn't time. I ought to read out, as leading back to it from 'The Schoolboy', 'Infant Sorrow', 'A Little Boy Lost', 'The Garden of Love', and 'The Lily'. But there isn't time, and, in any case, to stop at 'Ah! Sunflower' would be arbitrary. As things are, with my case to enforce about the nature of *Songs of Innocence and of Experience*, I can only hope to have suggested to some effect how one would proceed with a student-group that is devoting a number of meetings to Blake.

In that work he offers no solution of the problems it presents. But one mustn't suggest that he does no more than convey his sense of the complexity. He does that with an insight and a power that make it plain why he should have incurred his indebtedness to Shakespeare: no other writer could have served him, in his formative years, so well. For, as Eliot puts it, he had a 'profound interest in human emotions', and the 'profound knowledge' of them that Eliot credits him with was inevitably a profound insight into the complexity of human relations. In 'Innocence' these are a simple matter, and love is trust and security. But in 'Experience' love involves the complexities of sex; it is the 'rose', and the rose is the prey of the invisible worm that flies in the night, in the howling storm. Love, and not merely sexual love, tends in its diverse forms to possessiveness, and jealousy is for Blake an inexhaustible theme; it plays a major part in the 'howling storm' that one thinks of as raging through the prophecies. Blake, nevertheless, who sees that belief in energy, which is dangerous, goes necessarily with belief in life, stands up with angry spontaneity for desire, the anger being directed against priests, their religion, and moral codes in general.

Songs of Innocence and of Experience does indeed present human life as a frightening problem. What, then, can one say to enforce one's judgement that the effect of the poetry is very far from the inducing of an acceptance of human defeat? One can testify that the poet himself is not frightened, and, further, that there is no malevolence, no anti-human animus, no reductive bent, in his realism: nothing could be more unlike the effect of Swift. The answer is to be found *there*. Blake believes in human creativity, as Eliot in *Four Quartets* so paradoxically – and significantly – does not. His belief is not a mere matter of explicit affirmation; it is implicit in the art. There is explicitness, too, again and again, in that – in the poetic presentation; the implicit and the explicit confirm and enforce one another. So there need be no hesitation about invoking the explicitly formulated as, in the collected volume, one finds it in other than creative forms.

Though Eliot says '*The Marriage of Heaven and Hell* is naked philosophy', the comprehensive statement of Blake's 'philosophy' I might be expected to conclude with couldn't be drawn from what is found there – a summary of the substance wouldn't provide it. I put 'philosophy' in quotation marks because I don't like the word in this use of it: Blake is peculiarly exposed to falsifying expectations and wrong-headed cults that it may very well encourage. Let me say bluntly that I am not grateful to Yeats for inaugurating the kind of Blake research of which Miss Kathleen Raine is the recognized high-priestess in our time. Blind to Blake's genius, it generates blindness, and perpetuates a cult that, whatever it serves, doesn't serve Blake or humanity. The notion that by a devout study of Blake's symbolism a key can be found that will open to us a supreme esoteric wisdom is absurd; and to emphasize in that spirit the part played in his life's work by Swedenborg, Boehme, Paracelsus, Orphic tradition, Gnosticism, and a 'perennial philosophy' is to deny what makes him important.

He was very intelligent and kept his mind constantly informed and in training, showing more than competence in relation to what was then modern thought – the thought of his time, as well as mastery of his own, which was astonishingly – and centrally – original. His habitual use of the names of Newton and Locke was not the expression of *une manie*; it was an insistence on human creativity – the creativity of life; a necessary insistence that is not less in place today. He insisted in an age of Lockean common sense that perception was not passive, and that there was a continuity from the inherent creativity of perception to the creativity, trained and conscious, of the artist. 'Jesus was an artist,' he says. That remark implies, of course, a conception of art different from either Pater's or T. S. Eliot's – a conception that seems to me sound; at any rate, I share it. It implies a conception of human creativity that is at the same time a conception of human responsibility; and one aspect of Blake's living importance is that he compels us to realize fully and clearly what 'human responsibility' means.

I must here refer to the distinction he makes between the 'identity' and the 'selfhood' in the individual human being. He was never in danger of forgetting that only in the individual being is life concretely 'there'. The 'selfhood' is that which asserts itself and seeks to possess from within its self-enclosure. The 'identity' is the individual being as the disinterested focus of life; it was as 'identity' that Lawrence's Tom Brangwen 'knew he did not belong to himself'. Blake was voicing the same recognition when he said of his paintings and designs: 'Though I call them mine, I know that they are not mine.' The reply made to Crabb Robinson's inquiry 'in what light he viewed the great question concerning the Divinity of Jesus Christ' is a parallel formulation: 'He said – *He is the only God* – But then he added – "And so am I and so are you".'* Crabb Robinson goes on: 'Now he had just before (and that occasioned my question) been speaking of the errors of Jesus Christ.' Blake, who knew he wasn't infallible, had no tendency to mistake himself for God.

It was in this combined clarity and intensity of conviction that the sense of human responsibility he so signally represents was manifested. There is no paradox here – or in what follows: it is a question of giving the due force to the phrase 'human responsibility'. The conviction was a creative drive, and it led him, in his most ambitious attempts, the major prophecies, into difficulties that defeated his art. He takes up in them a challenge so formidably presented in the totality of *Songs of Innocence and of Experience*. He commits himself to what it is customary to describe, with a good deal of reason, as epic treatment, although Shakespeare counts for essentially more in it than Milton does: it is not merely the verse that is positively un-Miltonic.

There is a book – one of the few guides to which one can concede a certain credit balance of usefulness – called *Blake's Humanism*.† The word 'humanism', at any rate at Cambridge, suggests a form of hubristic enlightenment ('Cambridge Humanism'), but what the author intends by it is to emphasize (rightly) the characteristic of Blake's thought expressed in his insistence that Man, concretely 'there' only in the individual human being and governed by his knowledge that he doesn't belong to himself, is responsible for determining what his responsibility is. That is indistinguishable from determining what he himself is in relation to what he ought to be (according to the *ahnung*, the divination, he at the same time develops, tests, and sharpens). It was Blake's genius to be – I impose an anti-positivist, or anti-pseudo-scientific, sense on the word 'psychology' – a great psychologist. The characters, then, in his attempts at Shakespearian epic, are separated aspects, or constitutents, or potentialities of complete human nature, which is thought of as the whole inclusive essential Man. The difficulty besetting such an undertaking is that characters in dramatico-epic action and interaction must inevitably be imaginable as actors – that is, as full human persons. The consequence for Blake's long poems is that, while specialist scholars offer to guide us diagrammatically through their bewildering complexities, no diagram provides the

* G. E. Bentley Jr., *Blake Records*, Oxford, 1969, p. 310.
† John Beer, *Blake's Humanism*, Manchester, 1968.

help we need: the fissions, coalescences, doublings, overlappings, and psychologico-symbolic subtleties of changing interrelation wear down our powers of attention.

To make this criticism is in a way to pay Blake a compliment: he has a profound insight into human nature and *la condition humaine*, and is the master of an incomparably subtle psychological realism. Only the novel as represented by the concept one adduces with the names of Dickens, George Eliot, Tolstoy, Conrad, and Lawrence could have rendered such anti-Cartesian insight and psychological mastery in successful art, and to blame Blake for not having invented the subsequent 'modern novel' would be absurd. As it is, the effect to which he learnt from Shakespeare is a marvel of genius.

But it was not by the problem of 'Life and lives' alone that Blake was beaten in his major works. An irreconcilable foe to the 'positive culture', yet not accepting human defeat, he inevitably in that age, having to explain to himself the necessity of the creative battle he preached and practised, invoked the Christian tradition of the Fall. The τέλος in view, the goal and upshot he posited as the end that gave the battle its meaning, was the reversal of the Fall. In the variously presented action that makes the poems epic, it ensues on the culminating Apocalypse. But Blake can no more know, or imagine, what follows the reversal of the Fall than he can what preceded it. In essence as he posits it (and, for all his offers of a transcendentalizing ecstasy, he can do no more than posit), it is the restoration of the Eternal Man – who is also Woman, for in Eternity the sexes are abolished. It is in keeping with the Blakean habit of symbolism that Jerusalem, the Eternal Man, is a city too.

For us, of course, it isn't the supreme reality attained at last, the really real; it is a plunge into wordy and boring unreality. Human reality, the human condition to which art belongs, is inescapably a matter of individual human beings in their relations with one another, the only conceivable way in which Man could be 'there'. Whatever the promptings of religious or metaphysical thought may be, the creative agents of human insight and wisdom must resist them when they incite to the presentation of the unimaginable. That is what Lawrence meant when he said: 'Blake was one of those ghastly obscene knowers'. The immediately relevant point I have to make is that, in postulating a τέλος, *a terminus ad quem*, Blake was involving himself in a fundamental contradiction. In his insistence on a human creativity that means human responsibility he was repudiating all forms of determinism; to posit an ultimate end ('In my beginning is my end') that gives significance to the creative effort, being its final cause, is to gainsay the repudiation.

My emphasis is not on the adverse criticism, but on the magnificent, and (for us) very timely, rightness this leaves exposed and clear for recognition. The creative *nisus* is essentially heuristic; the *ahnung* that informs it is not to be identified with the apprehension of a τέλος or ultimate goal. The new knowledge and the new sense of the real to which it leads involve a new apprehension of possibility, creative impulsion, and goal. Blake's reaction against Newton and Locke represents the really momentous new development associated with the complex spiritual and cultural eruption that we call the Romantic Revolution – eruption of ideas, impulsions, and intransigently conscious human needs. His compellingly presented conception of an ultimate human responsibility that, while the reverse of hubristic, manifests itself in human self-reliance – bold, yet deferential towards the life whose source is not to be possessed (though we may cut ourselves off from it and perish) – recommends itself peculiarly to our needs at this crisis of human history.

The crisis to which I refer is, in one very important aspect, that which Marjorie Grene points to here, in the introduction to *The Knower and the Known*:

We have come, or are coming, at last to the end of this epoch, the epoch presided over by the concepts of Newtonian cosmology and Newtonian method. We are in the midst of a new philosophical revolution, a revolution in which, indeed, the new physics too has had due influence, but a revolution founded squarely on the disciplines concerned with life: on biology, psychology, sociology, history, even theology and art criticism. Seventeenth-century thinkers had to free themselves from the bonds of scholastic discipline, and we have had to free ourselves from the bonds of Newtonian abstraction, to dare, not only to manipulate abstractions, to calculate and predict and falsify, but to *understand*. The revolution before us is a revolution of life against dead nature, and of understanding as against the calculi of logical machines.

I should add of course (and underline) to Marjorie Grene's list of disciplines the discipline of thought that belongs to intelligent literary study – philosophers are always weak in dealing with language. My own preoccupation is not focused for any intellectual realm or specialist discipline such as the word 'philosophy' suggests – though Marjorie Grene herself intimates that the revolution she has in mind must involve very much more than philosophy. We may study the essentially Blakean conception that is peculiarly relevant by focusing on Los as he figures in *Jerusalem*, and inquiring into the significance of his becoming, as he does, the central figure in that poem. Blake there, *almost* closing a firmly explicit grasp on the intuition that makes him so important to us, can represent Los, human creativity in the fallen human condition (for 'fallen' put 'rising'), as working creatively though unpossessed of any vision of an ultimate goal. But, as prophetic poet with Swedenborg, Boehme, and Milton behind him, he can't help feeling that he must himself aspire to a clarity and certitude of such vision. Yet the idea of possessing an achieved knowledge of ultimate solutions and ultimate goals is not for poets or artists, or for those among us who, figured by Los, know that their business is to get the conscious and full human responsibility that the crisis of the human world calls for awakened and vindicated.

I ought then in closing to be quite explicit about that conception of our responsibility which, given in Los, represents the essential insight that makes Blake so important to us now. For Blake, the enemy of Locke and Newton, might have inspired Marjorie Grene's account of our need, and brings a good deal more than endorsement to the wisdom of Michael Polanyi, the scientist-philosopher whose pupil Marjorie Grene was. Few educated persons will dispute the reasonableness of the assumption that there was once a time when there was, in the world of nature, no life. Life emerged, and no scientist or philosopher has begun to explain how, or by what causation – apart from the persistent offer to explain it away. Though we have to recognize that Darwin's life testifies to the existence of intelligence and purpose, his theory of evolution offered to dispense with the need for those words. Nevertheless Collingwood, a very intelligent and conscientious and well-informed witness, reported only (so to speak) the other day:

This at any rate seems clear: that since modern science is now committed to a view of the physical universe as finite, certainly in space and probably in time, the activity which this same science identifies with matter cannot be a self-created or ultimately self-dependent activity. The world of nature or physical world as a whole, on any such view, must ultimately depend for its existence on something other than itself.*

* *The Idea of Nature*, Oxford, 1945, p. 155.

That would seem to be closely related to the intuition, unmistakably and inevitably asking to be called 'religious' as the great writer conveys it, expressed in Blake's insistence that he does not belong to himself.

Essential or Blakean responsibility manifests itself in the full accepting recognition that the directing *ahnung* implicit in life and the *nisus* that has led to the achieving of mind and anticipatory apprehension and initiative are to be thought of as, in the world we know (Los's world), pre-eminently represented by humanity. They *are*, as Blake conceives it, human responsibility. There is all the difference between that and the cock-a-hoop euphoria of those who tell us that Man has conquered nature, and that there is now nothing that emancipated human purpose can't achieve – not excepting the creation of life. What human creativity *has* created, and continually re-creates in response to change, is the human world, and it entails of its very nature the recognition that (in Collingwood's words) it 'must ultimately depend for its existence on something other than itself'. For, as Polanyi insists, true creativity, like perception, is never arbitrary, but always seeks the real – which it knows that it can never with complete certainty, still less exhaustively or finally, know.

I am very much aware that there is too much assertion in what I have contrived to say about Blake in an hour. But my aim itself was limiting. For I think that some such initial presentment of one's claim for Blake, and of the supporting critical argument, would be necessary, whether what was to follow proposed itself as a book, or as a series of student sessions with the volume of Blake in front of us. The thorough grounding, testing, and refining of critical judgement and conclusion in a scrutiny of the data, a process necessarily long-drawn-out and distractingly complex, would thus be made possible.

WORDSWORTH:

THE CREATIVE CONDITIONS

That Wordsworth is a great poet seems to me certain. That he was in the nineteenth century, and still in my childhood, a very important influence – such an influence as only a great poet could be – is, I think, unquestionable. I haven't, all the same, read any account of the nature of the influence that I found satisfying, and I myself couldn't be glib (or shall I say fluent?) about it. But then, here we have a major critical datum: the greatness itself is hard to give a satisfying account of.

Let me state the spirit of my own critical approach. If Wordsworth is a great poet, then one ought to be able to urge convincingly that he should be current – that is, known, frequented and appreciated among the cultivated – now. I think this is true in respect of every great writer – every writer whom one sincerely and actively believes to be great. Great literature has its life in the present, or not at all. Where there is so much claiming permanent value, inert concurrence in conventional valuations and reputations is to be challenged: they get in the way of life.

There is too much of the merely conventional; perhaps it will be said that there is too much literature. Most certainly it can be said with indisputable justice that there is too much Wordsworth. You can't tell a student to look through his copy of the Wordsworth in the Oxford Standard Authors and mark the poems that in his opinion are worth going back to. There are nine hundred small-print double-column pages. Wordsworth had a long life, and, though he didn't finish his great philosophic poem, he went on indefatigably practising his art. There are those acres of sonnets, and a great deal else. That formidable mass of printed paper contains things we wouldn't be without, as well, no doubt, as things we should have called memorable if we had ever found them.

There is a consensus, of course, that the great Wordsworth, the Wordsworth of decisive creativity, is the Wordsworth of a very limited phase of his life, and that the triumphantly innovating poet lost his drive early. But what *was* the great Wordsworth? What can we say by way of defining his innovating power, its importance, and the nature of his originality?

These questions are not easy to answer – which doesn't mean that they shouldn't be asked. It means rather that the effort at answering will be a profitable one: it is the critic's business, and I, as is fairly widely known, believe in the critic's business. If I make such obvious points it is in order to express, not only my sense of the difficulty, but my conviction that while, in the nature of the case, no neat formulations worth having will be found, the complexities of a real answer will immensely enhance the critical value of the judgement that the Wordsworth of decisive creativity was the Wordsworth of a limited phase of his life. Critical value: I am interested in explanations and genetic accounts only insofar as they enable one to appreciate more intelligently and fully the creative achievement and to realize the importance of the poet. And this is the point at which to adduce the criticism of Wordsworth I have found most use for. It is Shelley's in 'Peter Bell the Third' (1819).

Shelley's commentary there on Wordsworth is, in its way, fellow to Eliot's on Donne and his school in the essay on 'Metaphysical Poets.' In it Shelley shows that he has turned on Wordsworth the intensity of interest and critical intelligence that one poet turns on another from whom, he perceives, he has something essential to learn. What is so significant is the nature of the emphasis. Here are four stanzas from Part the Fourth:

> He had a mind which was somehow
>   At once circumference and centre
> Of all he might or feel or know;
> Nothing went ever out, although
>   Something did ever enter.
>
> He had as much imagination
>   As a pint-pot; – he never could
> Fancy another situation,
> From which to dart his contemplation,
>   Than that wherein he stood.

> Yet his was individual mind,
>   And new created all he saw
> In a new manner, and refined
> Those new creations, and combined
>   Them by a master-spirit's law.
>
> Thus – though unimaginative –
>   An apprehension clear, intense,
> Of his mind's work, had made alive
> The things it wrought on; I believe
>   Wakening a sort of thought in sense.

In the next stanza, as the opening lines intimate, he returns to his adverse and limiting criticism –

> But from the first 'twas Peter's drift
> To be a kind of moral eunuch

– returns, since no one reading can have failed to note the unsympathetic element. As the 'unimaginative' brings out, what he means by the first two stanzas is that Wordsworth hadn't a Shelleyan imagination. Shelley, in fact, is registering his perception of the differences between himself and Wordsworth. The stanzas, with those extra two lines added, touch decisively on the two differences that come out when one looks at almost any three or four lines of the other. Wordsworth seems static; poised above his own centre, contemplating; Shelley always moving headlong – eagerly, breathlessly, committed to pursuing his centre of gravity lest he should fall on his face. The two lines from the starza I don't quote in fu.'l give the characteristic temperature difference – Shelley always seems to *have* a temperature – the effect is given by the pervasiveness in his verse of erotic suggestion, overt or implicit. Naturally he finds Wordsworth subnormal – cold, frigid; and, however unfair he may be, he does point to a Wordsworthian characteristic I shall have to refer to later on as very important. There is in Wordsworth a notably un-Shelleyan absence of suggestions of embracing, caressing, fondling – of erotic warmth – in the habit of sensibility expressed in his verse. I mean, this is what you note when you make the comparison and ask what lies behind the temperature difference. I don't endorse the implications of Shelley's way of registering the difference.

He does register the difference – the differences. And let me here make an observation about the nature of influence – influence as, in the important kind of case, it is exerted by one great poet upon another; or rather, about the way in which the beneficiary of 'influence' *is* influenced. It will be largely a matter of its being brought home to him how different he is – in what ways he is different, and so having his sense of his own essential idiosyncrasy, his own expressive need, sharpened. Of course, if there had been only difference, Shelley wouldn't have been drawn to read Wordsworth with that devoted intensity; and what draws him he states with significantly felicitous precision in the line of the passage that begins with 'Yet'. I will lead up to it again so as to give the 'Yet' its proper force:

> He had as much imagination
>   As a pint-pot; – he never could
> Fancy another situation,
> From which to dart his contemplation,
>   Than that wherein he stood.
>
> Yet his was individual mind...

There you have it; there you have what made Wordsworth decisive for the later poets of the Romantic period. They were very different from one another, and from Wordsworth; what they had in common was the need to escape – positively – from the habits and conventions of expression handed down to them by the eighteenth century. These made the expression of 'individual mind' impossible; they laid all the emphasis on 'social.' What is meant by this is a matter for discussion. For the present purpose, meaning enough, I think, will be conveyed to make *this* worth saying: Wordsworth's success in expressing creatively an intensely and profoundly individual sensibility gave later contemporary poets the impulsion they needed.

I recall here an observation of T. S. Eliot's. He says of 'certain poets' of the eighteenth century: 'They had not the consciousness to perceive that they felt differently, and therefore must use words differently.' Shelley in 'Peter Bell the Third' arrives at an essentially kindred formulation in paying *his* tribute to Wordsworth's genius; I will quote the stanzas leading up to the formulation I have in mind. I shall so, while bringing out with what responsiveness Shelley had frequented Wordsworth, ensure that the brief formulation has a suitable charge of definitive suggestion; for, like Eliot's, it has its focus on words – the use of words – and 'word,' in respect of the question what the object it points to, or evokes, *is*, is a disconcertingly elusive word: some intimation of what Shelley registers as the purpose, or spirit, of Wordsworth's 'using' helps. Here, then, is 'Peter Bell the Third,' Part the Fifth (Peter, of course, is Wordsworth, and the 'subtle-souled psychologist' is Coleridge):

> Among the guests who often stayed
>   Till the Devil's petits-soupers,
> A man there came, fair as a maid,
> And Peter noted what he said,
>   Standing behind his master's chair.
>
> He was a mighty poet – and
>   A subtle-souled psychologist;
> All things he seemed to understand,
> Of old or new – of sea or land –
>   But his own mind – which was a mist.
>
> This was a man who might have turned
>   Hell into Heaven – and so in gladness
> A Heaven unto himself have earned;
> But he in shadows undiscerned
>   Trusted – and damned himself to madness.
>
> He spoke of poetry, and how
>   'Divine it was – a light – a love –
> A spirit which like wind doth blow
> As it listeth, to and fro;
>   A dew rained down from God above;
>
> A power which comes and goes like dream,
>   And which none can ever trace –
> Heaven's light on earth – Truth's brightest beam.'
> And when he ceased there lay the gleam
>   Of those words upon his face.
>
> Now Peter, when he heard such talk,
>   Would, heedless of a broken pate,
> Stand like a man asleep, or balk
> Some wishing guest of knife or fork,
>   Or drop and break his master's plate.
>
> At night he oft would start and wake
>   Like a lover, and began
> In a wild measure songs to make
> On moor, and glen, and rocky lake,
> And on the heart of man –

And on the universal sky —
 And the wide earth's bosom green —
And the sweet, strange mystery
Of what behind these things may lie
 And yet remain unseen.

For in his thought he visited
 The spots in which, ere dead and damned,
He his wayward life had led;
Yet knew not whence the thoughts were fed
 Which thus his fancy crammed.

And these obscure remembrances
 Stirred such harmony in Peter,
That, whensoever he should please,
He could speak of rocks and trees
 In poetic metre.

For though it was without a sense
 Of memory, yet he remembered well
Many a ditch and quick-set fence;
Of lakes he had intelligence,
 He knew something of heath and fell.

He had also dim recollections
 Of pedlars tramping on their rounds;
Milk-pans and pails; and odd collections
Of saws and proverbs; and reflections
 Old parsons make in burying-grounds.

But Peter's verse was clear, and came
 Announcing from the frozen hearth
Of a cold age, that none might tame
The soul of that diviner flame
 It augured to the Earth:

Like gentle rains, on the dry plains,
 Making that green which late was gray,
Or like the sudden moon, that stains
Some gloomy chamber's window-panes
 With a broad light like day.

For language was in Peter's hand
 Like clay while he was yet a potter . . .

There you have it. Shelley as critic of Wordsworth is, to use Eliot's word, the 'practitioner'. I won't now examine the felicities of his evocation of the great poet who mattered so much to him; the point that takes the stress at the moment is that Shelley's commentary comes to a close – which is the kind of conclusion the 'For' makes it – in this:

> For language was in Peter's hand
> Like clay when he was yet a potter...

I am reminded of another dictum of Eliot's; it comes from the same essay: 'Sensibility alters in everybody, whether we will or no; but expression is only altered by a man of genius'. Wordsworth, for Shelley – for his younger contemporaries in general – was the genius who had triumphantly 'altered expression', thus making it possible for *them* to achieve the means of expressing their own instinctive sensibilities. I'll not now discuss, either, the relation between 'sensibility' as referred to in the sentence of Eliot I quoted – in what sense is there a period sensibility? – and the 'sensibility' of that last phrase; but it would repay some inquiry in seminar conditions. Meanwhile there is no problem that need hold up discourse.

The Wordsworth of the period of 'decisive creativity', to take up the phrase I threw out, is the Wordsworth who earned the tribute paid him in 'Peter Bell the Third' (a tribute the more impressive for being accompanied by severe adverse and limiting judgements). That period, in 1819, is already well in the past. The defining formulation I've just given doesn't enable us to set an end date to the great creative phase, but it does help us to think perceptively about the oddity of the creative Wordsworth represented by the early decline. The point of that, as I've said, wouldn't be that it satisfied an itch for 'explanation' as such, but it led to a better perception of the nature of his genius and so to a fuller realization of the value of what he achieved.

When in the 1920's I heard Herbert Read, as Clark Lecturer, defining his approach to Wordsworth, his subject, I reflected (very relevantly) that the oddity I've just referred to is not merely that Wordsworth started to decline as a creative power early, but that he started to be a poet late. This latter fact is the odder because if ever a young man was early convinced that he was a poet by vocation it was William Wordsworth. He was so determined to be a poet that he refused – his neglect amounted to that – to acquire the professional qualifications for earning a living. He was born in 1770. The first work that tends to justify his sense of vocation, and actually it justifies it transcendently, is 'The Ruined Cottage'.

I can't think that anything he had written before would have been found to show much promise of the writer's turning out to be a great poet, an original genius, if the fact of his later demonstration that he *was* one hadn't been there among the data the critic or scholar started with. But 'The Ruined Cottage' is an utterly convincing creative achievement. Jonathan Wordsworth, writing about it in his recent book *The Music of Humanity*, adduces me as having said that it is Wordsworth's greatest poem. When I wrote about it, thirty-five years or so ago, the accepted datum was that Wordsworth wrote it in 1795–96 – a datum that made me recall a phrase from 'Tradition and the Individual Talent': 'he who would continue to be a poet after his twenty-fifth year' – it being the 'Romantic' idea of the poet that Eliot is glancing at (critically). The date for the original drafting given now is 1797–98, which gives us a Wordsworth who was beginning to be a poet in his twenty-eighth year.

I reflected on the late start as I listened to Herbert Read forty-five years ago because, though he was discussing the significance of the early decline, he made no reference to the complementary fact – which, it seemed to me, ought, where significance was in question, to be thought of as essentially complementary. He was intent on providing an explanation of the early decline: the petering-out of the triumphant creativity celebrated, we have seen (I think it should be a locus classicus), by Shelley. Since I was alive in the 1920's and coeval with Read, and knew something of his work, I could have forecast the terms of his explanation. The discoveries of Harper and Legouis about the affair with Annette Vallon were then quite recent. Further, the invocation of Freud by non-specialist intellectuals had become a familiar, though still 'modern', practice in the cultivated world. Read explained the case of Wordsworth in terms of Annette and the illegitimate daughter. Wordsworth, the argument goes, was tormented by guilt over this surrender to passion and over the consequences of it, and, after a betraying attempt or two to deal with passion and guilt in poetry, closed down on passionate love and eliminated it from the world of his creative interests; that is, repressed in his own life what is represented by the theme. The inevitable result was the petering-out of his creativity.

Read, you perceive, might have adduced Shelley in support; at any rate, he doesn't reject as I do the implications of 'But from the first 'twas Peter's drift / To be a kind of moral eunuch'. For I think Shelley, in a very Shelleyan and self-ignorant way, was wrong there (the whole passage amounts with related things in the poem to a very drastic privative judgement). And where Herbert Read's explanation is concerned I stand by the reply I made so long ago in written criticism: his theory, invoking as it does repression, is obviously false – demonstrably so, I'm inclined to say. Repression, surely, would manifest itself in an avoidance of the explicit theme and an oblique and disguised insistence by the repressed 'interest', or vital potency, on its clandestine presence. Actually Wordsworth showed not the slightest tendency to shy away from the theme of erotic passion. On the contrary, strikingly uninhibited utterances are reported of him (they may reasonably be called characteristic) – utterances that are quite inconceivable in a repressed man, or in what Shelley meant by 'moral eunuch' and 'solemn and unsexual man'. The 'coldness' that Shelley registers as contrasting with the sensibility expressed in his own poetic texture certainly means that Wordsworth was a different kind of man from Shelley. There is nothing at all to suggest that it indicates repression or unsexual solemnity; it goes with the fact that creativity in Wordsworth is impelled by the pressure of deeply and intensely experienced preoccupations – emotional problems that are at once personal and impersonal (that is, moral) – in relation to which erotic passion plays only a minor part.

And this brings me to 'The Ruined Cottage', the poem in which the creativity that earned the tribute paid by Shelley manifested itself with such convincing power, manifested itself for the first time, superlatively. 'The Ruined Cottage' as it appears in the collected poems is incorporated in Book I of *The Excursion*. I had almost said, constitutes Book I; but in the form in which we have it there it has been much extended. The original completed poem, or what may reasonably be taken as that, can be found in the book by Jonathan Wordsworth that I have mentioned. If you compare it with Book I of *The Excursion* you will see at once, even without considering the other data produced by Mr Wordsworth, how he comes to be discussing another poem, 'The Pedlar', amalgamation with which gives us (this is substantially the case) the text we now read as the opening of *The Excursion*. I, for my purposes here, shall refer to and quote from the text that is accessible in the Oxford Standard Authors. I shall do that, not merely because Book I of *The Excursion is* so accessible, but because I think that the form in which 'The Ruined Cottage' ought to be current – ought in general to be read.

My reasons will come out as I explain the view of 'The Ruined

Cottage' that Mr Wordsworth doesn't actually endorse, and my reasons for holding it. My reasons are an account of the conditions of – the conditions behind or implicit in – this supreme initial manifestation of the great poet's creativity; that it *is* a supreme manifestation Mr Wordsworth agrees. My account lays an essential emphasis on the significance of the dramatic mode of presentation that, in an obvious way, distinguishes 'The Ruined Cottage' from 'Michael', that other poetic classic on the theme of 'silent suffering' and one which, I think, is considered to be the more characteristically Wordsworthian. And there is, indeed, a sense in which 'The Ruined Cottage' may be said to be *not* characteristic: its essential distinction is to have a disturbing immediacy that makes it, in its major way, unique. That distinction, the poignant disturbingness, is inseparable from the mode of presentation – from the fact that, while the tale is told by the Pedlar, the poet himself (William Wordsworth) is so insistently and effectively a presence for us that the sensibility *we* share is felt as very personally his.

Let me illustrate. The Wanderer (as the Pedlar is called here) visits the Cottage at a time when 'two blighting seasons' and 'the plague of war' have brought desolation on it. Margaret's husband, Robert, who – stores running out – has tried in vain to get work, hasn't yet left home, and behaves with the profoundly disturbing oddness of a man reduced to impotent despair:

> 'One while he would speak lightly of his babes,
> And with a cruel tongue: at other times
> He tossed them with a false unnatural joy:
> And 'twas a rueful thing to see the looks
> Of the poor innocent children. "Every smile",
> Said Margaret to me, here beneath these trees,
> "Made my heart bleed."'
>   At this the Wanderer paused;
> And, looking up to those enormous elms,
> He said, ''Tis now the hour of deepest noon.
> At this still season of repose and peace,
> This hour when all things which are not at rest
> Are cheerful; while this multitude of flies
> With tuneful hum is filling all the air;
> Why should a tear be on an old man's cheek?
> Why should we thus, with an untoward mind,
> And in the weakness of humanity,
> From natural wisdom turn our hearts away;

> To natural comfort shut our eyes and ears;
> And, feeding on disquiet, thus disturb
> The calm of nature with our restless thoughts?'

The passage exemplifies the completeness with which, in this poem, in 1797–98, Wordsworth has suddenly achieved his 'alteration of expression' ('expression is only altered by a man of genius'). I don't mean that it is comprehensively exemplary. In the body of memorable Wordsworthian poetry you can distinguish a remarkable range of styles or manners. But this is, very significantly, at the centre of the range; it gives us, in all its power, a poetic that represents, or manifests, an achieved major originality. We have here the great Wordsworth who is qualified to be a decisive influence. I must not attempt to discuss now the relation of Wordsworth's achievement of 'altered expression' to the confused and ineffective, though not essentially unintelligent, arguments about Poetic Diction in the Preface; I will merely point to the obvious facts that the style of 'The Ruined Cottage' is intensely Wordsworthian, *not* the language of humble and rustic life or trying to be, and not Miltonic, and that it couldn't for a moment be mistaken for Akenside.* It accommodates readily and naturally the representation of natural speech, sensitively rendered.

Take, for instance:

> 'Every smile,'
> Said Margaret to me here beneath these trees,
> 'Made my heart bleed.'

The heart-piercing immediacy of that is brought out by the ensuing abrupt transition:

> At this the Wanderer paused;
> And, looking up to those enormous elms,   •
> He said...

What he says brings home to us that *his* heart is not now bleeding; for him the historical fact is 'recollected in tranquillity'. We note this, because the effect of 'made my heart bleed', notwithstanding the past tense, is one of present intensity of feeling, present and disturbing. I am not making a criticism, but calling attention to the inner organic, the emotional moral-spiritual, structure or economy

* See Nichol Smith's preface to *The Oxford Book of Eighteenth Century Verse* (Oxford: Clarendon, 1926). He quotes (p. x) a dozen lines of blank verse, and says triumphantly: 'Not Wordsworth, but Akenside'.

of the poem – on which its distinctive power depends. The avowed 'I' and the Wanderer are both Wordsworth. The 'I' is the actual Wordsworth, for whom, at this crucial moment of his creative career (indistinguishably, for him, of his life – his greatness as a poet is given in that identity), the thought of the poor woman's suffering is not a matter of 'emotion recollected in tranquillity'. The Wanderer, of whom we have been told, with the diagnostic verb italicized, 'He could *afford* to suffer/With those whom he saw suffer', is the ideal Wordsworth he aspires, in an effort of imaginative realization, to be. So little can the actual Wordsworth achieve such assured tranquillity that he is tormented by a compulsion that makes him expose himself to the contemplating he can hardly endure. The compulsion, the whole complex state, is evoked for us in the consummate passage – dramatically immediate, surprising and inevitable – that follows on from where I stopped:

> He spake with somewhat of a solemn tone;
> But, when he ended, there was in his face
> Such easy cheerfulness, a look so mild,
> That for a little time it stole away
> All recollection; and that simple tale
> Passed from my mind like a forgotten sound.
> A while on trivial things we held discourse,
> To me soon tasteless. In my own despite,
> I thought of that poor Woman as of one
> Whom I had known and loved. He had rehearsed
> Her homely tale with such familiar power,
> With such an active countenance, an eye
> So busy, that the things of which he spake
> Seemed present; and, attention now relaxed,
> A heart-felt chilliness crept along my veins.
> I rose; and, having left the breezy shade,
> Stood drinking comfort from the warmer sun,
> That had not cheered me long – ere, looking round
> Upon that tranquil Ruin, I returned,
> And begged of the old Man that, for my sake,
> He would resume his story.

Any detailed commentary aimed at enforcing the judgement 'consummate' I threw out before quoting the passage I must, again, leave to a different occasion. But one can here observe the way in which the utter unattainableness for Wordsworth of the Wanderer's 'easy cheerfulness' is brought home to us, and the significance of 'In my own despite'. The talk about 'trivial things' can't hold him, the effort at self-distraction peters out, and the compulsion reasserts its power. Such is Wordsworth's emotional involvement that he is physically affected, and has to get up and stand in the sun, which 'hasn't cheered him long' before he begs the old man that he will, 'for my sake', resume the story.

When he says

> In my own despite,
> I thought of that poor Woman as of one
> Whom I had known and loved

some who share Herbert Read's exegetical bent may exclaim: 'Annette!' But there is nothing in the context, or in what is known of the biographical facts, to support such an interpretation. The Wanderer's comment further down the column is more to the point: ''Tis a common tale,/An ordinary sorrow of man's life'. It is the condition incident to human life in general, the condition made concretely present in the story of Margaret, that Wordsworth can't think of without profound emotional disturbance. And if we ask what is the traumatic experience behind the compulsion, we have the hint that gives it a name in the account of the Wanderer's advantages that, in Book I of *The Excursion,* precedes his tale:

> In his steady course,
> No piteous revolutions had he felt,
> No wild varieties of joy and grief.
> Unoccupied by sorrow of its own,
> His heart lay open; and, by nature tuned
> And constant disposition of his thoughts
> To sympathy with man, he was alive
> To all that was enjoyed, where'er he went,
> And all that was endured; for, in himself
> Happy, and quiet in his cheerfulness,
> He had no painful pressure from without
> That made him turn aside from wretchedness
> With coward fears. He could *afford* to suffer
> With those whom he saw suffer.

The point of this is that it reminds us – or conveys to us – that Wordsworth *had* suffered wild varieties of joy and grief; he *had* known piteous revolutions. We can't, in fact, help telling ourselves that he was prompted with that last word, 'revolutions', by the great historic event concerning which he could testify later, in *The*

Prelude: 'Bliss was it in that dawn to be alive, / But to be young was very heaven'. He was not volatile – he was very different from Shelley; but he committed himself in that spirit to the revolutionary cause. Earnest, responsible, and loyal by nature, he identified himself with the Revolution, and the Revolution developed in the way it did. He witnessed, close at hand, hopes frustrated, suffering entailed upon the innocent and helpless, and diverse kinds of human deterioration, he being very young. His own innocent assumptions and his exalted faith were brutally questioned by actualities; the Revolution, in the accepted phrase, devoured its children; his own country declared war on revolutionary France; and after no great passage of time France invaded Switzerland, the home of liberty.

That chapter of Wordsworth's history is well enough known. Back in England, he eludes for a while the close confident knowledge aspired to by the modern biographer. Certainly he suffered a moral and emotional crisis; the haunting question was, how could he reconcile himself to life? When we find him again, living in the country, he has – tacitly, at least – come to one decision: he has renounced the centres and activities of political man and 'the storm / of sorrow barricadoed evermore / within the walls of cities'. And drawing on memories and habits of childhood and boyhood, he is bent on identifying the desired emotional-moral balance ('equipoise', the Wanderer calls it) with a devotion to 'Nature' – something which the student of Wordsworth has to try to define.

But the trauma is there; even if it were possible in the country to escape the spectacle of that 'wretchedness' from which the Wanderer does *not* 'turn aside with coward fears', the 'painful pressure', the compulsion to 'feed on disquiet', is there. The urgent personal problem is what Wordsworth is wrestling with in 'The Ruined Cottage'; his preoccupation with technique, 'poetic diction', versification, as he writes and ponders, identifies itself in his mind – and his fingers – with that. It is by reason of the inner 'pressure' during his 'wrestle with words and meaning' that (if you add the after all well-grounded conviction of his that a poet was what he was meant to be) he achieves, in that poem, his 'alteration of expression'. 'The Ruined Cottage', essentially representative of the major Wordsworth as it is, is unique; it is the one poem of that kind – that vital equivocalness, that kind of tense equipoise – in his *oeuvre*. Of course, he wrote much other poetry; poetry in various ways vitally Wordsworthian, building up the body of work that, in its diversity, made him a major presence, a living force and an influence. But the decisive 'alteration of expression', the release of creativity, is achieved in 'The Ruined Cottage'; the conditions of the achievement are so clearly manifested in it that we can say: 'Wordsworth becomes a great poet here'.

He had solved his personal problem for good, in the sense that there are (I think) no signs later in his work of the 'painful pressure' that had, as the Wanderer puts it, made him 'feed on disquiet'. In the nature of the success, however, he had not solved for good his creative problem, the problem of being a poet. The evoked Wanderer, plainly enough, is no more a poet potentially than he *is* one in his serene actuality. It was because the Wordsworth of 1797 was so different that he longed to be the Wanderer.

The 'equipoise' of 'The Ruined Cottage', then, is *not* the 'equipoise' that Wordsworth attributes to the Wanderer. Its poignant livingness unsays any promise of finality, of permanence, the poem may seem to offer – to say which is to point to the peculiar poetic vitality of the poem, even while we note, knowing of course what is to happen, the poet's strong impulse towards the Wanderer's state. He can't hold this tense and difficult poise very long.

What, with no relapse, he settles down to is, in that phrase of his from the 1800 Preface, 'emotion recollected in tranquillity', and, what goes with it, 'natural wisdom'. This latter phrase is of course from 'The Ruined Cottage', where it is associated with and supported by others – 'natural comfort', for instance, and 'the calm of nature'. Heaven forbid that I should be thought to be suggesting that there can be any simple comment on that Wordsworth. He is often a great poet. If I were faced with undertaking a critical discourse on that theme I might very well start from a passage which, in the close of 'The Ruined Cottage', he attributes to the Wanderer. Though, as the vibration tells us, it *belongs* to 'The Ruined Cottage', it has an essential relevance to the theme of the tranquil Wordsworth:

> Why then should we read
> The forms of things with an unworthy eye?
> She sleeps in the calm earth, and peace is here.
> I well remember that those very plumes,
> Those weeds, and the high spear-grass on that wall,
> By mist and silent rain-drops silvered o'er,

As once I passed, into my heart conveyed
So still an image of tranquillity,
So calm and still, and looked so beautiful
Amid the uneasy thoughts which filled my mind,
That what we feel of sorrow and despair,
From ruin and from change, and all the grief
That passing shows of Being leave behind,
Appeared an idle dream . . .

Judgements about that passage taken in isolation cannot, of course, be secure or final; we have seen how complex the emotional-moral situation registered in the poem is. But we can make some comments on manifest potentialities.

'She sleeps in the calm earth, and peace is here' – if we are to distinguish between the Wordsworth of the poem and the Wanderer, that is the Wanderer. But then, the Wordsworth we know *includes* the Wanderer; and further, we can say that, in terms of 'The Ruined Cottage', both parts in the dialogues (if that is the right description of the relation between the two personae) are to be heard in this passage: 'and looked so beautiful / Amid the uneasy thoughts which filled my mind' – that is unmistakably the young, troubled Wordsworth. And *his* presence in the distinctive vibration of the passage counters the complacent potentialities of 'She sleeps in the calm earth, and peace is here'. We feel the troubled Wordsworth in the emphasis on 'here'. The Wanderer has helped him to that; and there *is* a sound wisdom in the Wanderer's admonitions: life has to be lived. There *is* a refusal to accept that can be reasonably stigmatized as 'feeding on disquiet'. But no simple formulation, no easily summarizable doctrine, can be adequate to the human state – which is what the poem implicitly says.

I don't suppose that Wordsworth *intended* irony when he italicized the 'afford' in 'He could *afford* to suffer / With those whom he saw suffer'; but when we come to it in the account of the Wanderer we inevitably see irony, for we know Wordsworth's own history. As he achieved the longed-for equipoise, and the equipoise became more and more assured, he became more and more the Wanderer. I repeat, everyone admiring Wordsworth's genius must recoil from the idea of simplifying in an account of it. 'The Ruined Cottage' is unique, but between it (that is, the state out of which it issues) and the lapse of creativity we have poetry (more diverse, I think, than gets due recognition) that makes him the classical

39

presence for us he is – or ought to be. But that there *was* a lapse of creativity no one disputes.

One can see the movement that way in the characteristic Wanderer-Wordsworth phrase (not, actually, from 'The Ruined Cottage'), 'natural piety'. It would be hard to determine and fix the 'nature' of 'natural' in an excluding definition, and 'piety' is a word that becomes of great importance to Wordsworth as – time doing its work – the equipoise settles into security (and security, remember, is on the way to inertness). There is nothing insincere or censurable, so far as I can see, in his development into the Tory Anglican. One can see the movement that way in the Christian explicitnesses he worked in when he turned 'The Ruined Cottage' into Book I of *The Excursion* – one follows on from where I stopped and completes the sentence:

> all the grief
> That passing shows of Being leave behind
> Appeared an idle dream that could maintain,
> Nowhere, dominion o'er the enlightened spirit
> Whose meditative sympathies repose
> Upon the breast of Faith.

Though these Christian explicitnesses obviously don't belong, there is nothing obtrusively and offensively insincere about them: the transition was so easy for Wordsworth.

It was natural that, as in his reaction against the idea of revolution he fostered his equipoise, he should think of the village church as a focus of piety, and there could be no incongruity, no sharp separation, between that piety and the religious apprehensions that came to him among the mountains and in the presence of nature. But his poet's sensibility, his creative organization, a matter of painful growth, was *not* focused upon the village church. And when, with his gift of piety, he had arrived at affording to suffer with those whom he saw suffer as easily and securely as the Wanderer did, there wasn't much to save his creativity from lapsing into habit, or the Wanderer's philosophic calm. It had lost its intransigence. It had lost, that is, its creativeness.

COLERIDGE

IN CRITICISM

That Coleridge was a rarely gifted mind is a commonplace. It is perhaps equally a commonplace that what he actually accomplished with his gifts, the producible achievement, appears, when we come to stocktaking, disappointingly incommensurate. That 'perhaps' registers a hesitation: judges qualified in the religious and intellectual history of the past century might, I think, reply that actually Coleridge was a great power, exercising influence in ways that must be credited to him for very notable achievement, and that we cannot judge him merely by reading what is extant of him in print.* My concern, however, is with the field of literary criticism. That his performance there justifies some disappointment is, I believe, generally recognized. But I believe too that this recognition stresses, in intention, rather the superlativeness of the gifts than shortcoming in the performance. The full disparity, in fact, doesn't get clear recognition very readily; there are peculiar difficulties in the way – at least, these are the conclusions to which, after reconsidering the body of Coleridge's work in criticism, I find myself brought.

The spirit of that reconsideration had better be made plain at once. Let me start, then, by reminding the reader of the introduction to the standard scholarly edition of *Biographia Literaria*. The ninety

* *cf.* J. S. Mill's witness in 1840: 'The name of Coleridge is one of the few English names of our time which are likely to be oftener pronounced, and to become symbolical of more important things, in proportion as the inward workings of the age manifest themselves more and more in outward facts. Bentham excepted, no Englishman of recent date has left his impress so deeply in the opinions and mental tendencies of those who attempt to enlighten their practice by philosophical meditation.' *Dissertations and Discussions*, Vol. I, 'Coleridge'.

41

pages or so are devoted almost wholly to discussing Coleridge's relation to Kant and other German philosophers. Now it seems clear to me that no head of study that involves discussions of Coleridge's indebtedness to, or independence of, Kant, Schelling, the Schlegels or Fichte has any claims on the attention of the literary student; it is from his point of view a solicitation to unprofitable expenditures. If in a work recommended to him as directly relevant to the problems of literary criticism any such solicitations seem likely to engage or confuse him he had better be warned against them. It follows then, if this is so, and if J. Shawcross's introduction is relevant to the work it precedes, that the docile student ought certainly to be warned against a large part of *Biographia Literaria*. It may be that, as Shawcross suggests, 'Coleridge's philosophy of art' has not 'received in England the consideration which it deserves'. But Coleridge's philosophy of art is Coleridge's philosophy, and though no doubt he has an important place in the history of English thought, not even the student of philosophy, I imagine, is commonly sent to Coleridge for initiations into key-problems, or for classical examples of distinguished thinking. And the literary student who goes to Coleridge in the expectation of bringing away an improved capacity and equipment for dealing critically with works of literature will, if he spends much time on the 'philosophy of art', have been sadly misled.

It is by way of defining the spirit of my approach that I assert this proposition, the truth of which seems to me evident. Actually, of course, its evidence gets substantial recognition in established academic practice: the student usually starts his reading – or at least his serious reading – of *Biographia Literaria* at chapter XIV. Nevertheless, since the appropriate distinction is not formulated and no sharp separation can be made in the text, the common effect of the perusal can hardly be clarity – or clear profit. It is certain, on the other hand, that Coleridge's prestige owes a great deal to the transcendental aura; his acceptance as a master of 'theoretical criticism' is largely an awed vagueness about the philosophy – a matter of confused response to such things as

The primary IMAGINATION then, I consider, to be the living power and prime agent of all human Perception, and as a repetition in the finite mind of the eternal act of creation in the infinite I AM.

The essential distinction ought to be plain enough to us, but that

Coleridge himself should not have made it sharply and have held firmly to it cannot, given the nature of his genius, surprise us; on the contrary, even if he had been a much more orderly and disciplined worker than he was we still couldn't have expected in his work a clear separation between what properly claims the attention of the literary critic and what does not. 'Metaphysics, poetry and facts of mind,' he wrote, 'are my darling studies.' The collocation of the last two heads suggests the sense in which Shelley's phrase for him, 'a subtle-souled psychologist', must often, when he impresses us favourably in the literary-critical field, seem to us an apt one, and, on the other hand, it is difficult not to think of the first head as a nuisance. Yet we can hardly suppose that we could have had the psychologist without the metaphysician; that the gift of subtle analysis could have been developed, at that date, by a mind that shouldn't also have exhibited something like the Coleridgean philosophic bent. But that makes it not less, but more necessary to be firm about the distinction that concerns us here.

I had better at this point indicate more fully the specific equipment that might seem to have qualified Coleridge for great achievements in literary criticism – to be, indeed, its modern instaurator. The 'subtle-souled psychologist', it seems not superfluous to emphasize, was intensely interested in literature. He was, of course, a poet, and the suggestion seems to be taken very seriously that he indulged the habit of analytic introspection to the extent of damaging the creative gift he turned it upon. However that may be, it is reasonable to suppose that the critic, at any rate, profited. The psychological bent was associated with an interest in language that expresses itself in observations such as lend colour to I. A. Richard's enlistment of Coleridge for semasiology. But, as in reviewing in these pages *Coleridge on Imagination* I had occasion to remind Dr Richards, who lays stress on those of Coleridge's interests which might seem to fall outside the compass of the literary critic, these interests went, in Coleridge, with a constant wide and intense cultivation of literature:

O! when I think of the inexhaustible mine of virgin treasure in our Shakespeare, that I have been almost daily reading him since I was ten years old – that the thirty intervening years have been unintermittingly and not fruitlessly employed in the study of the Greek, Latin, English, Italian, Spanish and German *belle lettrists*, and the last fifteen years in addition, far more intensively in the analysis of the laws of life and reason as they exist in man – and that upon every step I have made forward in taste, in acquisition of facts from history or my own observation, and in knowledge of the different laws of being and their apparent exceptions from accidental collision of disturbing forces, – that at every new accession of information, after every successful exercise of meditation, and every fresh presentation of experience, I have unfailingly discovered a proportionate increase of wisdom and intuition in Shakespeare . . .*

The 'analysis' and the 'laws' mentioned hardly belong to literary criticism, but it is easy to assemble an impressive array of characteristic utterances and formulas that promise the literary critic's own concern with principle:

The ultimate end of criticism is much more to establish the principles of writing than to furnish *rules* how to pass judgment on what has been written by others; if indeed it were possible that the two should be separated.' [*Biographia Lit.* c.XVIII]

You will see, by the terms of my prospectus, that I intend my lectures to be, not only 'in illustration of the principles of poetry,' but to include a statement of the application of those principles, 'as grounds of criticism on the most popular works of later English poets, those of the living included.' [*Coleridge's Shakespearean Criticism, II,* p. 63]

It is a painful truth that not only individuals, but even whole nations, are ofttimes so enslaved to the habits of their education and immediate circumstances, as not to judge disinterestedly even on those subjects, the very pleasure arising from which consists in its disinterestedness, namely, on subjects of taste and polite literature. Instead of deciding concerning their own modes and customs by any rule of reason, nothing appears rational, becoming, or beautiful to them, but what coincides with the peculiarities of their education. In this narrow circle, individuals may attain to exquisite discrimination, as the French critics have done in their own literature; but a true critic can no more be such without placing himself on some central point, from which he may command the whole, that is, some general rule, which, founded in reason, or the faculties common to all men, must therefore apply to each – than an astronomer can explain the movements of the solar system, without taking his stand in the sun. And let me remark, that this will not tend to produce despotism, but, on the contrary, true tolerance, in the critic. [See Raysor, *Coleridge's Shakespearean Criticism,* Vol. I, p. 221]

These things seem the more significant for being thrown out by the way, suggesting a radical habit of mind, the literary critic's concern to 'ériger en lois' – his proper concern with the formulation

* I quote from the Everyman volume, *Essays and Lectures on Shakespeare,* but see T. H. Raysor, *Coleridge's Shakespearean Criticism,* Vol. I, p. 210.

of principle. They add greatly to the impressiveness of the account that can be elaborated of Coleridge's qualifications for a great achievement in criticism. My own experience is that one can easily fill a lecture on Coleridge with such an account, and that the impressiveness of the qualifications has a large part in one's impression of a great achievement. The qualifications are obvious but the achievement isn't readily sized up.

What, in fact, can be said of it after a resolute critical survey? Asked to point to a place that could be regarded as at the centre of Coleridge's achievement and indicative of its nature, most admirers would probably point to the famous passage on imagination at the end of chapter XIV of *Biographia Literaria:*

> The poet, described in *ideal* perfection, brings the whole soul of man into activity, with the subordination of its faculties to each other, according to their relative worth and dignity. He diffuses a tone and spirit of unity, that blends, and (as it were) *fuses*, each into each, by that synthetic and magical power, to which we have exclusively appropriated the name of imagination. This power, first put into action by the will and understanding, and retained under their irremissive, though gentle and unnoticed, control (*laxis effertur habenis*) reveals itself in the balance or reconciliation of opposite or discordant qualities: of sameness, with difference; of the general, with the concrete; the idea, with the image; the individual, with the representative; the sense of novelty and freshness, with old and familiar objects; a more than usual state of emotion with more than usual order; judgment ever awake and steady self-possession, with enthusiasm and feeling profound or vehement; and while it blends and harmonizes the natural and the artificial, still subordinates art to nature; the manner to the matter; and our admiration of the poet to our sympathy with the poetry.

It is an impressive passage – perhaps too impressive; for it has more often, perhaps, caused an excited sense of enlightenment than it has led to improved critical practice or understanding. The value we set on it must depend on the development and illustration the account of imagination gets in such context as we can find for it elsewhere in Coleridge and especially in his own critical practice. The appropriate commentary according to general acceptance would, I suppose, bear on the substitution by Coleridge of an understanding of literature in terms of organism, an understanding operating through an inward critical analysis, for the external mechanical approach of the neo-classic eighteenth century. That Coleridge has a place in literary history to be indicated in some such terms is no doubt true. And yet we ought hardly to acquiesce happily in any suggestion that the subsequent century exhibits a general improvement in criticism. What in fact this view – the academically accepted one, I believe – of Coleridge amounts to is that, of the decisive change in taste and literary tradition that resulted from the Romantic movement, Coleridge is to be regarded as the supreme critical representative.*

And it has to be recognized that, in effect, his 'imagination' does seem to have amounted to the Romantic 'creative imagination'. This much, at any rate, must be conceded: that, though justice insists that Coleridge's account of the creative process is not that given by Shelley in his *Defence of Poetry*, nevertheless Coleridge's influence did not, in the subsequent century, avail to make the Romantic tradition, of which he was an acclaimed founding father, aware of the difference. From whom, for instance, does that 'soul' descend in which, according to Arnold (who – and it is one of his claims to honour – was much less satisfied than Coleridge with the notion of poetry as the product of the inspired individual), 'genuine poetry' was 'conceived and composed'? Arnold can hardly be said to have favoured Shelleyan notions, and yet, if we conclude that it descends from the soul 'brought into activity' by the poet who is described in chapter XIV of *Biographia Literaria*, we are hardly recommending Coleridge.

In any case, Coleridge's historical importance isn't at the centre of my concern. My concern is with the intrinsic interest of his extant critical work – with his achievement in that sense. A critic may have an important place in history and yet not be very interesting in his writings: Dryden seems to me a case in point. Coleridge, on the other hand, may be more interesting than the claims made for him as an influence suggest. What credit we give him for the interesting possibilities of that passage on imagination depends, as has been said, on the way the account is developed and illustrated.

The Fancy-Imagination contrast hardly takes us any further. Coleridge does little with it beyond the brief exemplification that cannot be said to justify the stress he lays on the two faculties he distinguishes. I. A. Richards's attempts in *Coleridge on Imagination*

---

* *cf.* Mill: 'The healthier taste, and more intelligent canons of poetic criticism, which he was himself mainly instrumental in diffusing, have at length assigned to him his proper rank, as one among the great, and (if we look to the powers shown rather than to the amount of actual achievement) amongst the greatest, names in our literature.'

to develop the distinction is a tribute not to Coleridge but to Bentham. The best that can be said for Coleridge is that, though he was undoubtedly serious in positing the two faculties, actually the distinction as he illustrates it is a way of calling attention to the organic complexities of verbal life, metaphorical and other, in which Imagination manifests itself locally: Fancy is merely an ancillary concept. And Coleridge certainly gives evidence of a gift for critical analysis:

> Look! how a bright star shooteth from the sky;
> So glides he in the night from Venus' eye!

How many images and feelings are here brought together without effort and without discord, in the beauty of Adonis, the rapidity of his flight, the yearning, yet hopelessness, of the enamoured gazer, while a shadowy ideal character is thrown over the whole. [See *Coleridge's Shakespearean Criticism*, Vol. I, p. 213]

A good many passages of this kind could be quoted, showing a capacity for a kind of sensitive analytic penetration such as will hardly be found in any earlier critic.

But 'capacity' – again it is evidence of qualifications we are adducing. What corresponding achievement is there to point to? The work on Shakespeare constitutes the nearest thing to an impressive body of criticism, and everyone who has tried to read it through knows how disappointing it is. Coleridge didn't inaugurate what may be called the Bradley approach but he lends his prestige to it. Of course, his psychologizing is pursued with nothing of Bradley's system – he never carries through anything with system. On the other hand he has things to offer that are beyond Bradley's range. The subtle-souled psychologist appears to advantage, for example, in the analysis, if not of Hamlet's character, of the effects, at once poetic and dramatic, of the opening of the play. There are various notes of that kind and a good many acute observations about points in the verse. In short, when we take stock of what there is to be said in favour of the Shakespeare criticism, we again find ourselves considering, not achievement, but evidence of a critical endowment that *ought* to have achieved something remarkable. Even those who rate it more highly would, I imagine, never think of proposing the work on Shakespeare to the student as a classical body of criticism calculated to make much difference to his powers of appreciation or understanding.

What is, I suppose, a classical document is the group of chapters on Wordsworth in *Biographia Literaria*. But if they are that it is at least partly for reasons of historical interest, because Coleridge on Wordsworth is Coleridge on Wordsworth, and not because of achieved criticism of a high order contained in them. The treatment of the poetry, however interesting, hardly amounts to a profound or very illuminating critique. The discussion of poetic diction provides, of course, more evidence of Coleridge's peculiar gifts, especially in the argument about metre in chapter XVIII. That Coleridge perceives certain essential truths about poetic rhythm and metre – truths that are not commonplaces, at any rate in academic literary study – is plain. But anything approaching the satisfactory treatment of them that he seems preeminently qualified to have written he certainly doesn't provide. His virtue is represented by this:

Secondly, I argue from the EFFECTS of metre. As far as metre acts in and for itself, it tends to increase the vivacity and susceptibility both of the general feelings and of the attention. This effect it produces by the continued excitement of surprise, and by the quick reciprocations of curiosity still gratified and still re-excited, which are too slight indeed to be at any one moment objects of distinct consciousness, yet become considerable in their aggregate influence. As a medicated atmosphere, or as wine during animated conversation; they act powerfully, though themselves unnoticed. Where, therefore, correspondent food and appropriate matter are not provided for the attention and feelings thus aroused, there must needs be a disappointment felt; like that of leaping in the dark from the last step of a staircase, when we had prepared our muscles for a leap of three or four.

This fairly earns the tribute that I. A. Richards pays Coleridge in *The Principles of Literary Criticism*, in the chapter on 'Rhythm and Metre' (one of the useful parts of that book). But though the paragraph quoted tends to confer redit upon the context of technical-looking analysis, it doesn't really gain anything from that context, the rigorously and ambitiously analytic air of which doesn't justify itself, despite an element of interesting suggestion.

And this seems the moment to make the point that Coleridge's unsatisfactoriness isn't merely what stares at us in the synopsis of *Biographia Literaria* – the disorderliness, the lack of all organization or sustained development: locally too, even in the best places, he fails to bring his thought to a sharp edge and seems too content with easy expression. Expression came, in fact, too easily to him; for a man of his deep constitutional disinclination to brace himself to sustained work at any given undertaking, his articulateness was fatal. He could go down to the lecture-hall at the last minute with a marked copy of Shakespeare and talk – talk much as he talked anywhere and at any time. And what we read as Coleridge's writings comes from that inveterate talker, even when the text that we have is something he actually wrote, and not reported discourse.

Perhaps the habit of the lecture-hall accounts for such things as the definition of a poem in chapter XIV of *Biographia Literaria:*

> The final definition then, so deduced, may be thus worded. A poem is that species of composition, which is opposed to works of science, by proposing for its immediate object pleasure, not truth; and from all other species (having *this* object in common with it) it is discriminated by proposing to itself such delight from the *whole*, as is compatible with a distinct gratification from each component *part.*

That, I am afraid, is representative of a good deal in Coleridge, though it seems to me quite unprofitable. And at the end of the same chapter is this well-known pronouncement:

> Finally, GOOD SENSE is the BODY of poetic genius, FANCY is its DRAPERY, MOTION its LIFE, and IMAGINATION the SOUL that is everywhere, and in each; and forms all into one graceful and intelligent whole.

It comes, characteristically enough, just after the famous passage on imagination, which is of another order altogether.

The immediately succeeding chapter (XV) seems to me to show Coleridge at his best. It is headed, 'The specific symptoms of poetic power elucidated in a critical analysis of Shakespeare's Venus and Adonis and Lucrece', and this heading is significant: it suggests with some felicity the nature of Coleridge's peculiar distinction, or what should have been his peculiar distinction, as a critic. He speaks in his first sentence, referring no doubt mainly to the passage on imagination, of 'the application of these principles to purposes of practical criticism'. Actually, principle as we are aware of it here appears to emerge from practice; we are made to realize that the 'master of theoretical criticism' who matters is the completion of a practical critic. The theory of which he is master (in so far as he is) doesn't lead us to discuss his debt to Kant or any other philosopher; it comes too evidently from the English critic who has devoted his finest powers of sensibility and intelligence to the poetry of his own language.

This commentary is prompted by, specifically, the second head of the chapter:

A second promise of genius is the choice of subjects very remote from the private interests and circumstances of the writer himself. At least I have found that, where the subject is taken immediately from the author's personal sensations and experiences, the excellence of a particular poem is but an equivocal mark, and often a fallacious pledge, of genuine poetic power.

The general considerations raised are immediately relevant to that central theme of T. S. Eliot's criticism, impersonality. But they are presented in terms of particular analysis, and the whole passage is a fine piece of practical criticism:

In the 'Venus and Adonis' this proof of poetic power exists even to excess. It is throughout as if a superior spirit more intuitive, more intimately conscious, even than the characters themselves, not only of every outward look and act, but of the flux and reflux of the mind in all its subtlest thoughts and feelings, were placing the whole before our view; himself meanwhile unparticipating in the passions, and actuated only by that pleasurable excitement, which had resulted from the energetic fervour of his own spirit in so vividly exhibiting, what it had so accurately and profoundly contemplated. I think, I should have conjectured from these poems, that even then the great instinct, which impelled the poet to the drama, was secretly working in him, prompting him by a series and never broken chain of imagery, always vivid and, because unbroken, often minute; by the highest effort of the picturesque in words, of which words are capable, higher perhaps than was ever realized by any other poet, even Dante not excepted; to provide a substitute for that visual language, that constant intervention and running comment by tone, look and gesture, which in his dramatic works he was entitled to expect from the players. His 'Venus and Adonis' seem at once the characters themselves, and the whole representation of those characters by the most consummate actors. You seem to be told nothing, but to see and hear everything. Hence it is, that from the perpetual activity of attention required on the part of the reader; from the rapid flow, the quick change, and the playful nature of the thoughts and images; and above all from the alienation, and, if I may hazard such an expression, the utter *aloofness* of the poet's own feelings, from those of which he is at once the painter and the analyst; that though the very subject cannot but detract from the pleasure of a delicate mind, yet never was poem less dangerous on a moral account. Instead of doing as Ariosto, and as, still more offensively, Wieland has done, instead of degrading and deforming passion into appetite, the trials of love into the struggles of concupiscence; Shakespeare has here represented the animal impulse itself, so as to preclude all sympathy with it, by dissipating the reader's notice among the thousand outward images, and now beautiful, now fanciful circumstances, which form its dresses and its scenery; or by diverting our attention from the main subject by those frequent witty or profound reflections, which the poet's ever active mind had deduced from, or connected with, the imagery and the incidents. The reader is forced into too much action to sympathize with the merely passive of our nature. As little can a mind thus roused and awakened be brooded on by mean and indistinct emotion, as the low, lazy mist can creep upon the surface of a lake, while a strong gale is driving it onward in waves and billows.

It will have been seen that, incidentally, in the sentence about 'the perpetual activity of attention required on the part of the reader' and the further observations about the 'action' into which the reader is forced, Coleridge has given an account of the element of 'wit' that is in *Venus and Adonis*.

Though the other heads of the chapter contain nothing as striking, we tend to give full credit to what is best in them. In the first and third, for instance, Coleridge makes it plain (as he has already done in practical criticism) that the 'imagery' that matters cannot be dealt with in terms of 'images' conceived as standing to the verse as plums to cake; but that its analysis is the analysis of complex verbal organization:

It has therefore been observed that images, however beautiful, though faithfully copied from nature, and as accurately represented in words, do not of themselves characterize the poet. They become proofs of original genius only as far as they are modified by a predominant passion; or by associated thoughts or images awakened by that passion; or when they have the effect of reducing multitude to unity, or succession to an instant; or lastly, when a human and intellectual life is transferred to them from the poet's own spirit.

But there would be little point in further quotations of this kind. Such imperfectly formulated things hardly deserve to be remembered as classical statements, and nothing more is to be adduced by way of justifying achievement than the preceding long quotation. And there is nowhere in Coleridge anything more impressive to be found than that. We are left, then, with the conclusion that what we bring from the re-survey of his critical work is impressive evidence of what he might have done.

A great deal more space, of course, could be occupied with this evidence. Some of the most interesting is to be found in *Coleridge's Miscellaneous Criticism* (T. H. Raysor's collection) where, in the form of marginalia, odd notes, table talk and so on, there are many striking judgements and observations. There are, for instance, the pages (131 ff.) on Donne – pages that incline one to comment that if Coleridge had had real influence the vogue of Donne would have started a century earlier than it did. (Of *Satire* III, e.g., he says: 'If you would teach a scholar in the highest form how to *read*, take Donne, and of Donne this satire.' He is sound on Beaumont and Fletcher: 'Beaumont and Fletcher write as if virtue or goodness were a sort of talisman or strange something that might be lost without the least fault on the part of the owner' – and he refers to 'the too poematic-minus-dramatic nature' of Fletcher's versification. He is good on Swift: 'In short, critics in general complain of the Yahoos; I complain of the Houyhnhnms.' He is acutely severe on Scott. In fact, the volume as a whole repays exploration. Elsewhere there are the various notes on dramatic and poetic illusion, of which those in *Coleridge's Shakespearean Criticism,* Vol. I (pp. 199 ff) should be looked up, though the best-known formulation, 'that willing suspension of disbelief for the moment, which constitutes poetic faith', occurs in *Biographia Literaria* (c. XIV).

But to revert to the depressing conclusion: Coleridge's prestige is very understandable, but his currency as an academic classic is something of a scandal. Where he is prescribed and recommended it should be with far more by way of reservation and caveat (I have come tardily to realize) than most students can report to have received along with him. He was very much more brilliantly gifted
Arnold, but nothing of his deserves the classical status of
ld's best work.

ARNOLD AS CRITIC

'And I do not like your calling Matthew Arnold Mr Kidglove
Cocksure. I have more reason than you for disagreeing with him and
thinking him very wrong, but nevertheless I am sure he is a rare
genius and a great critic.'*

The note of animus that Hopkins here rebukes in Bridges is a
familiar one where Arnold is concerned: it characterizes a large part
of recorded comment on him. Raleigh's essay in *Some Authors* is (if
we can grant this very representative *littérateur* so much distinction)
a convenient *locus classicus* for it and for the kind of critical
injustice it goes with. But one may be quite free from such animus or
from any temptation to it – may welcome rather than resent that in
Arnold by which the Raleighs are most antagonized – and yet find
critical justice towards him oddly difficult to arrive at. He seems to
present to the appraising reader a peculiarly elusive quantity. At
least, that is my experience as an admirer, and I am encouraged in
generalizing by the fact that the experience of the most important
literary critic of our time appears to have been much the same.

In *The Sacred Wood*, speaking of Arnold with great respect, Mr
Eliot calls him 'rather a propagandist for criticism than a critic', and
I must confess that for years the formula seemed to me
unquestionably just. Is Arnold's critical achievement after all a very
impressive one? His weaknesses and his irritating tricks one
remembers very well. Is it, in fact, possible to protest with any
conviction when we are told (in the later essay, 'Arnold and
Pater')? –

* *The Letters of Gerard Manley Hopkins to Robert Bridges, XCVIII.*

Arnold had little gift for consistency or for definition. Nor had he the power of connected reasoning at any length: his flights are either short flights or circular flights. Nothing in his prose work, therefore, will stand very close analysis, and we may well feel that the positive content of many words is very small.

And yet, if the truth is so, how is it that we open our Arnold so often, relatively? For it is just the oddity of Arnold's case that, while we are apt to feel undeniable force in such judgements as the above, we nevertheless think of him as one of the most lively and profitable of the accepted critics. Let us at any rate seize on the agreement that as a propagandist for criticism he is distinguished. On the view that has been quoted, the first two essays in *Essays in Criticism: First Series* would be the texts to stress as exhibiting Arnold at his strongest, and they have, indeed, seemed to me such. And re-reading confirms the claim of 'The Function of Criticism at the Present Time' and 'The Literary Influence of Academies' to be remembered as classical presentments of their themes. The plea for critical intelligence and critical standards and the statement of the idea of centrality (the antithesis of 'provinciality') are made in memorable formulations of classical rightness:

whoever sets himself to see things as they are will find himself one of a very small circle; but it is only by this small circle resolutely doing its own work that adequate ideas will ever get current at all.

All the world has, or professes to have, this conscience in moral matters... And a like deference to a standard higher than one's own habitual standard in intellectual matters, a like respectful recognition of a superior ideal, is caused, in the intellectual sphere, by sensitiveness of intelligence.

... not being checked in England by any centre of intelligence and urbane spirit...

M. Planche's advantage is ... that there is a force of cultivated opinion for him to appeal to.

... a serious, settled, fierce, narrow, provincial misconception of the whole relative value of one's own things and the things of others.

– Arnold's distinction as a propagandist for criticism cannot be questioned. At the same time, perhaps, it must be admitted that these essays do not involve any very taut or subtle development of an argument or any rigour of definition. They are pamphleteering – higher pampleteering that has lost little of its force and relevance with the passage of time.

Yet it must surely be apparent that the propaganda could hardly have had its virtue if the pamphleteer had not had notable qualifications in criticism. The literary critic, in fact, makes a direct appearance, a very impressive one, in the judgement on the Romantics, which, in its time, remarks Mr Eliot* (who elsewhere justly pronounces it incontrovertible) 'must have appeared startlingly independent'. It seems plain that the peculiar distinction, the strength, represented by the extracts given above, is inseparable from the critical qualifications manifested in that judgement: the sensitiveness and sure tact are essentially those of a fine literary critic.

But does any actual performance of Arnold's in set literary criticism bear out the suggestion at all convincingly? Again it is characteristic of his case that one should be able to entertain the doubt. How many of his admirers retain very strongly favourable impressions of the other series of *Essays in Criticism*? – for it is to this, and to the opening essay in particular, 'The Study of Poetry', that the challenge sends one back. For myself, I must confess to having been surprised, on a recent re-reading of that essay, at the injustice of my recollection of it. The references to Dryden and Pope tend (in my experience) to bulk unfairly, and, for that reason and others, there is a temptation to talk too easily of the essay as being chiefly memorable for having standardized Victorian taste and established authoritatively what, in the academic world, has hardly ceased to be the accepted perspective of poetic history. And it is, actually, as a review of the past from the given period angle that the essay claims its classical status. But it is classical – for it truly is – because it performs its undertaking so consummately. Its representative quality is of the highest kind, that which can be achieved only by the vigorously independent intelligence. If it is fair to say that Arnold, in his dismissal of Dryden and Pope by the criterion of 'soul' and his curious exaltation of Gray, is the voice of the Romantic tradition in his time, we must note too that he is the same Arnold who passed the 'startlingly independent' judgement on the Romantics. And with whatever reservations, protests and irritations we read 'The Study of Poetry', it is impossible in reading it (I find) not to recognize that we have to do with an extraordinarily distinguished mind in complete possession of its purpose and

* *The Use of Poetry and the Use of Criticism*, p. 104.

pursuing it with easy mastery – that, in fact, we are reading a great critic. Moreover, I find that in this inconsequence I am paralleled by Mr Eliot. He writes in *The Use of Poetry and the Use of Criticism* (p. 118), in the mainly depreciatory chapter on Arnold:

> But you cannot read his essay on *The Study of Poetry* without being convinced by the felicity of his quotations: to be able to quote as Arnold could is the best evidence of taste. The essay is a classic in English criticism: so much is said in so little space, with such economy and with such authority.

How is this curious inconsistency of impression – this discrepancy of report which, I am convinced, many readers of Arnold could parallel from their own experience of him – to be explained? Partly it is, I think, that, taking critical stock at the remove from the actual reading, one tends to apply inappropriate criteria of logical rigour and 'definition'. And it is partly (a not altogether separable consideration) that the essay 'dates' in various ways; allowances have certainly to be made with reference to the age to which it was addressed, certain things 'date' in the most damaging sense, and it is easy to let these things infect one's general impression of the 'period' quality of the essay.

The element that 'dates' in the worst sense is that represented by the famous opening in which Arnold suggests that religion is going to be replaced by poetry. Few now would care to endorse the unqualified intention of that passage, and Arnold as a theological or philosophical thinker had better be abandoned explicitly at once. Yet the value of the essay does not depend on our accepting without reservation the particular terms in which Arnold stresses the importance of poetry in those introductory sentences, and he is not disposed of as a literary critic by pointing out that he was no theologian or philosopher; nor is it proved that he was incapable of consistency and vigour of thought. Many who deplore Arnold's way with religion will agree that, as the other traditions relax and social forms disintegrate, it becomes correspondingly more important to preserve the literary tradition. When things are as already they were in Arnold's time, they make necessary, whatever else may be necessary too, the kind of work that Arnold undertook for 'Culture' – work that couldn't have been done by a theologian as such. No doubt Arnold might have been able to do it even better if he had had the qualifications that actually he hadn't; he would at any rate have known his limits better, and wouldn't have produced those writings of his which have proved most ephemeral and which constitute the grounds on which Mr Eliot charges him with responsibility for Pater.* But his actual qualifications were sufficiently remarkable and had their appropriate use. His best work is that of a literary critic, even when it is not literary criticism: it comes from an intelligence that, even if not trained to some kinds of rigour, had its own discipline; an intelligence that is informed by a mature and delicate sense of the humane values and can manifest itself directly as a fine sensibility. That the specific qualifications of the literary critic have an important function some who most disapprove of Arnold's religious position readily grant. Failure to recognize – or to recognize unequivocally – an admirable performance of the function in 'The Study of Poetry' may be partly explained by that opening of the essay: Arnold, after all, issues the distracting challenge, however unnecessarily.

The seriousness with which he conceived the function and the importance he ascribed to poetry are more legitimately expressed in the phrase, the best-known tag from the essay, 'criticism of life'. That it is not altogether satisfactory the animadversion it has been the object of must perhaps be taken to prove: at best we must admit that the intention it expresses hasn't, to a great many readers, made itself satisfactorily clear. Nevertheless Arnold leaves us with little excuse for supposing – as some of his most eminent critics have appeared to suppose – that he is demanding doctrine or moral commentary on life or explicit criticism. Nor should it be necessary to point out that all censure passed on him for having, in calling poetry 'criticism of life', produced a bad definition is beside the mark. For it should be obvious to anyone who reads the phrase in its context that Arnold intends, not to define poetry, but, while insisting (a main concern of the essay) that there are different degrees of importance in poetry, to remind us of the nature of the criteria by which comparative judgements are made.

Why Arnold should have thought the insistence and the reminder worth while and should have hit on the given phrase as appropriate for his purpose is not difficult to understand if we think of that Pater with whom, as noted above, he has been associated:

'Art for Art's sake' is the offspring of Arnold's Culture; and we can hardly

* See the essay 'Arnold and Pater' in *Selected Essays*.

venture to say that it is even a perversion of Arnold's doctrine, considering how very vague and ambiguous that doctrine is.

At any rate, we can certainly not say that 'Art for Art's sake' is the offspring of Arnold's 'criticism of life'. In fact, Arnold's phrase is sufficiently explained – and, I think, vindicated – as expressing an intention directly counter to the tendency that finds its consummation in 'Art for Art's sake'. Aestheticism was not a sudden development: the nature of the trend from Keats through Tennyson and Dante Gabriel Rossetti was, even in Arnold's mid-career, not unapparent to the critic who passed the judgement on the great Romantics. The insistence that poetry must be judged as 'criticism of life' is the same critic's reaction to the later Romantic tradition; it puts the stress where it seemed to him that it most needed to be put.

In so far as Arnold ever attempts to explain the phrase, it is in such terms as those in which, in the essay on Wordsworth, he explains why it is that Wordsworth must be held to be a greater poet than the 'perfect' Gautier. But with no more explanation than is given in *The Study of Poetry* the intention seems to me plain enough for Arnold's purposes. To define the criteria he was concerned with, those by which we make the more serious kind of comparative judgement, was not necessary, and I cannot see that anything would have been gained by his attempting to define them. His business was to evoke them effectively (can we really hope for anything better?) and that, I think, he must be allowed to have done. We may, when, for example, he tells us why Chaucer is not among the very greatest poets, find him questionable and provoking, but the questions are profitable and the provocations stimulate us to get clear in our own minds. We understand well enough the nature of his approach; the grounds of his criticism are sufficiently present. Pressed for an account of the intention behind the famous phrase, we have to say something like this: we make (Arnold insists) our major judgements about poetry by bringing to bear the completest and profoundest sense of relative value that, aided by the work judged, we can focus from our total experience of life (which includes literature), and our judgement has intimate bearings on the most serious choices we have to make thereafter in our living. We don't ordinarily ask of the critic that he shall tell us anything like this, or shall attempt to define the criteria by which he makes his major judgements of value. But

Arnold appears to challenge the demand and so earns reprobation for not satisfying it. By considering the age to which he was addressing himself we are able to do him justice; but if in this way he may be said to 'date', it is not in any discreditable sense.

There is still to be met the pretty general suspicion to which Mr Eliot gives voice when he says* that Arnold 'was apt to think of the greatness of poetry rather than of its genuineness'. It is a suspicion that is the harder to lay because, with a slight shift of accent, it turns into an unexceptionable observation:

> The best of Arnold's criticism is an illustration of his ethical views, and contributes to his discrimination of the values and relations of the components of the good life.†

This very fairly accords due praise while suggesting limitations. We have, nevertheless, to insist that, but for Arnold's gifts as a literary critic, that criticism would not have had its excellence. And when the suspicion takes such form as the following,‡ some answer must clearly be attempted:

> Yet he was so conscious of what, for him, poetry was *for*, that he could not altogether see it for what it is. And I am not sure that he was highly sensitive to the musical qualities of verse. His own occasional bad lapses arouse the suspicion; and so far as I can recollect he never emphasizes this virtue of poetic style, this fundamental, in his criticism.

Whatever degree of justice there may be in these suggestions, one point can be made at once: some pages of 'The Study of Poetry' are explicitly devoted to considering 'genuineness' – the problem of how the critic makes those prior kinds of judgement, those initial recognitions of life and quality, which must precede, inform and control all profitable discussion of poetry and any evaluation of it as 'criticism of life'. Towards the close of the essay we read:

> To make a happy fireside clime
> To weans and wife,
> That's the true pathos and sublime
> Of human life.

There is criticism of life for you, the admirers of Burns will say to us; there is the application of ideas to life! There is, undoubtedly.

---

* *The Use of Poetry, etc.*, p. 110.
† *Criterion*, Vol. III, p. 162.
‡ *The Use of Poetry, etc.*, p. 118.

And Arnold goes on to insist (in terms that would invite the charge of circularity if we were being offered a definition, as we are not) that the evaluation of poetry as 'criticism of life' is inseparable from its evaluation as poetry; that the moral judgement that concerns us as critics must be at the same time a delicately relevant response of sensibility; that, in short, we cannot separate the consideration of 'greatness' from the consideration of 'genuineness'. The test for 'genuineness' Arnold indicates in this way:

> Those laws [of poetic truth and poetic beauty] fix as an essential condition, in the poet's treatment of such matters as are here in question, high seriousness; — the high seriousness which comes from absolute sincerity. The accent of high seriousness, born of absolute sincerity, is what gives to such verse as
>
> > In la sua volontade è nostra pace...
>
> to such criticism of life as Dante's, its power. Is this accent felt in the passages which I have been quoting from Burns? Surely not; surely, if our sense is quick, we must perceive that we have not in those passages a voice from the very inmost soul of the genuine Burns; he is not speaking to us from these depths, he is more or less preaching.

This passage is old-fashioned in its idiom,* and perhaps 'high seriousness' should be dismissed as a mere nuisance.† But 'absolute sincerity', a quality belonging to the 'inmost soul' and manifested in an 'accent', an 'accent that we feel if our sense is quick' — this phrasing, in the context, seems to me suggestive in a wholly creditable and profitable way. And actually it has a force behind it that doesn't appear in the quotation: it is strengthened decisively by what has come earlier in the essay.

The place in question is that in which Arnold brings out his critical tip, the 'touchstone'. Whatever that tip may be worth, its

* Comparison with a passage in a more modern idiom may prove interesting:
'But unless the ordering of the words sprang, not from knowledge of the technique of poetry added to a desire to write some, but from an actual supreme ordering of *experience*, a closer approach to his work will betray it. Characteristically its rhythm will give it away. For rhythm is no matter of tricks with syllables, but directly reflects personality. It is not separable from the words to which it belongs. Moving rhythm in poetry arises only from genuinely stirred impulses, and is a more subtle index than any other to the order of the interests.'   I. A. Richards, *Science and Poetry*, p. 40. Arnold's 'accent', it will be shown, is intended to do much the same work as 'rhythm' in this passage.

† It is an insistent nuisance in the whole essay. But the suspicion that Arnold is demanding with it a Victorian nobility of *tenue* should have been disposed of by his remarks on Burns.

intention should be plain. It is a tip for mobilizing our sensibility; for focusing our relevant experience in a sensitive point; for reminding us vividly of what the best is like.

> Of course we are not to require this other poetry to resemble them; it may be very dissimilar.

> The specimens I have quoted differ widely from one another, but they have in common this: the possession of the very highest poetical quality.

It is only by bringing our experience to bear on it that we can judge the new thing, yet the expectations that we bring, more or less unconsciously, may get in the way; and some readers may feel that Arnold doesn't allow enough for the danger. But that he means to allow for it and envisages the problem with the delicate assurance of a fine critic is plain.

What, however, we have particularly to mark – the main point of turning back to this place in the essay – is what follows. Arnold, while protesting that 'It is much better simply to have recourse to concrete examples', ventures, nevertheless, to give some critical account, 'not indeed how and why' the characters of a high quality of poetry arise, 'but where and in what they arise'. The account is characteristic in its method and, I think, notably justifies it.

> They are in the matter and substance of the poetry, and they are in its manner and style. Both of these, the substance and matter on the one hand, the style and manner on the other, have a mark, an accent, of high beauty, worth, and power.

And the succeeding couple of pages might seem to be mainly a matter of irritating repetition that implicitly admits an inability to get any further. Nevertheless, there is development, and the varied reiteration of associated terms, which is certainly what we have, has a critical purpose:

> We may add yet further, what is in itself evident, that to the style and manner of the best poetry their special character, their accent, is given by their diction, and, even yet more, by their movement. And though we distinguish between the two characters, the two accents, of superiority, yet they are nevertheless vitally connected one with the other. The superior character of truth and seriousness, in the matter and substance of the best poetry, is inseparable from the superiority of diction and movement marking its style and manner.

It is plain that, in this insistent association of 'accent', 'diction' and 'movement' in the equally insistent context, Arnold is offering his equivalent of Mr Eliot's 'musical qualities of verse' and of the 'rhythm' of the footnote to page 60. His procedure is a way of intimating that he doesn't suppose himself to have said anything very precise. But he seems to me, all the same, to have done the appropriate directing of attention upon poetry – and that was the problem – not less effectively than the other two critics.*

Inquiry, then, into the main criticisms that have been brought against 'The Study of Poetry' yields reports decidedly in Arnold's favour. If he speaks in that essay with economy and authority, it is because his critical position is firmly based, because he knows what he is setting out to do, and because he is master of the appropriate method. The lack of the 'gift for consistency or for definition' turns out to be compensated, at his best, by certain positive virtues: tact and delicacy, a habit of keeping in sensitive touch with the concrete, and an accompanying gift for implicit definition – virtues that prove adequate to the sure and easy management of a sustained argument and are, as we see them in Arnold, essentially those of a literary critic.

However, it must be confessed that none of the other essays in that volume can be called a classic in English criticism. The 'Milton' is a mere ceremonial address. (But it may be noted at this point that the reader who supposes Arnold to have been an orthodox idolator of Milton will be surprised if he turns up in *Mixed Essays* the essay called 'A French Critic on Milton'.) The 'Gray' dates most of all the essays in the series – dates in the most damaging sense; though it may be said to have gained in that way a classical status as a document in the history of taste. Neither the 'Keats' nor the 'Shelley' makes any show of being a model critique of poetry; but nevertheless the rarely gifted literary critic is apparent in them. It is apparent in his relative placing of the two poets. 'Shelley,' he says, 'is not a classic, whose various readings are to be noted with earnest attention.' And the reasons he gives for his low valuation, though they are not backed with particular criticism, seem to me

---

* As a way of bringing home the difficulty of achieving anything more precise in the treatment of this problem, the reader may profitably compare with one another Arnold's passages, the footnote above from *Science and Poetry*, Mr Eliot's account of the 'auditory imagination' (*The Use of Poetry, etc.*, pp. 118–119), and Coleridge's remarks on 'the sense of musical delight' in chapter XV (head 1) of *Biographia Literaria*. Arnold's comparative adequacy will be apparent.

unanswerable. On Keats he is extraordinarily just, in appreciation both of the achievement and of the potentiality – extraordinarily just, if we think of the bias that 'criticism of life' is supposed to imply. The critic's quality comes out of some notable phrases:

> But indeed nothing is more remarkable in Keats than his clear-sightedness, his lucidity; and lucidity is in itself akin to character and to high and severe work.

> Even in his pursuit of 'the pleasures of song', however, there is that stamp of high work which is akin to character, which is character passing into intellectual production.

The 'Wordsworth', with all its limitations, is at any rate a distinguished personal estimate, and though by a Wordsworthian, and by the critic who spoke of poetry as the 'application of ideas to life', exhibits its salutary firmness about the 'philosophy'.

But what has to be stressed is his relative valuation of the great Romantics: Wordsworth he put first, then Byron (and for the right reasons), then Keats, and last Shelley. It is, in its independence and its soundness, a more remarkable critical achievement than we easily recognize to-day. (The passage on the Romantics in the 'Heine' essay should not be overlooked.)

If any other particular work of his is to be mentioned, it must be the long essay 'On Translating Homer'. It was, as Saintsbury points out,* an extraordinary original undertaking at the time, and it was carried out with such spirit and intelligence that it is still profitable reading.

The actual achievement in producible criticism may not seem a very impressive one. But we had better inquire where a more impressive is to be found. As soon as we start to apply any serious standard of what good criticism should be, we are led towards the conclusion that there is very little. If Arnold is not one of the great critics, who are they? Which do we approach with a greater expectation of profit? Mr Eliot himself – yes; and not only because his preoccupations are of our time; his best critical writing has a higher critical intensity than any of Arnold's. Coleridge's pre-eminence we all recognize. Johnson? – that Johnson is a living writer no one will dispute, and his greatness is certainly apparent in his

---

* 'Almost for the first time, too, we have ancient literature treated more or less like modern – neither from the merely philological point of view, nor with reference to the stock platitudes and traditions about it.' *Matthew Arnold*, George Saintsbury, p. 68.

criticism. Yet that he imposes himself there as a more considerable power than Arnold isn't plain to me, and strictly as a critic – a critic offering critical value – he seems to me to matter a good deal less to us. As for Dryden, important as he is historically, I have always thought the intrinsic interest of his criticism much overrated: he showed strength and distinction in independent judgement, but I cannot believe that his discussion of any topic has much to offer us. We read him (if we do) because of his place in literary history, whereas we read Arnold's critical writing because for anyone who is interested in literature it is compellingly alive. I can think of no other English critic who asks to be considered here, so I will say finally that, whatever his limitations, Arnold seems to me decidedly more of a critic than the Sainte-Beuve to whom he so deferred.

'GWENDOLEN HARLETH'

George Eliot called her last novel *Daniel Deronda*, so that to separate part of it off for publication under another title than her own might seem to be challenging the judgement, the deliberate and emphatic intention, of the author herself in the most questionable way. But there are two George Eliots, and they both – neither, it seems, embarrassed by consciousness of the duality – play dominating roles in the massive book: they dominate it together as if they were one. But the essential spirits in which they dominate are so much *not* one that the creatively vital of them by its mere presence as what it unmistakably is exposes the creative impotence of the other. That George Eliot should have been so unconscious of the incompatibility of the spirits she has in fact married together is one of the things that seem most to justify the usual dismissal of *Daniel Deronda*. It also makes the book in a special way a rewarding critical study, one that notably illuminates the nature of creativity. But my directing purpose here is not what such a statement suggests; it is to establish in the only way possible that there is a major classic, which may be suitably called 'Gwendolen Harleth', hidden from the general recognition it deserves in the voluminous mixed work that George Eliot published – a classic that it is incumbent on us to reclaim for English literature. It is Gwendolen Harleth who represents the great creative George Eliot – Gwendolen, together with the drama in which she is the focal character. The other George Eliot, to whom, respectful as we are bound to feel towards her, we must deny the insight, the disinterested intensity and the irresistible power of the major creative genius, gave for title to the novel the name of Daniel Deronda – on behalf, as it were, of both. It is a prompting that we have to defy. That is easily said; but the right kind of defiance isn't so easily determined and arrived at.

That George Eliot *is* great, and that her greatness is qualified by characteristic weaknesses – this is generally recognized. It is not perhaps a commonplace that, though not in an even way, and never achieving perfection, she went on advancing in her novelist's art to the end, and produced her most impressive work in her last novel. But it *is* so: the very substantial strong part of *Daniel Deronda* is itself, I hope it will be recognized, one of the major classics of the English tradition – it seems to me a greater novel than *Middlemarch*. Yet it is little read by the public that makes, or keeps, such judgements a live currency, accepted and effectively real. The trouble is that the insufferably boring stretches that the title insists on loom so large, and do in fact face the conscientious reader with a painful *corvée*. And the enlightened and kindly sprightliness of the Meyrick household, Mirah's refuge, hardly tends to compensate for the non-excitements of the long-unvindicated hope of finding and identifying Mirah's brother, for Mordecai's flow of prophetic eloquence, and for the complexities of family history that explain why Deronda had the opportunity to save Mirah from committing suicide in the Thames.

There can be few who have read *Daniel Deronda* to whom the idea has not occurred of freeing by simple surgery the living part of the immense Victorian novel from the deadweight of utterly different matter that George Eliot thought fit to make it carry: it promises on first thoughts to be a pretty easily effected disencumberment. But when one contemplates the challenge in a practical spirit a forbidding major difficulty presents itself – I speak as one who in the past has several times been moved to consider the idea as a possibility to the realising of which one ought, out of admiration for George Eliot, to apply oneself.

The difficulty lies in that 'thought fit'; she did, having no discordant perception or apprehension, think fit to unite the compellingly imagined human truth of Gwendolen Harleth's case history with the quite differently inspired presentation, the difference being radical and disastrous, of her Daniel Deronda in what is offered us as an organically conceived total work, a living single whole. The very opening of the first chapter intimates that we shall hardly find it possible to eliminate Deronda from the projected 'Gwendolen Harleth'. Not that we can point to anything in the initial episode that could have led us to foresee (but for our knowledge of what actually ensues) the kind of problem we should find ourselves faced with. Deronda and the essential relation between him and Gwendolen are introduced with all the inspired skill, the perfection of touch, of the great George Eliot. We arrive at realizing the full significance of this favourable judgment only a good deal later – when we have become familiar with a Deronda towards whom we can't feel in the way the novelist counts on us to feel, and when we know that the kind of interest she takes in him is something about which we can't be happy.

It is essential to the presentation of the Gwendolen whose naïvely egoistic confidence has been shattered, and who, having married Grandcourt, finds herself trapped in a torment of conscience and impotence, that she should have a lay father-confessor to resort to, an authoritative spiritual guide whom she trusts implicitly: the need is in and of her case. The observer whose ironically compassionate interest in her as she stands at the gaming table still strikes one when – knowing what developments are to come – one considers again the opening episode and its sequel, the prompt and offensive return to Gwendolen of the turquoise necklace she has pawned, as (in embryo) potentially the right confessor for her. There is certainly nothing in our sense of him to preclude that development: the deep-piercing imaginative intuition of the great creative George Eliot here is focused where the observing Deronda's (which *is* in fact hers) is – on the beautiful, young, reckless and proud Gwendolen and the fate she is defying.

But it was not in the plan of the novelist as elaborator of plots to actualize what we must see as the felicitous potentiality. I might have said that George Eliot the great genius, having begun what was to be a major work on a grand scale by associating Gwendolen with her future disciplinary guide in the ideal way, hands Deronda over to the other George Eliot if the 'hand over' wouldn't have implied a conscious duality. But, as I have said already, the extraordinary thing about George Eliot (who had been known as a distinguished *savant* until decidedly middle-aged) is that her novels yield no evidence of the least awareness of the radical difference. Yet the difference *is* radical; it entails the difference between the ability to draw on the deepest springs of creative life* and a confident lack of

---

* What Blake said of works of his own is relevant here: 'Tho' I call them mine, I know that they are not mine.'

that ability. And I have further to insist – having described Mary Ann Evans as a *savant* and remembering that she hobnobbed with the great intellects of the age and was known as the translator of Strauss and Feuerbach – that the creative genius was incomparably more *intelligent* than the other George Eliot. This is a point that oughtn't to have needed making, but it does – which is a sign of its crucial importance.

The difference matters to us and matters in relation to the recognized standing of the novelist: it is decidedly for us, at any rate, to cultivate and refine our consciousness of it and of the issues involved. It is in chapter XVI that we get the monitory hint of what actually is going to be done with Deronda. He appears before that in chapter XV. He is still, with Sir Hugo Mallinger, at Leubronn after Gwendolen's sudden departure, and in this conversational exchange about her we know unquestioningly that we have the Deronda of the opening chapter; it is the same distinctive kind of interest in the 'pretty gambler', evoked by the same creative sensibility:

When Sir Hugo and Deronda were alone, the baronet began –

'Rather a pretty story. That girl has some drama in her. She must be worth running after – has *de l'imprévu*. I think her appearance on the scene has bettered my chance of getting Diplow, whether the marriage comes off or not.'

'I should hope a marriage like that would not come off,' said Deronda, in a tone of disgust.

'What! Are you a little touched with the sublime lash?!' said Sir Hugo, putting up his glasses to help his short sight in looking at his companion.

'Are you inclined to run after her?'

'On the contrary,' said Deronda, 'I should rather be inclined to run away from her.'

'Why, you would easily cut out Grandcourt. A girl with her spirit would think you the finer match of the two,' said Sir Hugo, who often tried Deronda's patience by finding a joke in impossible advice. (A difference of taste in jokes is a great strain on the affections.)

'I suppose pedigree and land belong to a fine match,' said Deronda, coldly. 'The best horse will win in spite of pedigree, my boy. You remember Napoleon's *mot* – *Je suis un ancêtre*,' said Sir Hugo, who habitually undervalued birth, as men after dining well often agree that the good of life is distributed with wonderful equality.

'I'm not sure that I want to be an ancestor,' said Deronda. 'It doesn't seem to me to be the rarest kind of origination.'

'You won't run after the pretty gambler, then?' said Sir Hugo, putting down his glasses.'

'Decidedly not.'

This answer was perfectly truthful; nevertheless it had passed through Deronda's mind that under other circumstances he should have given way to the interest this girl had raised in him, and tried to know more of her. But his history had given him a stronger bias in another direction. He felt himself in no sense free.

It is the next chapter (XVI) that points forward to the complicating development, in relation to which we have to consider George Eliot's embarrassing duality. The scene is Sir Hugo's residence, the Abbey, and the chapter opens:

Deronda's circumstances, indeed, had been exceptional. One moment had been burnt into his life as its chief epoch – a moment full of July sunshine and large pink roses shedding their last petals on a grassy court enclosed on three sides by a Gothic cloister. Imagine him in such a scene: a boy of thirteen, stretched prone on the grass where it was in shadow, his curly head propped on his arms over a book, while his tutor, also reading, sat on a camp-stool under shelter. Deronda's book was Sismondi's *History of the Italian Republics*:- the lad had a passion for history, eager to know how time had been filled up since the Flood, and how things were carried on in the dull periods. Suddenly he let down his left arm and looked at his tutor, saying in purest boyish tones –

'Mr Fraser, how was it that the popes and cardinals always had so many nephews?'

The tutor, an able young Scotchman who acted as Sir Hugo Mallinger's secretary, roused rather unwillingly from his political economy, answered with his clear-cut, emphatic chant which makes a truth doubly telling in Scotch utterance –

'Their own children were called nephews.'

'Why?' said Deronda.

So he learns the meaning of the word 'illegitimate' and there 'darts into his mind with the magic of quick comparison the possibility that here was the secret of his own birth, and that the man he called uncle was really his father'. He is only thirteen, but his inner life from that moment is painfully intensified and complicated – a 'circumstance' that (we are to understand) helps to explain the preternatural wisdom, gravity and authority that later, though he is only a couple of years older than Gwendolen, lead her to make him her compassionate but largely unwilling and embarrassed confessor. The mystery of his birth is an essential ingredient in the 'Anti-Gwendolen Harleth' (we may call it) that fills about half of the immense Victorian novel. The mystery isn't cleared up until *Daniel*

Deronda is nearing its end, when Daniel turns out to be legitimate after all, and not a son of Sir Hugo, but a Jew. He gets his beauty and his distinction from his mother, the Princess Halm-Eberstein who, herself a Jew, had arranged with Sir Hugo to have him brought up as an English gentleman.

Among the unrealities and falsities that are confirmed or authorized by this discovery is that Deronda can now propose to Mirah (whose long-sought brother the prophetic Mordecai, it turns out, is) with the certainty of being, not – as before – rejected, but accepted; for Mirah, he can hardly help knowing, is devoutly in love with him, but naturally wouldn't think of marrying anyone but a Jew. I call all this an unreality because neither Deronda nor Mirah is real, while George Eliot's endorsing participation in Deronda's euphoria at being proved a Jew – it goes with resentment at having been so long kept out of the spiritual and moral advantages of his Jewishness – makes it a falsity too. In fact, the only interest – and it doesn't preclude boredom – yielded by the tedious Victorian web of plot-ingenuities leading, at great length, to the coincidence that brings Deronda to Genoa for his interview with the Princess, his mother, in time to be recognized by Gwendolen and Grandcourt at the *Italia*, and be at hand to take charge of Gwendolen after the marine disaster, is a study of George Eliot's own clear and self-committing sympathetic involvement and the nature of the duality to which this relates.

There is a pervasive unreality that contrasts with the vivid livingness and actuality of the persons, scenes and episodes that George Eliot the creative genius makes present to us. It is the unreality of self-indulgent day-dream, indulgence that passes unrecognized by the novelist for what it is. When she writes as the great genius her truly noble and compassionate benignity is controlled by the intelligence and insight it informs – or, more simply, it goes into the intelligence and insight and functions as these. But she has a profound need to feel benignly and compassionately disinterested, and sometimes this prevails as a kind of intoxication that licenses for self-indulgence the weak side of her femininity. The egoism and falsity of day-dream manifest themselves as sentimentality.

What deserves to be called genuine compassion is exemplified in the penetrating intelligence with which Gwendolen is given us: she is as unlike George Eliot herself as could well be, but the disinterestedness of sympathetic insight could hardly go further than in 'Gwendolen Harleth'. It looks as if the strain of maintaining this utterly unflinching and unsentimental realism, the strain of continued self-exposure to the reports of disinterested insight, does something to explain the paradox of *Daniel Deronda* – the collapse into day-dream self-indulgence.

The day-dream is a kind of fairy-tale, ending for Deronda in happiness and benign intoxication ever after. He is a fairy-tale hero-prince, irresistibly beautiful, absolutely altruistic, and a genius – for this last is what the letter Sir Hugo sends the Princess virtually says. In the Meyricks' Chelsea home, which provides a haven for Mirah (its proximity to the river has point), he is referred to as Prince Caramalzaman. True, the mode of reference is humorous in tone, but the humour has no astringency in it – it's a form of sentimentality. In fact, I find the whole Meyrick milieu, including the humorous and artistically irresponsible Hans, Deronda's Cambridge *protégé*-friend, insufferable. A certain astringency is seldom far away in the art of the great George Eliot; there is no astringency at all in the treatment of Deronda and the Deronda world.

The George Eliot of noble altruism offers to offset and authenticate the exalted Hebraism of the prophetic Mordecai – whom she implicitly endorses – with the indulgent low-life realism of the pawnbroker and his whole *ménage*, including the odious spoilt brat Jacob and little Adelaide-Rebekah, whom Deronda, unmistakably agent here of non-mother sentimental femininity, is made to kiss. The astringency of the creative genius can be wholly unreductive and is in any case free from superiority. In the portrayal of the admirable Mr Gascoigne it serves as defensive explanation of Gwendolen: his worldliness is necessary to the wisdom that George Eliot is far from treating as a debit-item against him. The inability of that wisdom to see that marriage to Grandcourt can only be disastrous is neither hateful conventionality nor stupidity; it is inevitable, and is registered as bringing out how virtually inevitable some painful misadventure is for a girl like Gwendolen in the world – the normal civilized world – into which she has been born. The astringency is strongly there in the portrayal of Klesmer, who – a great artist, standing up without compromise for the supreme importance of creativity – represents a basic value of the great George Eliot. It is the marriage of Miss Arrowpoint to Klesmer and not Deronda's to Mirah that gives us the significance, the authoritatively endorsed antithesis, of Gwendolen's to Grandcourt.

There isn't, and there couldn't be, either a Klesmer or a Miss Arrowpoint in anything inspired by the Deronda ethos. For Klesmer and Miss Arrowpoint together represent irrepressible creativity understood, immensely respected and truly valued by intelligence – its essential part in the living human world realized and consciously recognized. What is posited as supremely admirable in Deronda is not creativity, but rather its absence: he is noble altruism personified – it is made plain to us that the meaning of life resides for him in the exercise of noble compassion; we are told, as by George Eliot, that his extraordinary distinction manifests itself in the service of unfortunates who need succouring:

Persons attracted him, as Hans Meyrick had done, in proportion to the possibility of his defending them, rescuing them, telling upon their lives with some sort of redeeming influence.

The Deronda in George Eliot is not conscious that this ideal of noble altruism doesn't belong to the great writer who vindicated her insight and her faith by creating Klesmer and Miss Arrowpoint. It is actually a form of egoism; the day-dream self-indulgence and the unreality so apparent here are characteristic:

Since I began to read and know, I have always longed for some ideal task in which I might feel myself the heart and brain of a multitude – some social captainship, which would come to me as a duty, and not to be striven for as a personal prize.

Deronda's utterance is equally the novelist's – it exemplifies the day-dream self-identification, and what one notes is the way in which it reduces the possibilities to a choice between 'duty' (fixed and known beforehand, and assumed to be authoritatively final) and a 'personal prize'. The artist's striving is of another kind than that which achieves 'personal prizes', and the effect of the reduction is to rule out the artist's distinctive responsibility, which is of an utterly different order from anything that the word 'duty' suggests.

I am not judging one way or the other the judgement regarding Zionism that George Eliot expresses through Deronda when in a final meeting he tells Gwendolen: 'That is a task which presents itself to me as a duty. . . . I am resolved to devote my life to it.' I am merely insisting that the George Eliot who presents us with a

Deronda whom she asks us to take as being real with a reality that qualifies him to exist in a world that contains Gwendolen, Grandcourt, Mr Gascoigne, Herr Klesmer and Miss Arrowpoint, is guilty of a radical confusion. It follows that the Deronda-wisdom derives no penetration or authority from the insight of the great creative George Eliot, and the confusion faces the would-be liberator of 'Gwendolen Harleth' with a difficulty. It is not only that Gwendolen as the insight of genius has presented her does need to be provided with a lay-confessor; there has also to be dealt with the problem constituted by the worst aspect of the confusion inherent in George Eliot's duality. The spiritual disciplinarian to a Gwendolen is, one may venture, necessarily a man, and one can hardly censure the imagination that conceived him as attractive. The shattering (for Gwendolen) irony of the close can't, then, be dispensed with – the blow dealt her by the unforeseen when her trusted and almost deified physician tells her, the patient, just as the consciousness of having fallen in love with him dawns in her, that he is about to marry someone else. The difficulty for the liberator is that the physician is Deronda, the significance of whose development is to be seen in its goal – Zionism – and the someone else in Mirah, the worthy sister of the prophet Mordecai; so that it is impossible to purge 'Gwendolen Harleth' completely of the voluminous clouds of Zionizing altruism and Victorian nobility that Deronda trails and emits – and for the most part *is*.

It should nevertheless be possible to produce a sufficiently self-contained 'Gwendolen Harleth' by excising the virtual half of the total work that seems to justify the title the novelist gave it – the half that is focused on Deronda and the process leading up to the proof of his Jewishness; and further, by reducing to the necessary minimum the confidential talks between Deronda and Gwendolen. Not to have done this last could only have been to emphasize the formal imperfection left by the excision of the unacceptable Deronda theme – most certainly unacceptable as a major something against which the theme of Gwendolen and Grandcourt is, in the novelist's invention, to be counterpointed.

I should make the penultimate chapter (with some elisions) of *Daniel Deronda* – significantly the next and last concerns Deronda's marriage to Mirah – the final chapter of 'Gwendolen Harleth'. It would have to be included, for it records his embarrassed last interview with Gwendolen, in which he has somehow to tell her of the approaching marriage. We read it as having its main focus on Gwendolen, and it closes with a truly fitting end for 'Gwendolen Harleth'. The efforts of the stricken girl to reassure her mother throw a light on essential characteristics of her own, and a comment on them can't but emphasize the paradox of George Eliot's duality. The closing paragraph runs:

> When he was quite gone, her mother came in and found her sitting motionless.
>
> 'Gwendolen, dearest, you look very ill,' she said, bending over her and touching her cold hands.
>
> 'Yes, mamma. But don't be afraid. I am going to live,' said Gwendolen, bursting out hysterically.
>
> Her mother persuaded her to go to bed, and watched by her. Through the day and half the night she fell continually into fits of shrieking, but cried in the midst of them to her mother, 'Don't be afraid. I shall live. I mean to live.'
>
> After all, she slept; and when she waked in the morning light, she looked up fixedly at her mother and said tenderly, 'Ah, poor mamma! You have been sitting up with me. Don't be unhappy. I shall live. I shall be better.'

It is a perfect close to the novel that, of all she wrote, seems to me the supreme product of the great George Eliot's genius. It can hardly be denied that egoism is one of Gwendolen's most prominent characteristics. But 'egoism' is a word that has a number of forces – the novelist herself is highly conscious that Grandcourt's egoism is very different from Gwendolen's. His is basic, ultimate, irremediable and evil. He is described as a 'used-up life'; and he has no satisfaction left but to feel superior to everyone and to dominate and make his power to do so felt – and he remains always bored. There is a remarkable coincidence with Lawrence when George Eliot refers to Grandcourt as a 'handsome lizard of a hitherto unknown species, not of the lively, darting kind'. I am thinking of the passage in *The Crown* (V) where Lawrence takes the snake and the newt, and reptilian creatures generally, as representing 'the opposite equivalent of creation'. And it is not for nothing that in the same pages I find an analysis confirming my remark that the noble altruism and the emphasis on duty as a sufficient end in itself of which the Zionizing George Eliot makes Deronda the representative is a form of egoism – of imprisonment in the ego. The Deronda-will to be subject to a fixed and all-commanding duty is anti-creative. 'We cannot,' says Lawrence, 'subject a divine process to a static will, not without blasphemy and loathsomeness.' It is no mere matter of artistic creation, though that it should be the great creative George Eliot who implicitly makes my point about her Gwendolen is significant. It is not merely that the prostrate Gwendolen's resolution to ease her mother's distress can hardly be called the will that is egoism. Lawrence's distinction between Will and Power is a necessary one; Gwendolen certainly has egoistic will, but she has something else too – she has Power: creative life that comes in from outside the enclosing ego. This truth about her is manifested in many ways; the Power that flows from beyond the ego is what Lawrence calls divine. That Gwendolen has it is again and again virtually stated too, as here:

Behind, of course, were the sad faces of the four superfluous girls, each, poor thing – like those many thousand sisters of us all – having her peculiar world which was of no importance to any one else, but all of them feeling Gwendolen's presence to be somehow a relenting of misfortune: where Gwendolen was, something interesting would happen...

This life-giving vitality of Gwendolen's, so different from Grandcourt's sinister will, makes her reduction to an abjectly complete loss of belief in herself and life peculiarly poignant. But the close of 'Gwendolen Harleth' strikes the right note – not happy, but intimating that the loss of Power was not final.

GERARD MANLEY HOPKINS:

REFLECTIONS

AFTER FIFTY YEARS

I couldn't have bought Hopkins's *Poems* when they came out, for that was in 1918, before the Armistice, and I was not in England. Nevertheless, I was able to buy a copy of the first edition, which, numbering 750, was not exhausted till 1928. I bought my copy well before that, though just when I can't recall. I think the prompting came from the review of the book Middleton Murry had done in *The Athenaeum* – not from the review as it appeared in that weekly, but from reading it among those included in the collection of Murry's reviews entitled *Aspects of Literature* (1920). I lectured at Cambridge on Hopkins along with Eliot, the Pound of *Hugh Selwyn Mauberley* and the Yeats of 'Sailing to Byzantium' in the 1920s – when, let me remind (or tell) you, the taste and criteria represented by Robert Bridges (poor Hopkins!) still prevailed and Dean Inge, John Donne's successor, could confidently call T. S. Eliot a 'literary Bolshevik'. The great change was yet to be consummated, and I had my relevant convictions, which I still think well-founded.

I open in this personal way because I have decided that a mode of discussion that is frankly personal and informal best suits the present occasion. Any special qualification I may have as a critic of Hopkins the poet is inseparable from the fact that I was contemporary with the beginnings and establishment of his reputation. That fact for me means that coming to terms with his work played an important part in my own development. The attendant advantages occurred to me as such when I was considering the problem that faced me as a result of my having accepted the invitation to give this lecture. Frankly, I have from time to time since I committed myself regretted that acceptance. I wrote what I intended for a concentrated essential critique of Hopkins nearly forty years ago, and a good many years later, at the time of the centenary of his birth, I wrote in *Scrutiny* my offer of a maturely considered estimate. I didn't contemplate repeating this, tactfully rephrased and rearranged, for the benefit of this evening's audience. Hopkins, you see, isn't Shakespeare, and the essential considerations are limited. But the approach by personal record I have in mind, while focused on Hopkins and essentially critical, entails a different distribution of emphasis and a different critical economy – at any rate, it makes the given distribution and the given economy natural and proper.

It enables me, for one thing, to say without seeming in any gross way indifferent to the proprieties that I regret the way in which Hopkins has been made into a minor academic industry. I do indeed fall short of gratitude for any extensive study made and published of his poetic, but, when I say that, it can pass as the forgivable grudgingness of the pioneer whose work has been superseded – who feels that what he has done was all that needed to be done. The subsequent Hopkins authority who called on me in the 1930s and asked some exploratory questions could, for example, if my present insistence on my attitude came to his attention, classify it in that way. One of his questions, I remember, was whether one ought to learn Greek in order to attain to a full understanding of Hopkins's prosodic peculiarities, and I remember my answer: 'No'. The obvious answer, and so very easy to remember.

The provocation to the question comes in the 'Author's Preface', where, in the course of his commentary on his own rhythmic experiments, Hopkins, among other things, refers to 'what the Greeks called a Logaoedic Rhythm'. I still think the firmness and finality of my 'No' right. In fact, I never myself found the Preface as a whole, though Hopkins's arguments don't really rest on any reference to the Greek, helpful. I never thought of sending anyone to it as an introduction that would ease the way to an attempt at reading out Hopkins's poetry. What I used to say was: 'Go to actual poems and use your intelligence, remembering that to use your intelligence is to free yourself from inappropriate habits of expectations'. Of course I had further help to give, starting with suggestions for the choice of poems, but that was the way in which I had reached and established my own convictions about Hopkins as a poet.

Even in those days, forty and more years ago, I had convictions also about the tendency of scholarship and academic specialization to put obstacles between the student and the understanding of creative literature. And I am not less convinced now that an insistence on a relation between Hopkins's poetry and Greek prosody – or, for that matter, the elaborated Welsh art – is academic in the bad sense. I'm inclined to add 'or insistence on prosody as such at all'. It isn't difficult, however, to see why Hopkins should have had to write that Preface, and some attention to the reasons is involved in the appreciation of his genius and originality. He and his friend Bridges had, as poets, much the same educational background: Public School and Grammar School Classics, and the great representative fact of Tennyson. Bridges, the Academy poet *par excellence*, was incapable of questioning the orthodoxy of taste and critical assumption in which he had grown up, and which was to bring him the Laureate crown. The genius of Hopkins manifests itself tragically in the contrast he presents to Bridges, the upholder of (I quote Bridges' own words) 'a continuous literary decorum' – a phrase that suggests fairly the nature of the poet-critic's assured conception of 'form'. I say 'tragically' because Hopkins, doomed in any case to suffer an acute sense of his human isolation, felt badly the invincible pertinacity of his friend's obtuseness. His creativity, like that of all original artists, had a profound need of encouragement, but had to be content with its own prompting and conviction.

You see how Hopkins served my turn in the 1920s and later – of what use he was to me critically and historically. He and his friend (who as editor had worthy successors in Claude Colleer Abbott and Charles Williams) gave us a classical situation. The nature of Bridges' complacent assurance was apparent enough in his editorial notes. When Hopkins's letters to Bridges came out the confirmation wasn't the less striking because one had to divine what he was answering. How poignantly the wry humour of this brings out the force of my 'tragically' (there is much more in the letters of the same significance):

You say you wd. not for any money read my poem again. Nevertheless I beg you will. Besides money, you know, there is love. If it is obscure do not bother yourself with the meaning but pay attention to the best and most intelligible stanzas, as the two last of each part of the narrative of the wreck. If you had done this you wd. have liked it better and sent me some serviceable criticisms, but now your criticism is of no use, being only a protest memorialising me against my whole policy and proceedings. (XXXVII)

Hopkins too, we see, was convinced, and *his* conviction was the conviction of genius. The prosodic exposition and argument of the Preface give us his way of strengthening his hold on his creative impulses and perceptions and justifying to himself as far as possible, in terms of his training, he being a contemporary of Bridges, his scandalous experiments. As I've said, the taste and critical orthodoxy represented by Bridges were still very strong in the 1920s – even at Cambridge. They, in their contemptuous confidence, had still to be fought – not merely on behalf of Hopkins. Hopkins in fact gave one a good military opportunity: an effective attack in that sector could tell in the campaign to get recognition for a greater poet – Eliot.

Form, music, melody – these are the words that point to the preconceptions, or habits of expectation, that made it impossible for Bridges, Dean Inge and the cultivated in general – the public of poetry-lovers – to recognize the presence of creative life in the poetry of their own time. I have specified Tennyson as a major power in the cultural background. His reputation was not at its zenith in the 1920s – indeed, I think he was little read; but the consequences of Tennyson remained unchallenged – that is what I meant by referring to him as the great fact in the background. Perhaps I had better add, as a correction to 'consequences', 'the significance of Tennyson remained unappreciated'. For 'consequences' suggests that he was a great originating poet, and, if such a description implies that his work challenged a marked effort of readjustment, of self-exposure to experience, he wasn't. If, however, one hesitates therefore to call him a major poet, one can hardly be happy in calling him a minor. My solution is to say that he was an Academy poet of genius – there was no genius in Bridges' case (and I should like to save the word 'talent' for cases in which one can see some genuine creativity). Tennyson's achievement was to give the Victorian age the consummate expression of the conventional poetic sensibility it was, after the Romantic period, ready to recognize as such, to share, and to enjoy.

It happens that there is an early poem of Hopkins's that enables one to insist effectively that Tennysonian poetry is Art in a restrictive sense that doesn't apply to any of the very diverse great 'Romantics'. I shall comment on it briefly later. Immediately I will note, once again, the consequence of what I will call the Tennysonian change: formal poetry in the Victorian age ceased to matter much. Dickens was an incomparably greater poet than all the formal poets of the age put together, his Shakespearian creativity being manifested, in diverse and irresistible ways, in his very handling of the English language.

What, with my eye on his relation to Tennyson, I used to say about Hopkins was that he brought back into poetry the distinctive speech-strength of English. Having had occasion later to consider Eliot's achievement I now see that something of a qualifying kind ought to follow that formulation. At the moment I will ask you to think of it as repeated; it points to the importance I saw in Hopkins, and the use I had for him, in those exhilarating years of the 1920s when it seemed that a new creative period in English poetry was opening. My eye, I've said, was on the background fact of Tennyson, and of Tennyson I used to say that his explicit ambition was to bring English as near as possible to the Italian, and that he achieved the ambition marvellously. I was asked the other day by a specialist scholar engaged in work on Tennyson where, regarding the alleged explicitness, I had found the authority for my statement, and I couldn't satisfy the inquirer. I may have picked it up from some Victorian commentator; in any case, it suggests with felicity the spirit of Tennyson's handling of English. And I remember that at Cambridge in the 1920s a lecturer for the English Tripos (he belonged primarily to Classics and was accounted brilliant and 'himself a poet') throwing out with approval the *mot*, 'he drove the geese out of the language'.

It wasn't only the sibilance that Tennyson was intent on mitigating; he made it an essential part of his creative aim to maintain a smooth canorousness, a quasi-musical play of vowels, in which English should be cured of its tendency to produce effects of consonantal 'harshness' requiring marked effort to pronounce — that is, be cured of its energy:

> The long day wanes: the slow moon climbs: the deep
> Moans round with many voices. Come, my friends...

> There lies a vale in Ida, lovelier
> Than all the valleys of Ionian hills.

> And some one pacing there alone,
> Who paced for ever in a glimmering land,
> Lit with a low large moon.

For epic style, Tennyson gives us this:

> So all day long the noise of battle roll'd
> Among the mountains by the winter sea...

Such a habit (it was second nature in Tennyson), such a preoccupation with poetic style, obviously entails, in relation to life and the possibilities of experience, a drastically exclusive specialization of poetic sensibility. It seems to me plain that the extremeness of Hopkins's experimenting was a response to the fact of Tennyson: he was determined to get back into poetry the resources of living – that is, spoken – English. When the *Letters to Robert Bridges* came out I was delighted to find (though – or because – it was hardly needed) explicit confirmation from Hopkins himself:

> So also I cut myself off from the use of *ere, o'er, wellnigh, what time, say not* (for *do not say*)), because, though dignified, they neither belong to nor ever cd. arise from, or be the elevation of, ordinary modern speech. For it seems to me that the poetical language of an age shd. be the current language heightened, to any degree heightened and unlike itself, but not (I mean normally: passing freaks and graces are another thing) an obsolete one. (LXII)

'The current language' – I have, where Hopkins's practice is concerned, still my qualification to offer, but that will wait. It seems to me that when I told my pupils to take to their encounter with him their intelligence together with their knowledge of their native language, I gave good advice. To these there also needed to be added the certitude that, formidable as his characteristic things might look, he was on producible evidence, a genuine poet with the gift and the skill necessary for convincing expression. By way of putting them in possession of such certitude I would have called their attention to certain of the poems—poems easy to read out at first approach.

I, years before I knew anything more of Hopkins, had been acquainted with one such. I had come on, during the war, *The Spirit of Man*, an anthology containing some French odds and ends along with the English poems and pieces, that Bridges had compiled with a view (I divined) to its being carried round in officers' pockets. However that may be, I picked it up somewhere or other in wartime

France, and, since no one else wanted it, got to know its contents pretty well. Among the unfamiliar poems, this one impressed itself on my memory – it appears in the volume of Hopkins's poems as 'Spring and Fall' (in reading it there I discovered that Bridges, before including it in *The Spirit of Man*, had excised the second couplet):

> Márgarét, are you gríeving
> Over Goldengrove unleaving?
> Leáves, líke the things of man, you
> With your fresh thoughts care for, can you?
> Áh! ás the heart grows older
> It will come to such sights colder
> By and by, nor spare a sigh
> Though worlds of wanwood leafmeal lie;
> And yet you wíll weep and know why.
> Now no matter, child, the name:
> Sórrow's spríngs áre the same.
> Nor mouth had, no nor mind, expressed
> What heart heard of, ghost guessed:
> It ís the blight man was born for,
> It is Margaret you mourn for.

We see the excision of that second couplet –

> Leáves, líke the things of man, you
> With your fresh thoughts care for, can you?

– as significant in the hint it gives of the nature of what Bridges calls his love of 'a continuous literary decorum'. I imagine the couplet gives no jolt to anyone here. We can see that its licence is unlicentious, going as it does with the effect, which it confirms, of the informal intimacy of the speaking voice. It is a manifestation in fact of an exquisite poetic skill – the 'exquisite' registering the perception that the skill is at once delicacy and precision. The sentence reads itself naturally with the slow, quietly pondering inwardness the maintaining of which all through the poet has ensured by putting accents here and there over words or syllables.

The characteristic Hopkins effect that we can put a finger on at once is in the penultimate couplet:

> Nor mouth had, no nor mind, expressed
> What heart heard of, ghost guessed:

– 'heart' here is the apprehending that precedes words, and the force of 'ghost' defines itself in turning (as it seems to do) into 'guessed': it is the spirit that intuits what the mind hasn't yet thought. I don't, in this commentary, suppose myself to be telling you what you couldn't perceive for yourselves, for the effect, like the whole poem to which it belongs, is compellingly successful. What I wanted to emphasize was that to be able to do *this* with the word 'ghost', and do it in a way that makes us take the whole effect as an unstrained and matter-of-course felicity is the mark of a truly creative poet (and whatever Bridges was, he wasn't that).

There is another poem, a very different one, that I should call attention to, adducing it also as clear proof of a rare poetic gift in Hopkins. It is one – the third – of the three 'Early Poems' that come first in the current Hopkins volume. This is the early poem I have already referred to. In reading it out, as I will now do, I shall stop half-a-dozen lines from the end. I shall do that in order to make plain the conscious restriction of my commentary on the poem. Seeing it is so decidedly a poem, it may be said to raise explicitly the question of the way in which his religious vocation (his actual theme) is related to his poetic creativity. That is a question which the literary critic must find a testing one: it demands of him some attention, but there is a point to push inquiry beyond which would be impertinent – the more so since it is unnecessary. I may say that I should feel that in talking to any audience. The poem is called 'The Habit of Perfection':

> Elected Silence, sing to me
> And beat upon my whorlèd ear,
> Pipe me to pastures still and be
> The music that I care to hear.
>
> Shape nothing, lips; be lovely-dumb:
> It is the shut, the curfew sent
> From there where all surrenders come
> Which only makes you eloquent.
>
> Be shellèd, eyes, with double dark
> And find the uncreated light:
> This ruck and reel which you remark
> Coils, keeps, and teases simple sight.
>
> Palate, the hutch of tasty lust,
> Desire not to be rinsed with wine:
> The can must be so sweet, the crust
> So fresh that come in fasts divine!

O feel-of-primrose hands, O feet
That want the yield of plushy sward...

The poet who wrote that was more like Keats than any other of the Victorian age – or any other that I know of. I am thinking of the power of sensuous concreteness that makes Keats's preoccupation with 'beauty' so utterly different a thing from what it becomes in the 'aesthetic' writers of the later century who derive from him (a derivation not to be laid to his responsibility). The Keatsian sensibility is announced in the 'lovely-dumb'. I am not thinking mainly of the compound adjective (prompted pretty obviously by Keats), but of the 'lovely', the suggestion of which gets its strikingly Keatsian realization in

> Palate, the hutch of tasty lust

– It is the thing nowadays to have much recourse to talk about 'imagery', but the concrete immediacy of that isn't easy to bring down to any specifiable 'images'. The imagery, then, that produces the effect of enjoying in vivid sensation the presented and shared is a matter of the co-operative play of a complexity of analogical suggestion, involving inseparably meaning and the muscular efforts required in the pronouncing of the significant succession of words. 'Palate', 'hutch', 'tasty' and 'lust', brought together in this way, combine to evoke a delighted luxury of indulgence that unites subtlety and fineness with rich substantiality. This is the Hopkins who helps one to enforce the point that Tennyson paid a heavy price for his 'perfection', a price the nature of which stands out when one compares any descriptive felicity of his that invites the attribution of richness with the major Keats.

I have, making the point in print somewhere, taken for my Keatsian sample the opening of the Autumn ode:

> Season of mists and mellow fruitfulness!
>> Close bosom-friend of the maturing sun;
> Conspiring with him how to load and bless
>> With fruit the vines that round the thatch-eaves run;
> To bend with apples the moss'd cottage-trees,
>> And fill all fruit with ripeness to the core.

– I needn't repeat here the obvious enough account of how the un-Tennysonian sensuous concreteness in which the factual plays so essential a part is evoked – how it entails the un-Tennysonian consonantal strength exemplified in the 'moss'd cottage-trees' of

> To bend with apples the moss'd cottage-trees

which has so potent an effect in the following line,

> And fill all fruit with ripeness to the core,

where, if we analyse *its* concreteness, we find it charged with the sensation of having bitten to the core a ripe apple, so that the flooding juice that starts from the luxurious bite fills the mouth: such, in the given Keatsian context, is the potency generated analogically in the pronouncing of the resistantly un-Tennysonian phrase.

A like co-presence of luxury and energy characterizes Hopkins's concreteness in 'The Habit of Perfection'. If, when we come to

> O feel-of-primrose hands, O feet
> That want the yield of plushy sward,

we are inclined to say that an 'aesthetic' luxuriousness prevails here, we have nevertheless not forgotten the striking manifestation of the Keatsian energy entailed in Hopkins's concreteness. And if we want internal evidence that, for all the difference, it was this poet who was to launch into the experimenting of 'The Wreck of the Deutschland', we have only to look again at

> This ruck and reel which you remark
> Coils, keeps, and teases simple sight

– lines which immediately precede

> Palate, the hutch of tasty lust,

an effect of consonantal energy that after all is not at odds with 'the yield of plushy sward'.

After these preliminaries I should suggest going straight on to 'The Wreck of the Deutschland'. Not that I find it, or ever found it – even in the 1920s – repellingly difficult in sum. But Bridges was – we have it as a datum – repelled by it, and, in relation to Hopkins's distinctive poetic, it is the great inaugural exercise. I will read out four stanzas from the opening of the second part:

> 'Some find me a sword; some
> The flange and the rail; flame,
> Fang, or flood' goes Death on drum,

And storms bugle his fame.
But wé dream we are rooted in earth – Dust!
Flesh falls within sight of us, we, though our flower the same,
Wave with the meadow, forget that there must
The sour scythe cringe, and the blear share come.

On Saturday sailed from Bremen,
American-outward-bound,
Take settler and seaman, tell men with women,
Two hundred souls in the round –
O Father, not under thy feathers nor ever as guessing
The goal was a shoal, of a fourth the doom to be drowned;
Yet did the dark side of the bay of thy blessing
Not vault them, the millions of rounds of thy mercy not reeve even them in?

Into the snows she sweeps,
Hurling the haven behind,
The Deutschland, on Sunday; and so the sky keeps,
For the infinite air is unkind,
And the sea flint-flake, black-backed in the regular blow,
Sitting Eastnortheast, in cursed quarter, the wind;
Wiry and white-fiery and whirlwind-swivellèd snow
Spins to the widow-making unchilding unfathering deeps.

She drove in the dark to leeward,
She struck – not a reef or a rock
But the combs of a smother of sand: night drew her
Dead to the Kentish Knock;
And she beat the bank down with her bows and the ride of her keel:
The breakers rolled on her beam with ruinous shock;
And canvas and compass, the whorl and the wheel
Idle for ever to waft her or wind her with, these she endured.

That is much the reading out I should have found myself giving
(say) forty years ago. I don't mean that I'm satisfied with my
performance; one rarely is when one takes from a poem or a passage
the implicit challenge to read out. But there's no special difficulty
there – no reason, surely, to baulk at the nature of the art or doubt
its substantial success. 'Traditional' is a tricky word, but there are
good grounds for describing the poetic as strongly traditional.
Remembering that behind Shakespeare there is not only the
Renaissance, but a continuity from Piers Plowman, and whatever
lies behind Piers Plowman, we can say Hopkins here belongs to the
Shakespearian in the complex poetic tradition of the English
language rather than to the Spenserian-Miltonic-Tennysonian. It is

to *that* in him – undisguised, and unconcerned for what Bridges, the Victorian Academy poet and critic, called 'decorum' – that Bridges can't be reconciled.

I said that we might properly call this poetry traditional in its strength; but 'traditional' isn't the first word that occurs to us as we read the first of those stanzas – nor is it 'idiosyncratic': the poetic creativity is such that we take in as central and unanswerable what is with that truth and weight evoked, and are too gravely affected to think of technique, convention, decorum or prosody. The stanza 'reads itself'; that is, the meaning takes charge and takes possession of us, so that we are conscious only of that. Had the accent over the fifth line been italics instead, that would have struck us, when we drew off to a commenting distance, as perfectly normal – a courtesy immediately acceptable because strictly speaking unnecessary, since the sense, which is commanding and unequivocal, gives the rhythm that places the major stress on 'we'. For the movement of the opening two lines Hopkins has relied on the sense and the reader's perception of the general rhythmic pattern and character. I will read the stanza again:

> 'Some find me a sword; some
> The flange and the rail; flame,
> Fang, or flood' goes Death on drum,
> And storms bugle his fame.
> But wé dream we are rooted in earth – Dust!
> Flesh falls within sight of us, we, though our flower the same,
> Wave with the meadow, forget that there must
> The sour scythe cringe, and the blear share come.

Hopkins's un-Swinburnian – or anti-Swinburnian – use of alliteration is well illustrated in the linkage across the line of 'flesh' and 'flower', and the whole poignantly telling, the spontaneous realizing development of the traditional imagery is Shakespearian. There is surely no exaggeration in that account of the sustained effect that rests for its insistent weighted close on the evoked scythe and plough-share. 'Cringe' is not merely a descriptive felicity, it gives the human recoil from the stark but inexorable and unaccepted fact, and it presents so potently the motion of scything that we don't need to be *told* of the plough-share's motion as, cold and metallically unrelenting, it turns up and over the earth that buries. Both adjectives, the 'sour' and the 'blear', have a pregnancy that tells at once, unanalysed, and without suggesting that the poet himself is ready with the analysis.

In the second of the stanzas we have, in 'The goal was a shoal', an instance of the internal rime that is as typical of Hopkins's poetic habit as alliteration, assonance and assonantal progression – all playing their part in the charged intensity of this poem, and all, in the stanzas I've read, obviously justified as belonging essentially to the expressive concentration and vividness they serve. In places in Hopkins the assonance or the internal rime may seem an opportunity too easily taken – a mere *procédé*, something too like a jingle. But here the charged gravity obviates any such suggestion; the rime, with its transmuting insistence, gives us the dreadful unforeseenness of the fact, and when, a little further on in the line, the word 'doom' comes, it is charged with the irony: not arrival at the port, but *this*; this the decreed end of the voyage – the end of the hazard of life. For a characteristic Shakespearian instance of the same kind of effect I have somewhere or other quoted from *Macbeth*:

> If it were done, when 'tis done, then 'twere well
> It were done quickly: if the assassination
> Could trammel up the consequence, and catch
> With his surcease success...

the parallel with 'The goal was a shoal' is close: 'surcease' *becomes* 'success'; analogically the significance, the catching (so infallible in the imagining, yet as prospective fact a dreadful hazard), is enacted.

But I mustn't spend time on analytic appreciation – which isn't, after all, necessary. Of the next stanza I'll merely remark, with my eye on Tennyson and decorum, that the habits and preconceptions they represent would have precluded before the conceiving any such Shakespearian creativity in the rendering of the storm and its edged and murderous cruelty. There is special point in the reiterated 'Shakespearian' here, because – without the imputation of derivativeness – one thinks of a place in *Lear*. Shakespeare's English language, which Shakespeare's genius did so much to strengthen, gets from Hopkins its creative vindication as the still continuing life the essential poet draws on – gets it in defiance of the Tennysonian climate (not made more congenial by the Swinburnian accentuation). For Swinburne's alliterative habit is hypnoidal, whereas all the formal or technical habits of Hopkins's poetic, where his genius is concerned, serve to intensify and enforce meaning; they organize, give edge and compel the realizing attention of the full waking mind. And the whole evocation of the monstrous and callous elemental fury is as obviously anti-Tennysonian as the insistent sibilance that gives us the northeaster:

> For the infinite air is unkind,
> And the sea flint-flake, black-backed in the regular blow,
> Sitting Eastnortheast, in cursed quarter, the wind;
> Wiry and white-fiery and whirlwind-swivellèd snow
> Spins to the widow-making unchilding unfathering deeps.

In the last of the stanzas I will point only to the rime-series:

> She drove in the dark to leeward,
>   night drew her
> Dead to the Kentish Knock;
>   these she endured.

The success of these rimes illustrates the force of Hopkins's statement about the need to feel his verse as *spoken* – which means to let one's ear and one's sense of natural English speech interpret, as one reads, what the eye gives them. Not only do 'leeward' and 'endured' rime perfectly; the time given by the passage from 'drew her' to the 'dead' of the next line satisfies the ear equally. It plays its part in the pattern with an unquestionable rightness, calling no attention to itself as a *tour de force*, but being duly, and no more, felt as we follow the movement of sense and the sound it informs. Hopkins elsewhere (as, for instance, the 'The Bugler's First Communion') permits himself rimes that are less unlike Browning's self-applauding acrobaticisms, but even then, unlike Browning, he doesn't mean such rimes to invite notice as feats strikingly brought off. He has simply – a penalty of isolation – been deserted by his sense of what can, and what can't, be assimilated into an effect that sounds natural and an inevitable registration of a creative significance.

This brings me to the question, why, after so convincing a demonstration of major potentiality, didn't a commensurate production of achieved poetry follow? For one can't do justice to Hopkins's impressive gift without constating the paradoxical meagreness. To attempt an answer to the question entails considerations of some delicacy, and I find it helpful to quote what Murry said at the end of his review:

There is no good reason why we should give characteristic specimens of the poet's obscurity, since our aim is to induce people to read him. The obscurities will slowly vanish and something of the intention appear; and they will find in him many of the strange beauties won by men who push on to the borderlands of their science; they will speculate whether the failure of his whole achievement was due to the starvation of experience which his vocation imposed upon him, or to a fundamental vice in his poetical endeavour. For ourselves we believe that the former was the true cause. His 'avant toute chose', whirling dizzily in a spiritual vacuum, met with no salutary resistance to modify, inform, and strengthen it.

I always, though I recoiled from something in him, thought Murry a good reviewer – until he reviewed my book on Lawrence (twice – once, if I guessed right, in the *Times Literary Supplement*, anonymously). The review of the *Poems* was written in 1919, and what I've just quoted seems to me intelligent. But there is a phrase that suggests a less acute consciousness in Murry of the considerations involved than I myself feel: 'His "avant toute chose", whirling dizzily in a spiritual vacuum'. Well, one of the essential *données* we have before us from the beginning is the duality of Hopkins – with Murry's phrase in front of me I will say, the duality of his spiritual energy. It is avowed in that early poem I adduced, and it gives him his peculiar thisness – his 'haecceity', to use Hopkins's word – as a poet, while entailing the at least tacit avowal in his poetry that to be a poet was not his main vocation.

In that early poem, 'The Habit of Perfection', he anticipates that his religious vocation will bring him an assured serenity. It didn't do that, of course. But as for the relation between his dedicated life and his poetry, how can anyone care to go behind this, written to Canon Dixon, for whom, I think, one must, after reading the letters from and to him, feel affection as well as respect:

The question then for me is not whether I am willing (if I may guess what is in your mind) to make a sacrifice of hopes of fame (let us suppose), but whether I am not to undergo a severe judgment from God for the lothness I have shewn in making it, for the reserves I may have in my heart made, for the backward glances I have given with my hand upon the plough, for the waste of time the very compositions you admire may have caused and their preoccupation of the mind which belonged to more sacred or more binding duties, for the disquiet and the thoughts of vainglory they have given rise to. A purpose may look smooth and perfect from without but be frayed and faltering from within. I have never wavered in my vocation, but I have not lived up to it.   (*Correspondence*, XXI)

I see that when, thirty-five years ago, I reviewed the *Correspondence of Gerard Manley Hopkins and Richard Watson Dixon*, I said: 'This says all that need be said'. My next sentence runs: 'At least, I do not think that any attempt to go behind, or to explain further and deeper, would bring any essential enlightenment to admirers of "The Windhover", "Spelt from Sibyl's Leaves" and the "terrible sonnets".' I still think as then. I do however see point in glancing at considerations that really confirm this recognition. Murry provides a pointer when he concludes his review by quoting the last five lines of the sonnet, 'To R.B.', that comes at the end of the finished poems as Bridges printed them. I will read the whole sonnet:

> The fine delight that fathers thought; the strong
> Spur, live and lancing like the blowpipe flame,
> Breathes once and, quenchèd faster than it came,
> Leaves yet the mind a mother of immortal song.
> Nine months she then, nay years, nine years she long
> Within her wears, bears, cares and combs the same:
> The widow of an insight lost she lives, with aim
> Now known and hand at work now never wrong.
>   Sweet fire the sire of muse, my soul needs this;
> I want the one rapture of an inspiration.
> O then if in my lagging lines you miss
> The roll, the rise, the carol, the creation,
> My winter world, that scarcely breathes that bliss
> Now, yields you, with some sighs, our explanation.

I think it worth remarking by the way that, if we look at Bridges' note on the sonnet we find this: 'In line 6 the word "moulds" was substituted by me for "combs" of original, when the sonnet was published by Miles; and I leave it, having no doubt that G.M.H. would have made some such alteration'. Bridges had no doubt – and Hopkins, who, though genuinely modest, was not recessive, wasn't there to resist, so 'moulds', though I didn't read it, stands as Hopkins's. We have here that complacent confidence characteristic of Bridges which completed the priest-poet's isolation – for I sense that Hopkins, though affectionately grateful, felt that Dixon's encouragement came from too kind a critic. The note exposes the confidence as invincible obtuseness: no one capable of perceiving Hopkins's genius could have supposed that he would have accepted Bridges' gift of 'moulds', a worse than inert word. It is worse than inert, because it blandly and blindly quarrels with the insistent imagery of gestation. The mother doesn't 'mould' the embryo. It may be that 'combs' is an audacity, but with the aid of the word 'proleptic' we might find it sufferable. For 'mould' I can see no defence. To thrust it into a context in which Hopkins has insisted so vividly that the rightness, the inevitability, of a poem is a matter of the poet's having, in the pursuit of his art, been strenuously faithful to a conception, a creative nucleus, that must be allowed to determine the development from within is to betray an extreme insensitiveness.

For as a poet too Hopkins felt – in the artist's way – that he 'didn't belong to himself': he would have understood Daniel Doyce's attitude. But, to come back to the (unless by Bridges) unquestionable *donnée*, his major, his compelling vocation was elsewhere. To justify creatively the interest he took in the expressive potentialities of the English language he would have had to devote to poetry immensely more of his life than he had to spare. As his letters show, he was superlatively intelligent and had a great capacity for experience and sympathetic human observation. Yet, gifted as he was for self-knowledge, there is a limitation in himself as poet that he unconsciously exposes – the unconsciousness being the significance – in these lines of the sonnet:

> I want the one rapture of an inspiration.
> O then if in my lagging lines you miss
> The roll, the rise, the carol, the creation...

There is, I think, a significant illusion here: the conception of poetry inspiring this is not a conception of the kind of poetry that would have made him the major poet he might have been had his vital economy left more to that side of him. 'The role, the rise, the carol' – the impulse that, innocently enough, produces that emphasis in such a context, it seems obvious to me, is to be explained by the effort and drag of his actual life. Hopkins, the realized major poet, could have developed the resources he perceived and loved in the English language only in a poetry adequate to the capacity for human experience that impresses and engages us so in the letters. His illusion is evidence of the completeness of his commitment to his religious vocation – of the unalterably marginal status (recognized as such by him) of poetry in his life; so little has he, from his inner fastness, turned his mind on what would be the actualities of becoming a major poet (for he has certainly no yearning to be a minor one) that he can refer to the creative career he has renounced in terms of 'the roll, the rise, the carol'.

I haven't forgotten the 'terrible sonnets', which I admire. They lead me to throw out some comparative observations about the two religious poets who were for me, in an important way, contemporary – Hopkins and Eliot. The comparative manoeuvre will, I hope, enable me to circumvent the delicacy that tends to inhibit me when it's a question of recognizing how it was that Hopkins's kind of complete religious conviction could hardly nourish a major poet's creativity. For I think that the diagnostic intention of the passage of Murry's I read out is in essence sound; it's the tone, the insouciance, of 'His "avant toute chose", whirling in a spiritual vacuum' I don't like. Let me say at once that in both poets one can't but be intensely conscious of the man, and, while I judge Eliot to be very much the greater poet, it's for Hopkins, man and personality, I feel respect, admiration, and affection.

I will find a licence for my remarks by attaching them to a comparative point that regards technique (or poetic). To that end, let me read one of the 'terrible sonnets':

> I wake and feel the fell of dark, not day.
> What hours, O what black hoürs we have spent
> This night! what sights you, heart, saw; ways you went!
> And more must, in yet longer light's delay.
>   With witness I speak this. But where I say
> Hours I mean years, mean life. And my lament
> Is cries countless, cries like dead letters sent
> To dearest him that lives alas! away.
>
> I am gall, I am heartburn. God's most deep decree
> Bitter would have me taste: my taste was me;
> Bones built in me, flesh filled, blood brimmed the curse.
>   Selfyeast of spirit a dull dough sours. I see
> The lost are like this, and their scourge to be
> As I am mine, their sweating selves; but worse.

That should bring home to everyone how convincingly the major poet can manifest himself. I needn't comment in detail on how immensely, though both poems sign themselves Hopkins, the late inwardly personal sonnet differs from 'The Windhover' (which, let me say, I have never found successful). The point I have to make about the sonnet is that it brings out so clearly the force of

Hopkins's contention that what to Bridges are his oddities, his audacities, and his offences against 'literary decorum' become natural and acceptable when one refers them to the spirit of living spoken English.

What, however, comparison with Eliot does is to make us note as a significant fact that there is one important power inherent in speech, and to be found in (say) Shakespearian poetry, which makes its essential appeal to the intelligent attentive ear, that can't be said to characterize even Hopkins's best work: delicate command of shifting tone, tempo and movement. To make quite plain what I mean I will remind you of a poem I have discussed elsewhere – the first poem in *Ash-Wednesday*; and I will repeat, in immediately appropriate form, certain of the observations I have made before. Because this poetry is irresistibly canorous and because the presence in it of liturgical and biblical suggestion and reminiscence is so potent, people – without telling themselves so – are apt to read it as if it were hypnoidal, and in this way to reinforce a conventional preconception of its significance. Actually it demands a more than ordinary attention of the delicately alert thinking mind: apprehension of the significance depends on sensitive response to the tone, which shifts subtly, the poet's command of tone being conditioned by the fact that the prevailing spirit of this complex and varying style is the spirit of spoken English. Only by appealing subtly as well as potently to the reader's sense of how things go naturally could a poet exercise such command.

I will now read out the first paragraph of *Ash-Wednesday*, and make my brief comments after doing so:

> Because I do not hope to turn again
> Because I do not hope
> Because I do not hope to turn
> Desiring this man's gift and that man's scope
> I no longer strive to strive towards such things
> (Why should the agèd eagle stretch its wings?)
> Why should I mourn
> The vanished power of the usual reign?

You will have noticed that the fourth line is, but for the 'gift' substituted for 'art', a quotation from one of the best-known Shakespeare sonnets:

> Desiring this man's art and that man's scope.

'Scope' rimes with 'hope', the repeated word that closes the repeated phrase of Eliot's first three lines. Recognizing that the line is quoted, the reader shouldn't need reminding that the mood, though depressed, of Shakespeare's sonnet is very different from the mood of Eliot's poem. I've found that he does often need telling that the point of the quoting lies in that, so that the line must, as it were, be spoken in inverted commas. In order that you may recall Shakespeare's mood vividly, let me give you a longer quotation from the sonnet:

> When in disgrace with fortune and men's eyes,
> I all alone beweep my outcast state,
> And trouble deaf heaven with my bootless cries,
> And look upon myself, and curse my fate,
> Wishing me like to one more rich in hope,
> Featured like him, like him with friends possest,
> Desiring this man's art, and that man's scope,
> With what I most enjoy contented least.

That defines a kind of hoping that for Eliot is hopelessly remote: 'The Hollow Men' is in the background of Eliot's poetry. His state – the inertness – in the poem I've just read the opening of is given in this from 'East Coker':

> I said to my soul, be still, and wait without hope,
> For hope would be hope for the wrong thing; wait
> > without love...

It isn't now the desperate paralysis of 'The Hollow Men'; he finds in himself an *ahnung*, or a nisus, which he knows he mustn't try to will into affirmation, but... – the wonder of the poetry is the way it conveys in its concreteness that 'but', or the 'but' together with the abstention in which it is an element.

To come back to *Ash-Wednesday*, there is another line in that paragraph requiring that we should register in rendering it a delicate effect of irony – the parenthesis:

> (Why should the aged eagle stretch its wings?).

There may be a hubris of humility, and this is Eliot's prophylactic recognition of that truth.

I will read the whole paragraph again:

> Because I do not hope to turn again
> Because I do not hope

Because I do not hope to turn
Desiring this man's gift and that man's scope
I no longer strive to strive towards such things
(Why should the agèd eagle stretch its wings?)
Why should I mourn
The vanished power of the usual reign?

Eliot no longer hopes to hope again. You mustn't however take that – you mustn't take any proposition in the poem – as carrying in itself a value you can rest on. Co-present in the total context are propositions, suggestions and implications that qualify and contradict. But I mustn't now go into the quasi-musical structure even of this one poem of *Ash-Wednesday*. I've said enough, I think, to make plain the essential nature of the contrast between Hopkins and Eliot as religious poets. Eliot's concern with technique, his whole poetic from *Ash-Wednesday* to 'Little Gidding', his astonishingly diverse and supple command of *procédé*, serves his desperate need to foster in himself a positive nisus in a pertinacious exploration of what it may mean or imply, while holding scrupulously back from unequivocal affirmation.

I say 'from *Ash-Wednesday* to "Little Gidding"' – in the latter, the concluding 'quartet' of the four, he has moved at last into a sustained and final affirmation, but it is here that my 'yes, but' – the form my response in general has taken – becomes an adverse judgement: it seems to me that here his heroic wrestling to discover what he is and what and how he believes has lapsed into self-deception. It is not conscious insincerity; that isn't the dangerous kind. But he has yielded to the insidious temptation his inner disunity exposes him to: he takes for the achieved clear-eyed humility of complete and sure self-knowledge what is not that. 'To be redeemed from fire by fire' – there is the possibility of equivocation there; and it is a possibility the treacherous weakness in Eliot takes advantage of.

If I hadn't set forth in carefully articulated criticism the justifying grounds, as I see them, for saying this I should not have said it now, and I adduce Eliot's case as a way of making with delicacy and force an important point about Hopkins. If Eliot's creative potentiality could find in preoccupations that were explicitly religious the fruitful challenge to the development of an astonishingly original and sophisticated poetic that success compels us to see as inevitable and right, it was because his desperate need was, for him, at the same time, the evasiveness – a near-impossibility – of the affirmation towards which it impelled him. Hopkins presents an antithesis to this plight – the plight that gave Eliot's creative gift the 'resistance' (Murry calls it, in pointing to the lack of such in Hopkins's case) that evoked that paradoxical great poetry – and it is in a unique way, and essentially, paradoxical. Hopkins's poetry presents no paradox. Who would suggest that even in the 'terrible sonnets' the anguish is in any way akin to that of 'The Hollow Men' – insufferable emptiness and the impossibility of any kind of affirmation? Hopkins, in a wholly unpejorative sense, was simple. There is nothing equivocal in his verse, and in the letters we see the simplicity as that of a man of high intelligence, fine human perception, irresistible charm and complete integrity.

HARDY THE POET

When *The Southern Review* honoured me with the invitation to contribute to this centennial issue I replied with the warning that I didn't share the generally accepted estimate of Hardy. I think, in fact, that it greatly overexalts him. I used once to say that I shouldn't have known he was a great novelist if I hadn't been told. After sufficiently dogged attempts to arrive at a less dissident valuation I am now convinced that he is not one. It will be interesting to see what persuasive new light will be thrown on the novels in this issue of *The Southern Review* – the desire not to stand in the way of possible new light ought, perhaps, to have made me resist the repeated invitation to write on the poetry. I should, at any rate, like to see what there is to be said about it by a critic who rates Hardy the poet higher than I do.

However, I must not pretend to be more modest than I am. And, moreover, the justice that I am convinced ought to be done is not merely a matter of deprivation: Hardy stands to gain by it – if, that is, I am right in my belief that his acceptance as a poet is almost wholly conventional. For though I shouldn't think of calling Hardy a great poet, I do believe that he wrote a certain amount of major poetry. And this major poetry is hardly ever represented in the anthologies that bring him in. It is a very small amount, though he wrote a great deal of verse: there are nine hundred and fifty pages in the collected volume, and to go through them again, as I did before writing this note, was to be, if possible, still more convinced of the need for a strictly discriminating justice. The judicious admirer wishing to ensure proper attention for Hardy would select a very small proportion indeed of that mass.

The best things are lost in it, and prolonged exploration is discouraging and blunting. Never did a writer of good poems show less promise and distinction in the common run of his work. It might have been produced by the 'Poet's Corner' Laureate of a Victorian country newspaper. One must add at once, however, that this Laureate would have been decidedly a character – a 'crusted character', in Hardyesque phrase. In saying that his characteristic verse has no distinction one is not intending to deny that it is characteristic: it is positively, even aggressively, so. Lack of distinction in Hardy becomes a positive quality. If one says that he seems to have no sensitiveness for words, one recognizes at the same time that he has made a style out of stylelessness. There is something extremely personal about the gauche unshrinking mismarriages – group-mismarriages – of his diction, in which, with naïf aplomb, he takes as they come the romantic-poetical, the prosaic banal, the stilted literary, the colloquial, the archaistic, the erudite, the technical, the dialect word, the brand-new Hardy coinage.

> Her death-rumour smartly relifted
>   To full apogee.

> Her bloom and bonhomie...

> Who now recalls those crowded rooms
>   Of old yclept 'The Argyle',
> Where to the deep Drum-polka's booms
>   We hopped in standard style?

> Your form has never darked its door,
> Nor have your faultless feet once thrown
> A pensive pit-pat on its floors.

> O they were speechful faces, gazing insistent,
>   Some as with smiles,
> Some as with slow-born tears that brinily trundled
>   Over the wrecked
> Cheeks that were fair in their flush-time, ash now with anguish,
>   Harrowed by wiles.

> 'I once had a friend – a Love, if you will –
> Whose wife forsook him, and sank until
>   She was made a thrall
> In a prison-cell for a deed of ill....'
> 'So my lady, you raise the veil by degrees....
> I owe this last is enough to freeze

The warmest wight!
Now hear the other side, if you please...'

These are representative; they give a fair idea of what one may expect to find at any opening of the collected Hardy. They scarcely, however, suggest how the assertive oddity of the Character can begin to look like the strength of a poet. He who handles words in this way, it might reasonably be concluded on such evidence (which could be multiplied indefinitely), couldn't possibly be a distinguished writer of any kind. Nevertheless, it is an unusually dull patch when half-a-dozen pages don't yield instances in which the same assertively characteristic hand achieves a decided expressive strength or vivacity.

To take what offers at a random turning-over of the pages, here is a stanza from a Swinburnian elegy on Swinburne (a typically innocent undertaking):

> – It was as though a garland of red roses
> Had fallen about the hood of some smug nun
> When irresponsibly dropped as from the sun,
> In fulth of numbers freaked with musical closes,
> Upon Victoria's formal middle time
> His leaves of rhythm and rhyme.

The odd prosaic qualifying of the Swinburnian afflatus in this passage strikes the reader, no doubt, as more characteristic than promising, yet the incongruously sensible prose directness of the 'smug nun' is closely related to equally characteristic effects elsewhere that are distinctly poetic. There are those fresh, sharply registered perceptions – direct perceptions of one who lives at first hand in a real world:

> Rain on the windows, creaking doors,
> With blasts that besom the green...

> Planing up shavings of crystal spray
> A moor-hen darted out
> From the bank thereabout,
> And through the stream-shine ripped his way...

> The rain imprinted the step's wet shine
> With target-circles that quivered and crossed
> As I was leaving this porch of mine...

– Not very impressive in themselves as quoted, perhaps; but they come pretty frequently, and are associated with related, but less quotable effects. And again and again we have instances of the characteristic diction in which something has happened to the familiar medley of ingredients, so that we can no longer call it insensitive or gauche; for example:

'Gone', I call them, gone for good, that group of local hearts and heads;
  Yet at mothy curfew-tide,
And at midnight when the noon-heat breathes it back from walls and leads,
They've a way of whispering to me – fellow-wight who yet abide –
  In the muted, measured note
Of a ripple under archways, or a lone cave's stillicide...

The whole poem from which this comes, 'Friends Beyond', is a success, and a representative one: there is a small handful that might fairly be classed with it, of which 'Julie Jane' is perhaps the most notable. They relate obviously to the novels, dealing with that rustic world of the novelist's most felicitous preoccupation, and, usually, with the passage of time. Along with them might be placed another handful of poems of a personal note, brooding and reminiscent:

I leant upon a coppice gate
  When Frost was spectre-gray,
And Winter's dregs made desolate
  The weakening eye of day.
The tangled bine-stems scored the sky
  Like strings of broken lyres,
And all mankind that haunted nigh
  Had sought their household fires.

– This is 'The Darkling Thrush'. 'Shut Out That Moon' begins:

Close up the casement, draw the blind,
  Shut out that stealing moon,
She wears too much the guise she wore
  Before our lutes were strewn
With years-deep dust, and names we read
  On a white stone were hewn.

These are the opening stanzas of 'The Night of the Dance':

The cold moon hangs to the sky by its horn,
  And centres its gaze on me;
The stars, like eyes in reverie,
Their westering as for a while forborne,
  Quiz downward curiously.

Old Robert draws the backbrand in,
The green logs steam and spit;
The half-awakened sparrows flit
From the riddled thatch; and owls begin
To whoo from the gable-slit.

Of things of these kinds one might find, perhaps, twenty or thirty pages deserving to be handed down; poems that present in quintessential form what is most living in the novels. But they would not of themselves have won for Hardy the repute of major poet. He owes this largely, no doubt, to his preoccupation with life's ironies and to his talk about the Immanent Will – to all those elements in his work which might encourage a belief that it conveys an impressive underlying metaphysic. But any real claim he may have to major status rests upon half-a-dozen poems alone: 'Neutral Tones', 'A Broken Appointment', 'The Self-Unseeing', 'The Voice', 'After a Journey', 'During Wind and Rain'.

There may be another one or two hidden in the collected volume: if so, in the exploration of those nine hundred and fifty pages my jaded eye has again and again rested on them without seeing. All half-dozen might, like the second group referred to above, be described as personal, brooding and reminiscent, but they are much more intense. They are all records of poignant particular memories – memories poignant in themselves or poignant by reason of the subsequent work of time. The quality of these poems is obvious, and I don't think there is much that needs saying about them. On 'A Broken Appointment' there is a brief commentary in Middleton Murry's *Problem of Style*, a book that most readers of this note will, I suppose, have read. I myself have discussed briefly the way in which in 'The Voice' Hardy's characteristic stiff provincial oddity is transmuted into something neither stiff nor odd. Since my book will have been read by few of my present readers, I may perhaps repeat the substance of that commentary here. This is the poem:

Woman much missed, how you call to me, call to me,
Saying that now you are not as you were
When you had changed from the one who was all to me,
But as at first, when our day was fair.

Can it be you that I hear? Let me view you, then,
Standing as when I drew near to the town
Where you would wait for me: yes, as I knew you then,

Even to the original air-blue gown!

Or is it only the breeze, in its listlessness
Travelling across the wet mead to me here,
You being ever dissolved to existlessness,
Heard no more again far or near?

 Thus I; faltering forward,
 Leaves around me falling,
Wind oozing thin through the thorn from norward,
 And the woman calling.

The first stanza might seem to threaten one of those crude popular lilts which Hardy is so fond of ('Any little old song will do'). Actually, the bare prosaic stating manner, which elsewhere would have been Hardy's characteristic gaucherie, turns the lilt into a subtle movement. This simplicity of bare statement, calling the maximum of attention to the sense, has by the end of the second stanza eliminated the sing-song from the rhythm; the shift of stress on the rhyme ('view you then,' 'knew you thén') has banished all danger of jingle. In the third stanza we have one of those Hardy coinages, 'existlessness'. In itself it might seem a typically awkward eccentricity, yet as it comes here it is peculiarly right, conveying vacancy in the sough of the breeze. Later Hardy changed it for 'wan wistlessness', which is now current as the final reading – he was not, one feels, an artist whose successes were associated with a refined critical consciousness. Yet it is an exquisite sureness of touch – hardly suggesting a naïf artist – that is manifested in the changed movement of the last stanza, with its effect as of a subsiding into the recognition of utter loss.

For a further illustration of the way in which in these poems the Hardy characteristics become poetic virtues the closing stanza of 'After a Journey' may be quoted:

 Ignorant of what there is flitting here to see,
  The waked birds preen and the seals flop lazily;
 Soon you will have, Dear, to vanish from me,
  For the stars close their shutters and the dawn whitens hazily.
 Trust me, I mind not, though Life lours,
  The bringing me here; nay, bring me here again!
   I am just the same as when
  Our days were a joy, and our paths through flowers.

The main reason for choosing this stanza lies in those last two lines.

For we come now to the question, what is meant by saying that in these poems Hardy is a major poet. Those lines –

> I am just the same as when
> Our days were a joy, and our paths through flowers

– perhaps help one to answer. Middleton Murry's answer, to be found in *Aspects of Literature* (reprinted reviews from *The Athenaeum* of twenty years back – those of Hardy had considerable influence), seems to me altogether too portentous.

Therefore we turn – some by instinct and some by deliberate choice – to the greatest; therefore we deliberately set Mr Hardy among these. What they have, he has, and has in their degree – a plenary vision of life. He is the master of the fundamental theme; it enters into, echoes in, modulates and modifies all his particular emotions, and the individual poems of which they are the substance. Each work of his is a fragment of a whole – not a detached and arbitrarily severed fragment, but a unity which implies, calls for and in a profound sense creates a vaster and completely comprehensive whole. His reaction to an episode has behind and within it a reaction to the universe. An overwhelming endorsement descends upon his words: he traces them with a pencil, and straightway they are graven in stone...

I see no need to invoke any 'comprehensive whole' of experience to explain the effect of 'overwhelming endorsement'. Hardy is notable for limitation rather than breadth. The effect is rather to be explained by the tenacious simplicity of character that enables him to say, 'I am just the same'. His preoccupation with time brings with it no sense of unreality; *panta rhei*, but not inside Thomas Hardy. What he valued forty years back was real and what he thought it was, and the valuing persists unchanged. In spite of time, the love and the loved object, equally real, are still present to him, and the recognition of loss is correspondingly complete and poignant. So it is that Hardy is able to render with such weight a central element in human experience. Moreover, the single-minded integrity of his preoccupation with a real world and a real past, the intentness of his focus upon particular facts and situations, gives his poetry the solidest kind of emotional substance. There is no emotionality. The emotion seems to inhere in the reality recognized and grasped. The effect is of a kind we call major in contrast with the specifically minor-poetical of 'Tears, idle tears' or 'Break, break, break', where the emotion is an intoxication and the poignancy a luxury. I don't think there is much more that need be said about Hardy's major status.

In any case, it is decidedly not as a philosophic poet that we grant it him. In his pessimistic ruminations he is very much himself, but he is not a poet. Not that his originality doesn't manifest itself in some impressive stylistic inventions, such as

> ... mindsight memory-laden,

and local effects, such as

> Souls have grown seers, and thought outbrings
> The mournful manysidedness of things. ...

But these are not representative of total effects; it is an uninspired and monotonous oddity that prevails for the most part in these generally-reflective compositions. As for the 'Life's Little Ironies' and the 'Satires of Circumstance', those pessimistic little anecdotes devised to enforce the Hardy *Weltanschauung* and illustrate the malice of Nescience, they are, though they again carry self-parody to unplausible lengths and abound in unintended risibilities, too monotonous in their *parti pris* to be read in bulk with anything but boredom.

An intense particular memory in control, that is the essential condition for one of Hardy's major successes. Even an obviously strong impulse from within, expressing a radical mood but lacking that kind of intensity, doesn't suffice for the fusing process of complete creation. The following, for instance, is representative of perhaps a dozen or a score of pieces that might be found for inclusion in the ideal 'Selected Hardy', but which are not altogether satisfactory poems:

> The day is turning ghost,
> And scuttles from the kalendar in fits and furtively,
> To join the anonymous host
> Of those that throng oblivion; ceding his place, maybe,
> To one of like degree.
>
> I part the fire-gnawed logs,
> Rake forth the embers, spoil the busy flames, and lay the ends
> Upon the shining dogs;
> Further and further from the nooks the twilight's stride extends,
> And beamless black impends.
>
> Nothing of tiniest worth
> Have I wrought, pondered, planned; no one thing asking blame or praise,

Since the pale corpse-like birth
Of this diurnal unit, bearing blanks in all its rays –
   Dullest of dull-hued Days!

   Wanly upon the panes
The rain slides, as have slid since morn my colourless thoughts; and yet
   Here, while Day's presence wanes,
And over him the sepulchre-lid is slowly lowered and set,
   He wakens my regret.

   Regret – though nothing dear
That I wot of, was toward in the wide world at his prime,
   Or bloomed elsewhere than here,
To die with his decease, and leave a memory sweet, sublime,
   Or mark him out in Time....

   – Yet, maybe, in some soul,
In some spot undiscerned on sea or land, some impulse rose,
   Or some intent upstole
Of that enkindling ardency from whose maturer glows
   The world's amendment flows;

   But which, benumbed at birth
By momentary chance or wile, has missed its hope to be
   Embodied on the earth;
And undervoicings of this loss to man's futurity
   May wake regret in me.
                    ('A Commonplace Day')

   This poem needs no long commentary. As the product of a genuinely individual sensibility it has a certain obvious impressiveness. No one but Hardy could have written it, and the Hardy who wrote it must be allowed to have shown a poet's originality of expression. Yet the touch, clearly, is far from perfect. Among other things, there is a certain strength that one feels to be of a wrong kind. For instance, one stops to question 'scuttles' in the second line. In conjunction with 'in fits and furtively' it suggests a spider, a beetle, or a rat, but hardly a ghost, or the process of 'turning ghost'. The effect is boldly idiosyncratic, but one's feeling that there has been something excessive, an unjustifiable violence, gets confirmation when, in the second stanza, 'the twilight's stride extends'. This produces a slow-motion effect that contrasts, in grotesque caricature, with the speed-up of 'scuttles' (the foot advances remorselessly to crush the day that scuttles to avoid it). That some touch of the grotesque was no doubt intended cannot justify the violence of what we actually get: this quarrels with the 'commonplace', the dreary ordinariness, well suggested in other parts of the poem, and in the title, as the main intention. Even readers who cannot be sure whether they agree with this criticism will hardly dispute that the 'Day's presence wanes' of the fourth stanza constitutes a damaging implicit commentary on 'scuttles'.

> Here, while Day's presence wanes,
> And over him the sepulchre-lid is slowly lowered and set...

– The boldness of the imagery of that last-quoted line, on the other hand, will probably be pronounced by most readers to justify itself. The whole stanza, in fact, like the one before (which takes no such risk) is successful. But the generally-reflective rest of the poem is poor stuff, though the final two lines might have been the close of something better.

If this account of Hardy is just, how did so gross an overestimate gain currency? I think that Middleton Murry's advocacy at a peculiarly favourable moment explains a good deal. Murry, immediately after the last war, as editor of *The Athenaeum* and then literary editor of *The Nation and Athenaeum*, had great influence, and justly: there is no comparable force in English critical journalism today (on the literary side *The New Stateman*, which absorbed *The Nation and Athenaeum*, is negligible and the group, largely Etonian, that controls most of the higher reviewing certainly doesn't owe its prerogatives to any critical distinction it commands). On the other hand, the prospect in contemporary poetry was mainly vacancy: while no intelligent observer could any longer suppose that the still continuing Georgian movement was a stir and promise of life, Eliot had not yet arrived as a major presence; so that Murry's projection of Hardy, helped by the dissent of the 'traditionalists', was readily seen by the enlightened and advanced as a solidly massive figure. Hardy's pessimism was, of course, congenial to the prevailing mood of the Chekhov period (Murry's Chekhov again).

Evidence corroborative of this account may be adduced from the Cambridge of those years: I remember that I. A. Richards, avowedly taking the cue from Murry (see *Science and Poetry*), was running Hardy as representative of the contemporary sense of 'the human situation' (Murry's phrase was 'the modern consciousness'), register of a specifically modern recognition of the 'neutralization of Nature' effected by Science, and type Major Poet.

At a lower academic level, too, there was – and is – much to be said for Hardy: there is so much to be said about him ('Victorian pessimism', 'Hardy's philosophy', his 'debt to Schopenhauer' or otherwise, and so on). And once a figure is established as Hardy was in the nineteen-twenties it has a fair chance of keeping its place for good. Some scores of pages of Hardy's poems were set for special study for the English Tripos at Cambridge in the subsequent decade; they included only one of the major poems. And a thoughtful teacher warns his pupils that if a Hardy poem appears on an examination paper for appraisal they must assume that it is there for 'appreciation' in the vulgar sense.

It is pleasant to be able to add as a concluding note that the *Chosen Poems* in the Macmillan *Golden Treasuries* series is, though much too large, a good selection, in so far as it contains all the major poems and, I think, all the others that a strictly judicious advocate of Hardy's claims would select.

JAMES AS CRITIC

The effect, if not the prime office, of criticism is to make our absorption and our enjoyment of the things that feed the mind as aware of itself as possible, since that awareness quickens the mental demand, which thus in turn wanders further and further for pasture. This action on the part of the mind practically amounts to a reaching out for the reasons of its interests, as only by its so ascertaining them can the interest grow more various. This is the very education of our imaginative life; and thanks to it the general question of how to refine, and of why certain things refine more and most, on that happy consciousness, becomes for us of the last importance. Then we cease to be only instinctive and at the mercy of chance, feeling that we can ourselves take a hand in our satisfaction and provide for it, making ourselves safe against dearth, and through the door opened by that perception criticism enters, if we but give it time, as a flood, the great flood of awareness; so maintaining its high tide unless through some lapse of our sense for it, some flat reversion to instinct alone, we block up the ingress and sit in stale and shrinking waters.

Henry James: 'The New Novel, 1914'

In every great novel, who is the hero all the time? Not any of the characters, but some unnamed and nameless flame behind them all.

D. H. Lawrence: 'The Novel', *Reflections on the Death of a Porcupine, and Other Essays*

Many of the books which now crowd the world, may be justly suspected to be written for the sake of some invisible order of beings, for surely they are of no use to any of the corporeal inhabitants of the world. Of the productions of the last bounteous year, how many can be said to serve any purpose of use or pleasure? The only end of writing is to enable the readers better to enjoy life, or better to endure it.

Samuel Johnson: Review of *A Free Enquiry into the Nature and Origin of Evil*

Henry James the critic has in recent years attained to something of classical standing. He even figures academically as prescribed reading for students of 'English' who are to take papers on Literary Criticism. It doesn't of course follow that this acceptance carries with it any just recognition of his strength and his limitations – of the qualities that make him worth study. In fact, there is an irony attending his acceptance as a distinguished critic that corresponds to the irony attending his recognized status among the great novelists. It is a characteristic of the age when 'English' has conquered Classics in the field of humane education, and an industry of specialized addiction on the part of academics to this and that modern author is acquiring an American aspect and scale in our universities, that the established 'appreciation' of the favoured authors should not uncommonly be conventional – flagrantly conventional, and not at all conducive to optimism in genuine admirers of the given author.

Thus, when there is question of James as critic, it is generally assumed that the Prefaces give us him at his most impressive and valuable, and that in the volume of the collected Prefaces we have a major critical classic. Yet few have read any considerable proportion of that volume, and very few indeed of those who have made pertinacious attempts to read it have brought much of value away. For the fact is, not only that it requires a great effort, but that the effort is not repaying. Those academics who take seriously the suggestion that it is the 'novelist's *vade-mecum*'* will indeed be drawing from it a new academicism, for that is what the attempt to establish a general interest and validity in it must yield. And one can only deplore any offer to deaden the undergraduate reading English with such a misdirection and such a *corvée*.

The preface the undergraduate might profitably be told to read, along with the novel itself, that to *Roderick Hudson*, is not commonly singled out for attention. Its examination of that strikingly promising early work is immediately intelligible and critically enlightening. The main point it makes explains – with a general critical profit for the reading of James – why the obvious weaknesses of the novel, the impossibility of making the postulated artistic genius anything but a postulate and the too rapid disintegrative effect on Roderick of the *femme fatale*, don't prevent *Roderick Hudson*'s being a distinguished success. 'The centre of

* Henry James: Letters to W. D. Howells, 17 August, 1908.

interest throughout *Roderick*,' James tells us, 'is in Rowland Mallet's consciousness, and the drama is the very drama of that consciousness.' And we see how the novel does in fact justify that account. But the Prefaces in general belong essentially to that phase of the late James in which they were written. One must not expect to find out from James's discussion of it how one is to take an example of his more difficult and problematic works. Those who assume naïvely that they *are* getting light (and it seems to be a not uncommon illusion) are likely to come away with some notable misconception. Thus, because of such a misadventure on the part of an influential commentator,* there has been a notion current that *The Awkward Age* is a comedy, though anyone who reads comprehendingly what is there (and the work is one of those in which the difficulty of the late James is triumphantly vindicated) sees that – if we are to talk in these terms – it is a tragedy. James's analytic discussion serves a special technical preoccupation, one that had for him an absorbing intensity characteristic of that late phase (and consider the given retrospective occasion!); and the resultant abstraction, with its inadvertent emphasis, suggests the false account of the novel that has been taken up (people don't expect to understand a late work of James unless they know beforehand on authority what they are to find). Of course, readers of the novelist who study him closely because of a genuine response to what he has written may very well find some critical interest in the Prefaces. What should certainly be found is reason for reflecting on the way in which, in the late James, what began as a short story or *nouvelle* will end as a two-volume novel.

If the collection of the Prefaces ought not to be prescribed as a critical classic, James nevertheless has his place among the classical critics. Like all great original artists, he was distinguished by critical intelligence where his art was in question. Coming when he did, and writing for an English-speaking public, he was inevitably concerned to insist that the novelist's art was, as seriously as any, an *art*. Not that its standing as such was not, in one sense – the most important, firmly established: there had been Jane Austen, Dickens, Hawthorne, Charlotte Brontë, and George Eliot. What James, of course, had to contend for was a general full recognition among the educated that creative talent – creative genius – was at least as likely to go into the novel as into any mode of art, and that for the critic

* Percy Lubbock: *The Craft of Fiction*, p. 193.

and the 'educated' reader to be innocent of their corresponding obligation was ignoble. The obligation was to be intelligent and to know that a novel might challenge all the intelligence and the most responsible judgement one could command. George Eliot had not waited to be assured that there would be a community capable of a perceptive response to the inventions of her genius, but towards the successors of George Eliot the public had none the less a duty. As James himself had, as time went on, his own poignant reason for knowing, the sense an artist has, or has not, that he may count on getting recognition from an intelligent public matters immensely to him – matters to him as an artist and a creative power.

James's distinctive position in criticism is given by these considerations: he, more than anyone else, was George Eliot's successor; he was an intimate of the Parisian literary world before he decided that he was irretrievably an Anglo-Saxon and must settle in England; the clear unignorable challenge for the novelist as artist, the vindicator of the artistic conscience in the art of fiction, was for him, inevitably, Flaubert, yet his decision that he was an 'Anglo-Saxon' was that which he rested in. He knew France, creative France, intimately and affectionately: his Anglo-Saxonism was fully conscious and fully informed: it cannot be charged with provincialism. The representative document is his appraisal of Flaubert; sympathetic, grateful, admiring, full of piety, but inexorable in its limiting judgement. This indeed is a classical piece of criticism, one that can be prescribed for the close attention of the literary student. What we have here, in the attack, the close relevance, the essential economy, the combined trenchancy and suppleness, the sensitiveness and the penetration, is the critical intelligence of the creative writer, the practising novelist – an intelligence trained and refined in the *atelier*; but there is nothing technical or esoteric about the critique. All that could propose itself to the student as something to be carried away for his own use is what can be derived from an example of convincingly relevant intelligence: he can take the incitement to try and be himself as intelligent. But the way in which James arrives at and makes his major value-judgement – the limiting or reluctantly qualifying judgement that is the upshot of his critique – has a general and central significance for criticism, a clear general bearing.

What we come to here is the basic matter of criticism that lies at the bottom of James's handling of the theme of 'morality'. The point of putting the word in inverted commas is that it covers more than one issue, and, even in what may be called *loci classici* for the discussion of 'art and morality', often, within one text, has a shifting force. It has more than one force, and (the student will perceive) some subtle transitions, in James's own reflections for which it provides the focus. In the commentary on Besant he is merely, or mainly, concerned to dismiss the idea that the novelist should be required to limit himself by the prohibitions and decorums of prudery, propriety and social convention. That his Anglo-Saxonism doesn't entail any lack of plainness, directness or completeness in this dismissal is put beyond question in his critique of Maupassant. But he has a criticism to make of this artist for whose un-Anglo-Saxon single-mindedness of devotion to art he is expressing an intense admiration. It is that Maupassant, militantly anti-sentimental vindicator of the right (or duty) of the novelist to render the whole of life as it presents itself to him, seems unaware of the part the moral sense actually plays in life. With the easy directness of a great Victorian Anglo-Saxon, James permits himself the gloss that Maupassant never, in his score of volumes, presents a gentleman.

But what basic to criticism is at issue under 'art and morality' doesn't get fairly suggested – or not suggested with any felicity – by the question, however much point it may have in the given context, as to whether the novelist's presentment of life allows adequately for the part we know to be played in life by the 'moral sense'. James, of course, was well aware of this. The important thing about his criticism as he deals with Maupassant is the way (it is at once firm, responsible and subtle) in which, defining his essential value-judgements – or, to put it in other terms, intimating as a literary critic his sense of the human significance of Maupassant's art – he invokes 'life'.

He is insisting – and this, perhaps, is the important thing in the given context – that in respect of any art one takes seriously one *has* to make value-judgements, since a real response entails this; it entails forming an implicit critical sense of the human significance of the art in question, and the demand of intelligence is that one should bring one's sense to conscious definition. In Maupassant he was dealing with that reaction against 'bourgeois' moralism (think of the prosecution of *Madame Bovary*) which denied any possible relevance of moral judgement to art. This meant the exaltation of art into something absolute, a self-justifying end in itself: *l'art pour l'art.* We don't, when Aestheticism is in question, think first of Maupassant, who was not addicted to Beauty; but he was (as James observes) the disciple of Flaubert, and for him too art was an absolute or ultimate: it was art for art's sake. You could say no more of a work than: 'This is perfect; this is perfectly done.' The critic could do no more than, within its own terms, point out the elements and structure of its perfection. It was irrelevant, supererogatory and presumptuous to ask questions about the value or significance (we need the words in association) of the perfectly done.

James discusses this implicit attitude of Maupassant. He points out, with his characteristic force of delicacy, that there is still the question of *interest*; the most resolute amoralism or anti-moralism doesn't eliminate that. He then asks of Maupassant: 'Is *this* all there is in life? Does life reduce to this? Has it no more than this in the way of interest to offer?' He brings home to his reader, that is, that there is no eliminating and no escaping the appeal to life, however much one may suppose oneself to believe in the ultimateness or self-sufficiency of art.

It doesn't take a great deal of reflection to establish that 'life' is a large word and doesn't admit of definition. But some of the most important words we have to use don't admit of definition. And this truth holds of literary criticism. Not only can we not, for instance, do without the word 'life'; any attempt to think out a major critical issue entails using positively the shifts in force the word is bound to be incurring as it feels its way on and out and in towards its fulfilment. And it would hardly be questioned that there is point in saying that a critic who would be intelligent about the novel must be intelligent about life: no discussion of the novel by any other kind of critic is worth attention.

When one remarks that the strength of James's criticism of the novel is his being himself a novelist one may complete the observation by noting how, in his own criticism, it is on the supreme need for the *novelist*, the novelist as artist, to be intelligent about life that the accent falls; always implicitly, explicitly in key places. There is nothing technical, it is worth repeating, in his examination of Flaubert, where, in criticism, we have a clear example of the consummate professional taking the challenge. And when he comes to the judgement that the masterpiece, *Madame Bovary*, is qualified by a default of intelligence in the master, the default of intelligence in the artist as artist *is* a default of intelligence about life. James, when he comes out with the explicit judgement, is considering in the first place Flaubert's heroine, Emma Bovary – 'Madame Bovary herself as a vessel of experience.* But the implicit effect of the whole approach is to bring the criticism against the Flaubertian exaltation of 'Art', for the mode and spirit of James's critique, with its essential appeal to life, implicitly challenges the contradiction represented by the Aesthetic way of exalting 'Art'. An intensity of addiction to an Art that is set over against life, an addiction that offers to manifest itself creatively in the rejection of life (subsumed under *la platitude bourgeoise*), must certainly be held to be a major default of intelligence. James doesn't actually say that, but his criticism, in its constant habit, conveys and enforces a refutation of Aestheticism as clear and basic as its dismissal of the opposite kind of fallacy. In many ways he expresses his charged sense that the creativity of art is the creativity of life – that the creative impulsion *is* life, and could be nothing else.

Addressing himself *ad hominem* to Maupassant, he points out that the cynic-sensualist's art is confined for its creative purposes to a sadly limited range of interests, since it leaves so much of life out. James's criticism, of course, is concerned for something more than range and variety: he can't conceive an artist, or (it follows) a critic, who is not concerned for significance. 'Significance', again, is a term that doesn't admit of close definition, and, again, the critic can't do without it. It points to the wholeness of a created work, to that which makes it one – to the principle of life that determines its growth and organization. Observations regarding significance are intimately bound up with judgements regarding 'value'; the two terms are in close attendance upon one another. Discussion of 'significance' entails in the most challenging way the anti-Aesthetic reference to life ('Art and Life' – we use the antithesis, knowing that we are not judging it to be meaningless, or anything but useful, when we remind ourselves that art is a manifestation of life or it is nothing). The creative writer's concern to render life *is* a concern for significance, a preoccupation with expressing his sense of what most matters. The creative drive in his art *is* a drive to clarify and convey his perception of relative importances. The work that commands the reader's most deeply engaged, the critic's most serious, attention asks at a deep level: 'What, at bottom, do men live *for*?' And in work that strikes us as great art we are aware of a potent normative

* From *Gustave Flaubert, 1902.*

suggestion: '*These* are the possibilities and inevitablenesses, and, in the face of them, *this* is the valid and the wise (or the sane) attitude.' Lawrence, asked, towards the end, about the creative impulsion in his own work, said: 'One writes out of one's moral sense; for the race, as it were.'*

'Moral' too is a difficult word and a necessary one. Lawrence's use of it here is special, but central and right. A great writer is a man impelled by a deep irresistible sense of responsibility, and he appeals to a deep sense of responsibility in us. A great work of art explores and evokes the grounds and sanctions of our most important choices, valuations and decisions — those decisions which are not acts of will, but are so important that they seem to make themselves rather than to be made by us. The tone (or *timbre*) of this kind of formulation is not, indeed, characteristic of James: for criticism, and statements of the grounds of criticism, in which (as in the utterance just quoted) the word moral has 'religious' in close attendance, the student will go to Lawrence.† But James in his way bears the same testimony, exemplifies the same truth. If not with the Laurentian astonishingness, the clairvoyant, deep-striking and wide-ranging genius, he is, as critic, finely and strongly central. For the student, his place in history adds to his value as that. His intelligence about the need of his time alerted and quickened by his Parisian initiation, he dealt firmly with Victorian moralism in the way the time — the state of British and American culture — required. On the other hand, strong in his un-British inwardness with France, he yielded no ground to the opposed fallacies of Aestheticism, which had so great an attraction for the would-be enlightened and unprovincial. He had achieved a centrality that made him strong to deal with all provincialisms. He expressed with a fine and irresistible sincerity his sense of Flaubert's place in the history of the novel, and of the indebtedness to Flaubert that should be felt by all practitioners. But, making his famous decision in favour of the country of George Eliot,‡ a decision that was a mature conscious realization of what for him was fact and necessity, he knew, while not the less

---

* Edward Nehls (ed.): *D. H. Lawrence, a Composite Biography*, Vol. 2, p. 414.

† The epigraph by Lawrence suggests how different his timbre is from James's.

‡ '...my last layers of resistance to a long-encroaching weariness and satiety with the French mind and its utterance has fallen from me like a garment. I have done with 'em, forever, and am turning English all over. I desire only to feed on English life and the contact of English minds.' Letter to William James, 29 July, 1876.

committed to go on developing his own post-Flaubertian conscience
of the *atelier*, that he belonged, not with Flaubert's associates and
disciples, but with George Eliot, Hawthorne, Dickens and Jane
Austen.*

That the sophisticated 'conscience of the *atelier*' had not the tendency
to make him less sensitively and supply responsive to great art in
the creation of which the artistic conscience engaged had been of a
different ethos from that characteristic of his own work – had been
(let us say) wholly English in genesis and habit – his 'Conversation'
on *Daniel Deronda* may serve as a demonstration. Even if one
registers a disagreement here or there, it is impossible to read this
critique, with its quick and witty sensitiveness of intelligence,
without some keen pleasure when one reflects that it was written as
a contemporary review. The conversation form, which lends itself to
the effect of ease and lightness and also permits a command of
varied tone, belongs to the critical method with which James
responds to the given challenge – one that he takes, it is clear, with a

---

* The 'post-Flaubertian' conscience of the *atelier* expresses itself in a way of talking
about 'form' and 'composition' that makes us a little uneasy sometimes – more than a
little when it goes with such a reference as we have here to Jane Austen: 'They all
represent the pursuit of a style, of the ideally right one for its relations, and would still
be interesting if the style had not been achieved. *Madame Bovary, Salammbô, Saint
Antoine, L'Education* are so written and so composed (though the last-named in a
minor degree) that the more we look at them the more we find in them, under this
head, a beauty of intention and of effect; the more they figure in the too often dreary
desert of fictional prose a class by themselves and a little living oasis. So far as that
desert is of the complexion of our own English speech it supplies with remarkable
rarity this particular source of refreshment. So strikingly is that the case, so scant for
the most part any dream of a scheme of beauty in these connections, that a critic
betrayed at artless moments into a plea for composition may find himself as blankly
met as if his plea were for trigonometry. He makes inevitably his reflections, which
are numerous enough; one of them being that if we turn our back so squarely, so
universally to this order of considerations it is because the novel is so preponderantly
cultivated among us by women, in other words by a sex ever gracefully, comfortably,
enviably unconscious (it would be too much to call them even suspicious) of the
requirements of form. The case is at any rate sharply enough made for us, or against
us, by the circumstance that women are held to have achieved on all our ground, in
spite of this weakness and others, as great results as any. The judgement is
undoubtedly founded: Jane Austen was instinctive and charming...'
That Jane Austen's art had made a deep and decisive impact on James is proved (if
that were necessary) by *The Europeans*. His being able to refer to her in such a
context as 'instinctive' proves that he himself as critic can be insufficiently conscious.
The passage might be noted by the student as a monitory *locus classicus* for the term
'form'.

warm and growing admiration and a proper kind of humility. He uses the conversation, with its different voices, representing a diversity of approaches and possibilities of response, to convey a due sense of the complexity both of the work and the critical recognition it calls for.

Those who have read (and there are authorities – James suffers much from authorities – who assert it as a patent truth) that Balzac is pre-eminently the master from whom he descends should consider how he deals with *La Comédie humaine*. He admires immensely and wonderingly the portentous energy, industry and courage of its creator, and the degree of success he has achieved. What he admires is the antithesis of himself. He reflects with a kind of envy on the conditions of an old civilization that made possible, in Balzac's attempt to 'faire concurrence à l'état civil', his 'solidity of specification', his effect of structure and density. The antithesis of the poverty that James, in a famous passage, notes as offered Hawthorne by the American scene* – that is what Balzac's France gave Balzac. But, without anything in the nature of envy, James is constating how different in *kind* Balzac's energy is from his own. For the upshot of James's critique is a drastic limiting or privative judgement, one that comes under the rubric of 'significance'.

The significance we look for in creative literature is a matter of the sense of life, the sense of the potentialities of human experience, it conveys. It may fairly be said that life in *La Comédie humaine*, life for the reader immersed in the 'comedy', is populous, an immensely demonstrative energy, and insistently 'actual', but that the 'life' that provides the themes and materials for Henry James's art hardly makes its presence felt. For all its populousness, Balzac's world strikes James as dauntingly empty. He conveys this judgement while his explicit emphasis falls on mass, weight and extent; the effect of 'solidity' or 'reality' he acclaims is significantly qualified in the acclaiming. 'A born son of Touraine, it must be said, he pictures his province, on every pretext and occasion, with filial passion and extraordinary breadth. The prime aspect in his scene all the while, it must be added, is the money aspect. The general money question so loads him up and weighs him down that he moves through the human comedy, from beginning to end, very much in the fashion of a camel, the ship of the desert, surmounted with a cargo. "Things" for him are francs and centimes more than any others, and I give up

* Henry James: *Hawthorne* (English Men of Letters), pp. 42–43.

as inscrutable, unfathomable, the nature, the peculiar avidity of his interest in them. It makes us wonder again and again what then is the use on Balzac's scale of the divine faculty. The imagination, as we all know, may be employed up to a certain point in inventing uses for money; but its office beyond that point is surely to make us forget that anything so odious exists. This is what Balzac never forgot; his universe goes on expressing itself for him, to its furthest reaches, on its finest sides, in the terms of the market. To say these things, however, is after all to come out where we want, to suggest his extraordinary scale and his terrible completeness. I am not sure that he does not see character too, see passion, motive, personality, as quite in the order of the "things" we have spoken of. He makes them no less concrete and palpable, handles them no less directly and freely. It is the whole business in fine – that grand total to which he proposed to himself to do high justice – that gives him his place apart, makes him, among the novelists, the largest, weightiest presence. There are some of his obsessions – that of the material, that of the financial, that of the "social", that of the technical, political, civil – for which I feel myself unable to judge him, judgement losing itself unexpectedly in a particular shade of pity. The way to judge him is to try to walk all round him – on which we see how remarkably far we have to go.'

There would be no point in summarizing the criticism or (it is hardly, the student will find, a separable thing) the way in which James makes it. The student will find a good and relatively simple illustration here of how James repays some attentive reading. A criticism of very much the same kind is brought against Arnold Bennett in the late essay, 'The New Novel'. And again the student should note the way in which the criticism is conveyed. James has his idiosyncrasy of expression, but his essential method, his approach and movement in criticism, can hardly be *imitated*. The learning that can be done by the reader is only of the right kind.

But there is no need to particularize further. The reader, aware enough of the distinction of James the critic to look with adverted interest through a varied collection of his criticism, will do his own exploring, picking-out and discriminating. For there *are*, of course, discriminations to be made: its interest doesn't invariably, or often wholly, lie in its convincing rightness and inevitableness. We turn up with some eagerness his review of *Our Mutual Friend*, and comment, perhaps, that he rightly judges it to be inferior and tired, and yet doesn't do it justice. To dismiss Bradley Headstone and Eugene Wrayburn in that way – is *that* right? Isn't there some subtle and convincing psychology that is at the same time penetrating insight into the conditioning civilization? Haven't we some strong Dickens in the waterside parts? And so on. We note his brief sentence on Lawrence in 'The New Novel'. And we may remind ourselves, observing how seriously he there takes Hugh Walpole, the type Book Society novelist of the time, that Walpole enjoyed great 'social' advantages, and was cultivating the old, lonely, recognition-starved James – in the same spirit that later (*via hommage* to Virginia Woolf) won him the entry into Bloomsbury and *The Criterion*.

Reading James on Whitman and Baudelaire, we comment that his being an intelligent novelist didn't help him here. But we don't feel superior – or oughtn't to: that is in and of the whole 'lesson', the total interest and profit of reading any representative collection of his criticism. Reading him on Baudelaire, for instance, though we may exclaim at his being able to rank Baudelaire below Gautier, we may find it salutary to explain to ourselves why it was natural, and almost inevitable, for him to do so. We might even, considering James's Baudelaire (whom he presents carefully), be led to ask whether in the post-Eliotic Baudelaire there doesn't perhaps tend also to be a deflection – of another kind.

JOYCE AND
'THE REVOLUTION OF
THE WORD'

To judge the *Work in Progress,* in any bulk, not worth the labour of reading is not necessarily to identify oneself with the late Poet Laureate (Robert Bridges). One may find some of the propositions with which the hierophants of the Mystic Logos seek to stagger the world commonplace – one may think Gerard Manley Hopkins the greatest poet of the Victorian Age – and yet regret the use to which James Joyce has put his genius since he finished *Ulysses.* There is no question of appealing to even the Oxford English Dictionary or even the most modern English Grammar as authorities. 'In developing his medium to the fullest, Mr Joyce is after all doing only what Shakespeare has done in his later plays, such as *The Winter's Tale* and *Cymbeline,* where the playwright obviously embarked on new word sensations before reaching that haven of peacefulness' etc. – in demurring to such a proposition, and replying that Mr Joyce is, after all, not doing only what Shakespeare has done, one's objection is not that he takes particular licences unprecedented in the plays.

Mr Joyce's liberties with English are essentially unlike Shakespeare's. Shakespeare's were not the product of a desire to 'develop his medium to the fullest', but of a pressure of something to be conveyed. One insists, it can hardly be insisted too much, that the study of a Shakespeare play must start with the words; but it was not there that Shakespeare – the great Shakespeare – started: the words matter because they lead down to what they came from. He was in the early wanton period, it is true, an amateur of verbal fancies and ingenuities, but in the mature plays, and especially in the late plays stressed above, it is the burden to be delivered, the precise and urgent command from within, that determines expression –

121

tyrannically. That is Shakespeare's greatness: the complete subjection – subjugation – of the medium to the uncompromising complex and delicate need that uses it. Those miraculous intricacies of expression could have come only to one whose medium was for him strictly a medium; an object of interest only as something that, under the creative compulsion, identified itself with what insisted on being expressed: the linguistic audacities are derivative.

Joyce's development has been the other way. There is prose in *Ulysses*, the description, for instance, of Stephen Dedalus walking over the beach, of a Shakespearian concreteness; the rich complexity it offers to analysis derives from the intensely imagined experience realized in the words. But in the *Work in Progress*, it is plain, the interest in words and their possibilities comes first. The expositors speak of 'Mr Joyce's linguistic experiments'; and: 'That he is following the most modern philological researches can be deduced from the passage...' (*Transition* 22, p. 103). We are explicitly told that 'words evoke in him more intense emotions than the phenomena of the outer world' (*Exagmination* etc., p. 153). Mustering his resources, linguistic and philological, (and, one hears, with the aid of an Interpreting Bureau), he stratifies his puns deeper and deeper, multiplies his associations and suggestions, and goes over and over his text, enriching and complicating.

'Few authors ever wrote a sentence with a more complete consciousness of every effect they wished to obtain' (*Exagmination* etc., p. 67) – but the wished effect (it would be self-evident, even without the successive versions extant of given passages) develops continually at the suggestion of the words: more and more possibilities of stratification and complication propose themselves. Working in this way, 'inserting his new ideas continually in whatever part of the supple text they are appropriate' (*Exagmination* etc., p. 164). Mr Joyce achieves complexities that offer themselves as comparable to Shakespeare's. But, achieved in this way, they betray at once their essential unlikeness. 'The obscurity of that passage, its prolixity and redundancy, all are deliberately and artistically logical' (*Exagmination* etc., p. 55). Nothing could be 'righter' than Shakespeare's effects, but they are irreconcilable with this kind of deliberate, calculating contrivance and with this external approach. They register the compulsive intensity and completeness with which Shakespeare realizes his imagined world, the swift immediacy that engages at a point an inexhaustibly subtle organization.

The contrast would still have held even if Shakespeare had had (as we are convinced he had not) to achieve his organization by prolonged and laborious experiment, and his immediacy with corresponding critical toil. The essential is that the words are servants of an inner impulse or principle of order; they are imperiously commanded and controlled from an inner centre.

In the *Work in Progress*, even in the best parts, we can never be unaware that the organization is external and mechanical. Each line is a series of jerks, as the focus jumps from point to point; for the kind of attention demanded by each one of the closely packed 'effects' is incompatible with an inclusive, coordinating apprehension. The kind of accent and intonation with which a pun announces itself refuse to be suppressed; they are persistent and devastating. Many of the effects are undoubtedly interesting; *Anna Livia Plurabelle* is in some ways a very striking – and, rendered by Joyce himself, one can believe, a pleasing – performance. But in anything resembling an integrated effect a very large part indeed of the intended complexity must be lost: 'It is possibly necessary to "trance" oneself into a state of word-intoxication, flitting concept-inebriation,' says one of the expositors (*Exagmination* etc., p. 114). The 'meaning', or an impressive amount of it, can always be worked out at leisure, just as it was worked in (the opportunities that the *Work in Progress* offers for knowing elucidation ensure it a certain popularity; it is surprising, Paris having long enough ago given the cue, that our undergraduate intellect stays content with the *Cantos*). But, at the best, the satisfaction provided even by *Anna Livia Plurabelle* is incommensurate with the implicit pretensions and with the machinery. It is significant that, for the English-speaking reader, so much of the satisfaction remains in the French translation published (with an amusing account of the method of translating) in the *Nouvelle Revue Française* (1931, vol. xxxvi, p. 633).

To justify a medium much less obtrusive in pretensions than that of the *Work in Progress* Joyce would have had to have a commanding theme, animated by some impulsion from the inner life capable of maintaining a high pressure. Actually the development of the medium appears to be correlated with the absence of such a theme – to be its consequence. For in the earlier work, in *Ulysses* and before, the substance is clearly the author's personal history and the pressure immediately personal urgency; the historical particularity is explicit enough and it is hardly impertinent to say that *Ulysses* is clearly a catharsis. But if one asks what controls the interest in technique, the preoccupation with the means of expression, in the *Work in Progress,* the answer is a reference to Vico; that is, to a philosophical theory.

'Vico proposed the making of "an ideal and timeless history in which all the actual histories of all nations should be embodied."' (*Exagmination* etc., p. 51). He also contemplated the formation of a 'mental vocabulary' 'whose object should be to explain all languages that exist by an ideal synthesis of their varied expressions. And now after two centuries, such a synthesis of history and language, a task which seemed almost beyond human achievement, is being realised by James Joyce in his latest work' (*Exagmination* etc., p. 54). A certain vicious bent manifested itself very disturbingly in *Ulysses,* in the inorganic elaborations and pedantries and the evident admiring belief of the author in Stephen's intellectual distinction, and the idea of putting Vico's theory of history into the concrete would seem rather to derive from this bent than to be calculated to control it.

In any case the idea would seem to be self-stultifying. The result in the *Work in Progress* of trying to put 'allspace in a notshall' – the 'ideal' (but concrete) 'and timeless history' in a verbal medium defying all linguistic conventions – is not orchestrated richness but, for the most part, monotonous non-significance. Forms, after all, in life and art, are particular and limiting, and *The Waste Land* probably goes about as far as can be gone in the way of reconciling concrete particularity with inclusive generality. Joyce's limitless ambition leads to formlessness, local and in survey. The 'ideal history' would seem to be chaos, that which precedes form – or swallows it. In it, 'movement is non-directional – or multi-directional, and a step forward is, by definition, a step back' (*Exagmination* etc., p. 22). H. C. E. (Humphrey Chimpden Earwicker) is glossed by 'Here Comes Everybody'; but a multi-directional flux, though it may be said to have something like universality, has not the universality of a mythical figure. Joyce's medium, likewise, is not in the end rich. It may be the 'esperanto of the subconscious'; if so, the subconscious is sadly boring.

As a matter of fact, Joyce's subconscious is worse than boring; it is offensively spurious. It is not that one objects to conscious management, which is inevitable. But conscious management in the

Work in Progress is not the agent of a deeply serious purpose; it serves in general an inveterate solemn ingenuity, and it is often the very willing pimp to a poor wit. 'Cosmic humour' there may be, as the expositors allege, in the *Work in Progress*; there is certainly a great deal of provocation for D. H. Lawrence's reaction: 'My God, what a clumsy *olla putrida* James Joyce is! Nothing but old fags and cabbage-stumps of quotations from the Bible and the rest, stewed in the juice of deliberate, journalistic dirty-mindedness – what old and hard-worked staleness, masquerading as the all-new!' There is more in the *Work in Progress* than that, but the spuriousness, the mechanical manipulation, is pervasive.

Lawrence, of course, objected to the whole thing; and his objection finds endorsement in the company Joyce keeps. It was fair to use the bits from his expositors quoted above, since it is not because he can get published nowhere else that he continues to appear in *Transition;* he, at any rate tacitly, encourages them. We are free to assume that the 'International Workshop for Orphic Creation' (as *Transition* now describes itself) is under his patronage, and that he does not dissociate himself from his expositors when they issue manifestos in favour of 'The Vertigral Age':

The Vertigral Age believes that we stand in direct line with the primeval strata of life.

The Vertigral Age wants to give voice to the ineffable silence of the heart.

The Vertigral Age wants to create a primitive grammar, the stammering that approaches the language of God.

Joyce (who gives 'such a picture of the entire universe as might be registered in the mind of some capricious god') is said to have 'desophisticated language' ('Vico applied to the problem of style'). It is, on the contrary, plain that the whole phenomenon is one of sophistication, cosmopolitan if not very subtle, and, so far from promising a revival of cultural health, is (it does not need Lawrence's nostril to detect) a characteristic symptom of dissolution. The 'internationalization of language' acclaimed by Joyce's apostles is a complementary phenomenon to Basic English; indeed, we note with a surprised and pleased sense of fitness that Mr C. K. Ogden has shown an active interest in the *Work in Progress*.

Their conception of the problem – 'I claim for *transition*,' says Mr Eugene Jolas, 'priority in formulating the problem on an international scope ... and in giving it a dialectical substructure' – is ludicrously inadequate. 'I believe,' says Mr Jolas, standing up for the artist, 'in his right to audaciously split the infinitive.' As if any amount of splitting infinitives, mimicking the Master, pondering Gertrude Stein and E. E. Cummings and connoisseuring American slang, could revivify the English language.

A brief reflection on the conditions of Shakespeare's greatness is in place here. He represents, of course, the power of the Renaissance. But the power of the Renaissance could never so have manifested itself in English if English had not already been there – a language vigorous enough to respond to the new influx, ferment and literary efflorescence, and, in so doing, not lose, but strengthen its essential character. The dependence of the theatre on both Court and populace ensured that Shakespeare should use his 'linguistic genius* – he incarnated the genius of the language – to the utmost. And what this position of advantage represents in particular form is the general advantage he enjoyed in belonging to a genuinely national culture, to a community in which it was possible for the theatre to appeal to the cultivated and the populace at the same time.

A national culture rooted in the soil – the commonplace metaphor is too apt to be rejected: the popular basis of culture was agricultural. Mr Logan Pearsall Smith shows how much of the strength and subtlety of English idiom derives from an agricultural way of life. The essential nature of the debt is well suggested by his notes on phrasal verbs. 'For when we examine these phrasal verbs, we find that by far the greater number of them also render their meanings into terms of bodily sensation. They are formed from simple verbs which express the acts, motions, and attitudes of the body and its members; and these, combining with prepositions like "up", "down", "over", "off", etc. (which also express ideas of motion), have acquired, in addition to their literal meanings, an enormous number of idiomatic significations, by means of which the relations of things to each other, and a great variety of the actions, feelings, and thoughts involved in human intercourse, are translated, not into visual images, but into what psychologists call "kinaesthetic" images, that is to say, sensations of the muscular

* ... considering how few other writers have added idioms to the language, it is a surprising proof, both of his linguistic genius and his popularity ...' Logan Pearsall Smith, *Words and Idioms*, p. 229. (The context – and, indeed, a great part of the essay – bears peculiarly upon the question under discussion.)

efforts which accompany the attitudes and motions of the body'
(*Words and Idioms*, p. 250).

This strength of English belongs to the very spirit of the language
– the spirit that was formed when the English people who formed it
was predominantly rural. Why it should be associated with a rural
order, why it should develop its various resources to the fullest
there, Mr Adrian Bell, illustrating the vigour and fineness of
rustic speech in the last number of *Scrutiny*,* suggested: he showed
'how closely the countryman's life and language grow together; they
are like flesh and bone'. They grow together just as mind and body,
mental and physical life, have grown together in those phrasal verbs.
And of how much richer the *life* was in the old, predominantly rural
order than in the modern suburban world one must go to the now
oft-cited George Bourne (under both his names) for an adequate
intimation. When one adds that speech in the old order was a
popularly cultivated art, that people talked (so making Shakespeare
possible) instead of reading or listening to the wireless, it becomes
plain that the promise of regeneration by American slang, popular
city-idiom or the inventions of transition-cosmopolitans is a flimsy
consolation for our loss.

It is an *order* that is gone – Mr Bell records its last remnants – and
there are no signs of its replacement by another: the possibility of
one that should offer a like richness of life, of emotional, mental and
bodily life in association, is hardly even imaginable. Instead we have
cultural disintegration, mechanical organization and constant rapid
change. There is no time for anything to grow, even if it would. If the
English people had always been what they are now there would have
been no Shakespeare's English and no comparable instrument: its
life and vigour are no mere matter of vivid idioms to be matched by
specimens of American slang (English, it may be ventured, has been
more alive in America in the last century than in England mainly
because of pioneering conditions, which are as unlike those of the
modern city as possible).

At any rate, we still have Shakespeare's English: there is indeed
reason in setting great store by the 'word' – if not in the
revolutionary hopes of Mr Jolas and his friends. With resources of
expression that would not have existed if Shakespeare's England
had not been very different from his own, Gerard Manley Hopkins
wrote major poetry in the Victorian Age. We have poets in our own

* June 1933.

day, and James Joyce wrote *Ulysses*. For how long a cultural tradition can be perpetuated in this way one wonders with painful tension. Language, kept alive and rejuvenated by literature, is certainly an essential means of continuity and transition – to what? We are back at the question, which has been raised in *Scrutiny* before and will be again, whether there can be a culture based on leisure, and if so, what kind.

We can demand no more than the certitude that there are certain things to be done and cared for now. The line of reflection indicated above leads one to the unanswerable questions raised innocently by scientists who (in romantic or journalistic moments) speculate as to the complete transformation, physical and psychological, that Science will effect in Man.

MEMORIES OF WITTGENSTEIN

I had better say at once that I didn't discuss philosophy with Wittgenstein; so that if any philosopher, attracted by my title, should be intending to read these 'memories' in the expectation of finding them charged with professional interest he is warned at the outset. Naturally I think that some of them ought to be recognized to have a significant bearing on Wittgenstein's intellectual approach and habit. But in the only one in which philosophic thought is explicitly referred to as such the reference is very general – as general as well could be. I will relate it at once, so as to have it, in its uniqueness, safely behind me (though that isn't, after all, the only reason for opening with it).

I was walking once with Wittgenstein when I was moved, by something he said, to remark, with a suggestion of innocent inquiry in my tone: 'You don't think much of most other philosophers, Wittgenstein?' – 'No. Those I have my use for you could divide into two classes. Suppose I was directing someone of the first to Emmanuel,' – it was then my college – 'I should say: "You see that steeple over there? Emmanuel is three hundred and fifty yards to the west-south-west of it." That man, the first class, would get there. Hm! very rare – in fact I've never met him. To the second I should say: "You go a hundred yards straight ahead, turn half-left and go forty" ... and so on. That man would ultimately get there. Very rare too; in fact I don't know that I've met *him*.' Thereupon I asked, referring to the well-known young Cambridge genius (who was to die while still young): 'What about Frank Ramsey?' – 'Ramsey? *He* can see the next step if you point it out.' I will give my reason later for assuming that he had a relatively high opinion of Ramsey. I associate with this memory so that I have the impression of his having said it to me too – though I am not sure – what I clearly remember having been told by someone else: 'Moore? – he shows you how far a man can go who has absolutely no intelligence whatever.'

The trait was highly characteristic of Wittgenstein; it was something one noticed at first encounter. Arrogance? I don't think that anyone who knew him would have rested on that as a suitable word. For the trait was a manifestation of the essential quality that one couldn't be very long with him without becoming aware of – the quality of genius: an intensity of a concentration that impressed itself on one as disinterestedness.

When one thought, as one often did, of 'singlemindedness' as a necessary descriptive word, there was apt to be some criticism in one's intention: 'He doesn't give one a chance.' From observation I conclude that that would have described my reaction if I had ever committed myself to a serious discussion with him. Argument once started, he exercised a completeness of command that left other voices little opportunity – unless (which was unlikely) they were prepared to be peremptory, insistent and forceful. In relation to philosophic discussion I heard it said: 'Wittgenstein can take all the sides himself; he answers before you've said it – you can't get in.'

I myself didn't offer to engage him in any serious argument of any kind, though I did on occasion take issue with him. And then I simply said, 'No, we mustn't do that,' and, if he pressed for a reason, dismissed the matter with a factual representation as settled – as far as possible unanswerably. This might perhaps seem to indicate that any arrogance there might be was mine. Actually, I think it would be a misleading word to use of either of us, though it seems to me to apply, if at all, to Wittgenstein rather than to me: if you were not by nature 'recessive', you had, on occasion at any rate, to be firm and final with him.

I was helped, no doubt, by my having no philosophic qualifications, a fact that must have been plain to Wittgenstein, though I met him first (before I knew who he was) at the house of my old friend, W. E. Johnson, the logician, who had 'supervised' him long before – as he had supervised all the Cambridge philosophers from Russell onwards. I may explain that I had been at school with Johnson's son, Stephen; but it was Johnson himself, a permanency in Cambridge, whom I continued to see over the years. It must have been in 1929, the year when Wittgenstein first came back to Cambridge after the outbreak of war in 1914. It was at Ramsey House, Barton Road, on a Sunday afternoon, when at tea-time Johnson and his sister, Miss Fanny, were 'at home' to lecturers for the Moral Sciences Tripos, distinguished old pupils, and visiting philosophers.

As I have indicated, I was not one of these, but it had become plain in the course of years that there was no tendency to regard me as an intrusive presence: I was, in fact, an established familiar in the little drawing-room, which was a quarter filled with the Broadwood grand on which the old logician used to take his exercise playing Bach. On this Sunday it was crowded, and I couldn't have named half the company. I wasn't, for instance, in a position, though I had heard of him, to identify the enlightened young viscount who (at his own request, I gathered) was known by his not uncommon surname, and was pledged to live – a matter of conscientious scruple – on an extremely small weekly expenditure. It was brought home to me that he was present, and that he was one of Johnson's pupils, when he was asked by name to sing something of Schubert's. What followed was the occasion of my first identifying Wittgenstein.

So far from the truth was the account old Johnson, with his benign sardonic twinkle, put into currency – 'When Wittgenstein and Leavis met they fell on one another's necks' – that it would be nearer to say that, moved to indignation, I offered to *fall on* Wittgenstein. It was what struck me as the cold brutality of his behaviour that provoked my anger. The young man, for whom the invitation was clearly an injunction, stood up – he seemed to me obviously very sensitive and very nice – and, looking across the room at the beautiful and stern face of (I assumed) the not so very much older man I had noticed as I came in, said nervously: 'Er, Wittgenstein will correct my German.' Wittgenstein, in a manner I can neither describe nor imitate, replied: 'How can I? How can I possibly?'

It was essentially meant to be routing. It had its effect, and when the unfortunate singer had finished, Wittgenstein triumphantly – so I thought – got up and left. The front door had hardly shut behind him when I, who had followed him out of the packed drawing-room as fast as I could make my way, opened it again. I caught him up on the Barton Road, which, the Johnson house standing at the corner of Millington Road, flanked one side of it, and, with my hands on my lapels as if (I later realized) I were about to take my coat off, said: 'You behaved in a disgraceful way to that young man.' He looked at me in surprise: 'I thought he was a foolish young man.' To which I returned, emphatically containing myself: 'You may have done, you may have done, but you had no right to treat him like that. You've no right to treat anyone like that.' It was my turn to be surprised. Putting his hand on my shoulder, he said: 'We must know one another.' Since he, we being at the bottom of the road, turned left towards the Backs and Cambridge, I, muttering 'I don't see the necessity,' turned right, towards the Grantchester footpath.

However, soon after, he actually appeared at my house, and began a practice of dropping in from time to time that he maintained for a couple of years. Often he suggested that we should go out, and it was while walking with him that I learnt a good deal about his past and himself. I learnt, for instance, that, although (it must have been in 1929 or the beginning of 1930) he was taken for an undergraduate at a Friday tea in my house at which he was present, he was then at least forty. For this datum I didn't need to depend on a characteristic ejaculation of his – 'I'm forty and a fool'; it was conveyed in a remark of his that began: 'When I was at Manchester before the war – ' To my interruption, 'At Manchester before Cambridge?' he replied yes, he *had* been – 'doing engineering', adding that he had gone from there to Cambridge 'to work with Russell'. He communicated no hint of any sense he might have had of Russell other than as the distinguished mind that had collaborated in *Principia Mathematica*.

I noted this because I was already coming more and more to a full awareness that I disliked Russell, and profoundly – the Russell to be divined in his books and publicities. I recall it vividly now because of the way in which, in his memoirs, Russell refers to his relations with Wittgenstein. He had no glimmering of Wittgenstein's immense superiority to him as a person – as a centre of life, sentience and human responsibility. Of course one knew that, in the nature of Russell, that must be so. It came as a shock, however, to register the tone – the amused and blandly conscious superiority – in which he recounts how he asked a patently troubled young Wittgenstein, who had come for an academic consultation, whether he was worrying about his work or his sins. Russell clearly still had no suspicion that in the brief unepigrammatically intended reply he reports – 'Both' – we have the difference between pupil and supervisor: the difference to examine which entails the drastic critical commentary to which Russell is exposed.

Wittgenstein was a troubled soul, a fact that he neither advertised nor concealed. It became apparent to me in many ways, and was not less significant of the essential man than the assurance, the two being intimately related. I suppose that I am not the only one who thought of the quality I have called assurance as having, going as it did with cultivation and quiet distinction, something aristocratic about it. I recall how once, at a crowded Friday tea-time, a sudden lull in the talk left Wittgenstein's voice clearly audible, and what I heard was: 'In my father's house there were seven grand pianos.' I thought: 'Ah! a Schloss.' I knew of the Princess Wittgenstein who figures in the annals of music, and had wondered whether our Wittgenstein was of that clan.

Actually, of course, he wasn't: I have gathered since he died that he was the son of a wealthy Austrian manufacturer, and that the immediate family background was partly Protestant, partly Catholic and partly Jewish. In any case, he was by nature intensely introspective and his habit of self-questioning was not restricted to any field in which the ethos of logic prevails. He was, in fact, as I have said, a troubled soul: no one could be with him long without discovering that. Not that he went in for intimate avowals, or was apt to drop explicit references to his inner state. The evidence was a matter of tone and passing or undeliberate implication, and so, for the present purpose, not easily conveyed.

I will relate a characteristic instance that, in the concrete, was for me profoundly impressive. I had a pupil, R., bearer of a distinguished Victorian name, who insisted on coming to me though he didn't belong to one of 'my' colleges. He soon got to feel that I didn't sufficiently appreciate his distinction, and I for my part thought that in his own estimate of that distinction, and of the critical authority which that gave him, his sense of the family connexion counted for too much. Anyway, we recognized that we were not congenial to one another, and the things said between us meant that the relation had come to an end. I can't remember what the young man's status was, but he was certainly not a first-year undergraduate, and I was not altogether surprised when I heard that he had gained admission to Wittgenstein's lectures. I *was*, however, surprised when Wittgenstein, quite inapropos of anything that had passed between us, said: 'R. thinks highly of you.' I replied: 'I don't really care what R. thinks of me.' 'You ought to care,' said Wittgenstein. Thinking this decidedly an instance of the Wittgenstein quality when it deserved rebuke as too like arrogance, or something closely akin, I retorted with marked quietness: 'Do you know what R.'s final remark to me was?' Then (for Wittgenstein only looked), reproducing as well as I could R.'s tone and intention: 'He said as he turned to go: "You're like Jesus Christ."' Wittgenstein's reaction to this exemplified a profound characteristic that had its bearing on one's judgement of the 'arrogance': 'That's an extraordinary thing to say!'

I can't, of course, render in writing the specific force of this ejaculation (nor, I ought to add, could I in speech – I am not Wittgenstein). It was a spontaneity of recoil, uttering a judgement expressive of the whole being. To know Wittgenstein was to recognize that tone, that force, again and again. I recognized it in the ejaculatory comment with which he received the answer to the question he once greeted me with: 'What is Basic English?' I told him. He said only: 'Would he do *that*!' – it left nothing in doubt regarding his attitude. I give only the words, being unable to do anything about the tone beyond using an interjection instead of a question mark.

I remember an occasion when the tone had more of wondering recognition in it, and less of adverse judgement. We were walking above Byron's Pool on the right bank of the Granta opposite Lingay Fen. In those days, just before the riverside thicket begins (or began) and about twenty yards back from the river there was a stretch of ground that had been furrowed and ridged as if a gigantic plough had been at work. At the bottom of each furrow, nine or ten feet down, there was standing water, held there by the clay which kept the furrows looking sharply cut as if the plough had made them last week. 'What's this?' Wittgenstein asked. I explained that the place had a good while ago been a resort of mammoths, with the result that, at the outbreak of the war, there were known exploitable deposits of coprolites there. Wittgenstein didn't need telling that coprolites had their use in the manufacture of munitions. What he said was, 'Did they do that!' – again I intimate the tone by closing the phrase with an exclamation mark.

Wonder, I suppose, always has an element of surprise in it, if only the surprise of new and sharpened realization: in this instance he was recognizing a reality he had clearly observed with insight and pondered a great deal. He was neither simple-minded nor self-exaltingly cynical about human nature, human possibilities and the human scene. Lawrence couldn't have applied to Wittgenstein what he told Russell in the days of the Union of Democratic Control: that he, the distinguished Bertrand Russell (who later, having recovered from the shock, was to cherish the affront with righteous indignation), suffered from the 'inexperience of youth'.

Wittgenstein, then, was very different from Russell; he was a complete human being, subtle, self-critical and un-self-exalting. When, in characterizing him, one touches on traits that seem to entail adverse or limiting judgements, one is not intending to impute defects in his potential full humanity.

This last uneasy sentence conveys my sense of the delicacy of what I have undertaken. I can't say several complementary and corrective things at once, and I haven't the opportunities that the scope and complexity of a novel would give for being just to Wittgenstein. I have to rely on the cumulative effect of 'memories' – an effect dependent on the order of rendering as well as on my commentary.

I remember – to resume my 'memories' – one summer evening when he called on me and suggested that we should go on the river. We walked the mile and a half to the boathouse in the garden of what is now the Garden House Hotel and took a canoe. We got in and Wittgenstein said: 'I'll do the paddling: I need exercise.' I thought that there was no reason why we shouldn't both take a paddle, and that I liked exercise too, but forbore to say it. After paddling up the Granta for a quarter of an hour he stopped the canoe under the bank opposite the University bathing place, and said, 'Let's get out and walk.' 'There's no footpath this side,' I replied, 'and, as a cross-country man, I can tell you that you'll find the going rough and rather difficult.' Since he seemed to regard the matter as decided in his sense, I got out with him, and devoted myself to steering him towards gates and hedge-gaps and helping him through barbed wire and across ditches.

We came finally to the plantation that bounds Trumpington Park on that side. 'Let's go in there,' he said, turning towards the fence. Night had come on by then, and I answered, 'No; it wouldn't be discreet.' 'Why not?' he asked challengingly. 'Because,' I said, 'the Hall is just behind – it's there as a screen.' 'Oh' came unconcessively from him, and we went along the cart-track that borders the wood, and emerged, by the stone bridge, on the road that runs from

Grantchester to Trumpington. Leftwards a noise as of steam-organs made itself heard in the middle distance, and there was a glow in the sky. 'What's that?' asked Wittgenstein. 'It must be Trumpington Feast,' I answered. 'Let's go,' he said. With a finality as unprovocative as I could make it I said, leaving the 'But Wittgenstein!' to be conveyed by the quiet firmness, 'It's by now about eleven.' 'I'm often out later than that,' he replied. 'Yes,' I said, 'but we've left a canoe by the river-bank a good way back, and then, considerably beyond that, there's a man waiting for us at the boathouse.' 'Oh!' he said in the same tone as before. But we turned and retraced our steps to where the springboard of the University Swimming Club pointed to our canoe. We got in; Wittgenstein took up his paddle, and we arrived at the Belle Vue boathouse towards midnight.

The man came forward and held our canoe as we got out. Wittgenstein, who insisted imperiously on paying, didn't, I deduced from the man's protest, give him any tip. I, in my effort to get in first with the payment, had my hand on some money in my trousers pocket and pulling it out, I slipped a couple of coins to the man. As we went away, Wittgenstein asked: 'How much did you give him?' I told him, and Wittgenstein said: 'I hope that is not going to be a precedent.' Not, this time, suppressing the impatience I felt, I returned: 'The man told you that he had been waiting for us a couple of hours – for us alone, and there is every reason for believing that he spoke the truth.' 'I,' said Wittgenstein, 'always associate the man with the boathouse.' 'You may,' I retorted, 'but you know that he is separable and has a life apart from it.' Wittgenstein said nothing.

Whatever I have illustrated here, it wasn't meanness. I think of him as having neither vices nor virtues that anyone would have called 'bourgeois'. It is true that the self-sufficiency, or robust singlemindedness, that figures in so characteristic a way in the whole episode I have just related, seems to me to involve certain limitations such as could incur at least one's tacit criticism, along with the immediate impulse of impatience. A relevant memory I recall is of his dropping in just after lunch one day and, volunteering the explanation that, having failed to find X, who lived (it seemed) close by, he proposed to wait with us for a while before trying again. Turning from a first glance through the window (from which, one gathered, he thought he might see X returning to his lodgings), he said: 'You've got a gramophone, I see – I don't suppose you've anything worth playing.' Then, with a marked change of tone, he exclaimed 'Ah!': from the repository just at hand he pulled out the album of Schubert's Great C Major symphony and put the first record on the machine. A moment after the music began to sound he lifted the tone-arm, altered the speed, and lowered the needle on to the record again. He did this several times, until he was satisfied. What was characteristic about the performance (Wittgenstein's) was not merely the aplomb with which he ignored our – my wife's and my – apprehensive presence, but the delicate precision with which he performed the manoeuvre. He was, in fact, truly and finely cultivated, and, as part of his obvious cultivation, very musical; and, having absolute pitch, had judged and acted instantaneously on hearing the opening bars.

I have not explained away the characteristic illustrated in these last two memories – the single-minded coolness so unambiguously apparent in 'I don't suppose you've anything worth playing,' and 'I always associate the man with the boathouse.' It was certainly there, a major trait in Wittgenstein, though one's sense of it varied with the circumstances and with the modifying accompaniments that composed with it a given total Wittgensteinian manifestation. When, once, he came to me and, without any prelude, said, 'Give up literary criticism!' I abstained from retorting, 'Give up philosophy, Wittgenstein!' largely because that would have meant telling him that he had been listening to the talk of a dominant coterie, and ought to be ashamed of supposing that Keynes, his friends and their *protégés* were the cultural *élite* they took themselves to be. That was too much to undertake and it would have profited very little. Besides, I respected Wittgenstein too much. When (being himself a remarkable linguist) he started to correct my spoken English, I didn't say, 'You're taking a modish manner of speech now in at King's as the standard, but it's a passing smart fashion, and goes in for what strike some of us as Cockney vowels.' I reflected, however, that the given trait of Wittgenstein's was sometimes decidedly Teutonic in its effect.

The fact is that the disinterested regardlessness in which his genius manifested itself was, as a matter of habit, apt to be a disconcerting lack of consideration; his 'single-mindedness' an innocent egotism. I have been asked to agree that Wittgenstein was cruel, but I think that description misleading, and I emphasize the 'innocent'. To call him 'childlike' would be certainly not less misleading; but the characteristics of genius had obviously asserted themselves very early, and compelled a tacit recognition from others that had, for life, established in him an element of childlike *prime-sautier* inconsiderateness. When he had a prompting he wasn't restrained from acting on it by the thought that to do so might be taken as a liberty.

No one, I think, would have charged him with complacency: the truth that I have expressed by saying that he 'had a troubled soul' was too apparent. There was a fundamental insecurity in him, though it hardly appeared to the world as that. It won't be taken as so paradoxical when I say that I think he was habitually unhappy. When I discovered that he was agoraphobic, I took it as a confirmation, whether validly or not. The agoraphobia he more or less avowed to me. We were walking one day on the Grantchester footpath when he said: 'Let's sit down.' Since the grass by the path, from which the meadows sloped down to the river, was obviously dry, and the slope began in a sharp drop that promised the sitter a comfortable posture, I sat down at once. Wittgenstein said: 'No, not here.' Getting up, I looked at him, and he explained: 'You'll think it strange, but I never sit down in the open.' I said, pointing, 'Look! there's a hawthorn tree halfway down by the ditch that drains into the river. That should be all right.' It was, and we went and sat under it. I associate this episode with his desire, on the occasion of our cross-country walk, to climb the fence bounding Trumpington Park and trespass in the plantation.

Whatever the agoraphobia might, or might not, have signified, there was certainly a profound insecurity in Wittgenstein. I recollect the evening when he called on me quite late, and sat talking for what seemed to me, who get up early, an inordinate while. I took some care not to betray impatience, for I knew that bouts of concentrated thinking left him exhausted spiritually and desolate, and I guessed that, for some reason or other, he had been severely taxing his endurance. But as midnight approached I said, as if suddenly recalling the fact: 'Didn't you tell me that you were reading a paper to the Aristotelian Society at Nottingham tomorrow?' I added, by way of reinforcing the stimulus: 'It's nearly twelve.' He exclaimed: 'I'm a bloody fool! – walk back with me.'

When we got outside my front gate, he turned, not to the left, as normally, but to the right, and said: 'Let's go this way.' 'This way' led to the Milton Road instead of to Chesterton Road, where G. E.

Moore lived, from whose house he sometimes came on to mine. It was the nearest way to his lodgings, as he can't have forgotten. I made no objection, since to go by Milton Road meant no more than a gratuitous hundred yards or so. When, however, as we very soon did, we got to it, Wittgenstein pointed away from Cambridge and said: 'Where does that go?' 'To Ely' – since he knew it went to Milton, I gave him the information I supposed him to be asking for. To my great surprise, he said: 'Let's go there!' With emphatic patience I replied: 'Ely is fourteen miles from here, and you're going to Nottingham tomorrow.' He said nothing as I took his arm, and we turned towards Cambridge.

After a few steps I realized that he *needed* my support, and that without it he could hardly walk. I thought of what he had told me of his exhaustion, his desperate need of sleep, during one of those interminable retreats on the Russian front. His exhaustion now, his need of sleep – certainly desperate, and probably too great for easy relaxing – was obviously the consequence of too sustained an effort of intellectual concentration and the rarefied abstractnesses to which it was applied. With him bearing heavily on me, he having surrendered to his fatigue, I did the steering as we went down Milton Road, along Chesterton Road and Chesterton Lane, across to Northampton Street, and then the length of the Backs to Silver Street, went by that opening, and then crossed the road to Malting House Lane. Facing us at the end of the lane was Frostlake Cottage, where he lodged.

Arrived at the front door, I knocked, and said to Wittgenstein: 'You'll go to bed at once, won't you?' He answered, with the inertness of exhaustion: 'You don't understand. When I'm engaged on a piece of work I'm always afraid I shall die before I've finished it. So I make a fair copy of the day's work, and give it to Frank Ramsey for safe-keeping. I haven't made today's copy.' I heard footsteps coming to the door, and left him, it being hardly possible to insist further.

Regarding the suggestion that he was cruel, I have said that that word, applied to him, would be very misleading. I must add something: to adduce at this point an illustration of a profound Wittgenstein characteristic is immediately relevant. I knew that he hadn't a high opinion of W. E. Johnson, who was his supervisor when he came to Cambridge before the war. In fact, I had both Wittgenstein's account of old Johnson, and Johnson's account of young Wittgenstein. Wittgenstein told me: 'I found in the first hour that he had nothing to teach me.' Johnson told me – he volunteered it in his quiet sardonic way: 'At our first meeting he was teaching me.' But when Johnson, always physically feeble when I knew him, began patently to break up, no one could have shown more sympathetic solicitude than Wittgenstein did. He went to Ramsey House, I gathered, if not every day, at any rate very frequently, to play chess with the old man and to be his audience for Bach on the Broadwood grand – which involved notable self-subordination on Wittgenstein's part; for Johnson, as Wittgenstein realized, still, though his weakness affected his command of his fingers, had to have a listener if he was to play.

Yet what may be called the basic lack of intellectual sympathy was mutual and undisguised. Two or three years before the time of which I have just spoken I had explicit confirmation from Johnson himself of what it required no great perspicacity to become aware of. This Ramsey House Sunday we were in the garden – it must have been a warm summer's day. There were many more present than there were deck-chairs to seat them, so that I was not the only one to be sitting on the grass of the small crowded lawn. The disadvantage of sitting on the ground is not so much that, if one hasn't room to sprawl, it's tiring, as that it very much limits one's power of looking behind one: I didn't, then, know who was in the chair that had been placed behind my shoulder while I talked with a young man I knew. The by then famous name having come up in the course of our conversation, I said: 'I think that Wittgenstein is a bad influence.' Before I could go on to explain what I meant and why I, not a philosopher, ventured to say it, a familiar voice not far from my ear broke in with: 'If *you* think that, what must *I* think!'

The vehemence was unusual, but a quick glance to the rear assured me that the voice *was* Johnson's. 'Here are these young men,' it went on; 'they go to Wittgenstein's lectures in their first week; and at the end of their three or four years they go down, and never know that some other people have done work in that field: there's Venn, there's Keynes, there's even my own work.'

Johnson put, from his professional point of view, and in his own way, the point that I myself had had it in mind to make. It was that the 'influence' represented by the immense vogue generated by Wittgenstein's genius, which was so manifest and so potent, wasn't in general the kind that has its proof in improved understanding of the influencer and his theme, or in fortified intellectual powers. And this is the point at which to avow that I can't believe Wittgenstein to have been a good teacher. It is not only that I knew very well some of the young men who were, or who professed to be, enthusiastic attenders at his lectures: I can't believe that most (at any rate) of even the mature and academically officed professionals who were present supposed that they could sincerely claim to have followed, in the sense of having been able to be even tacit collaborators (that is, serious questioners and critics), the discussions carried on by Wittgenstein.

As I have already intimated, Wittgenstein's discussions were discussions carried on *by* Wittgenstein. I say this with confidence, though I was never present when he was to be observed in action in professional company – in the company of philosophers and philosophy students. My confidence derives from my own experience of him, and my own very positive sense of the nature of his genius. I don't question that now and then some especially gifted, well-equipped and determined person did succeed in breaking into the battle and maintaining for a while something in the nature of an exchange. But what one has seen written and heard said a good many times seems to me well-founded: that the wonder and the profit for the lecture-audience lay in the opportunity to witness the sustained spontaneous effort of intellectual genius wrestling with its self-proposed problems. I was never present at one of those occasions, and I know, of course, that if I *had* been, the profit could hardly have been mine: I wasn't qualified by training and experience – or by interest in the mode of thought.

I had, however, as I have said, my experience of Wittgenstein, and my opportunities for what seems to me relevant observation. The kind of evidence that has led me to the conclusions I have just expressed is fairly represented by the following 'memory'. He dropped in one day very soon after lunch, and an unguarded polite reference I made to a paradox he had presented me with the last time we had met started him discoursing earnestly and energetically, for it turned out that the paradox for him was pregnant and crucial, and he meant to justify it, which would be to develop it. This became apparent as he continued. It was a Friday, the day on which my wife and I were known to be at home to the kind of company whose habit of meeting in this way was, before long, to make the successful launching of *Scrutiny* possible.

When, at about four, the first Friday guest arrived, Wittgenstein was still talking. Naturally, I was unable to attend steadily for the next hour and a half or so, but whenever I looked in his direction in order to convey politely to him that I was aware of his presence he seemed to be developing a serious argument. I recall that at one point, by way of ensuring full general attention, he picked up a book from the top of a pile that was within reach of the chair he was sitting in, held it up and, with quiet diagrammatic intensity, said: 'This is the world!' The hint of a suppressed snigger was audible in the room: printed large on the torn NRF paper cover, what we saw was the title: *Sodome et Gomorrhe.*

Whenever I had the chance to take note, he was still talking with the characteristic concentration and logical command, but I don't think that anyone was following. Finally the last of the tea-time guests departed, but Wittgenstein stayed on. I remember that he still talked, though I can't say whether or not it was in continuation of the argument he had begun at two o'clock: I have wholly forgotten the particulars of that rather embarrassing phase – I was dazed and tired and wanted him to go. Suddenly, at about eight o'clock, he realized the time and a pressing fact. He exclaimed: 'But I'm talking to the Moral Science Club this evening. Come down with me.' I did, and left him at the door of the meeting place. I heard afterwards that, apologizing for his lateness, he explained that he had been arguing all the afternoon with Dr Leavis.

I'm pretty sure that there was no conscious misrepresentation here. It's not that, in imputing to me an active part I had certainly not played, he thought of me as having a competence I was far from being able to exhibit. Indeed, in one of our actual exchanges he had, a good while before, thrown out a distinction between intelligence and character and made it (I thought) plain that he regarded me as representing character. I ought to add, though, that on the same occasion he said: 'Intelligence – you can pick it up in the street.' That is, he had found very few clever and willing persons who proved capable of engaging in real spoken exchange with him. Nevertheless he needed, as everyone does – geniuses are not exempt – a measure of collaborative human presence – presence of which he could be conscious as proof of a human interest other than his immediate personal own in the aims and methods he was verifying and refining as he battled with himself to make them acceptably articulate. The 'collaborative', of course, is implied in the 'own' – as it is in the 'make articulate' and the 'acceptably'. His 'lectures' were his discussions.

It is a commonplace that, to read, he is formidably difficult. I must confess that (such has been the inescapable economy imposed on me by life and my limitations) I can't claim to have made any show of a serious attempt on the later philosophy, which is what his most persuasive admirers have in mind when they exalt his achievement and influence. Nevertheless, I will avow my firm belief that university students of 'English' should be defended against the suggestion that they stand to benefit, at any rate on balance, by having lectures and seminars on Wittgenstein arranged for them. But it is not for me to present myself as a critic of Wittgenstein's philosophy – which I am not qualified to pronounce on. And if what I have just avowed, or anything else that I have said, seems to imply a more favourable actual sense on my part of my philosophic qualifications, my intention was to emphasize a necessary element in my account of my relations with him.

I had my strong conviction, which I think well-founded. As I have said, I didn't discuss philosophy with him; and I have recorded his coming to me and saying *tout court:* 'Give up literary criticism!' If I didn't reply 'Give up philosophy, Wittgenstein!' that – I will put it this way this time – was because Wittgenstein would have taken it for a mere retort, and my point would have been lost on him; it was so evident that, while (I thought) the easy aggressiveness of the injunction was the consequence of frequenting the Bloomsbury *milieu* in which he was 'Ludwig' to Keynes and company, he couldn't in any case imagine that literary criticism might matter intellectually. Even at that time I had an opposing conviction: it was, as it *is*, that the fullest use of language is to be found in creative literature, and that a great creative work is a work of original exploratory thought. With that conviction went the tendency towards the view I expressed recently, writing on Blake: 'philosophers are always weak on language.' So, while I had great respect for Wittgenstein, and he, I suppose, had some for me – for my character, perhaps, there was on both sides certainly some reserve in our sense of the other's intellect. For Wittgenstein my kind of addiction was hardly, if at all, more than pseudo-intellectual, and I, on my part, found myself at times thinking of his unmistakable genius as hardly more relevant to my own intellectual concerns than a genius for chess – though it was plain to me that *he* had character as well as genius.

Cultivated as he was, his interest in literature had remained rudimentary. He sometimes got me to read out to him parts, specified by him, of *The Uncommercial Traveller*, but I was unable to guess what it was in them that determined the choice – for he seemed to know them already. He knew *A Christmas Carol* by heart. To these works his interest in Dickens, so far as I could tell, was confined, and I never discovered that he took any other creative writing seriously. It may of course be that in German the range and quality of his literary culture were more impressive, but I can't give any great weight to that possibility.

There was, then, this tacitly accepted difference between us – potentially an intellectual incompatibility, and perhaps something like an antipathy of temperament. I will accordingly end on a memory that gives this fact an appropriate concluding emphasis. He said to me once (it must have been soon after his return to Cambridge): 'Do you know a man called Empson?' I replied: 'No, but I've just come on him in *Cambridge Poetry 1929*, which I've reviewed for *The Cambridge Review*.' 'Is he any good?' 'It's surprising,' I said, 'but there are six poems of his in the book, and they are all poems and very distinctive.' 'What are they like?' asked Wittgenstein. I replied that there was little point in my describing them, since he didn't know enough about English poetry. 'If you like them,' he said, 'you can describe them.' So I started: 'You know Donne?' No, he didn't know Donne. I had been going to say that Empson, I had heard, had come up from Winchester with an award in mathematics and for his Second Part had gone over to English and, working for the Tripos, had read closely Donne's *Songs and Sonnets*, which was a set text. Baulked, I made a few lame observations about the nature of the conceit, and gave up. 'I should like to see his poems,' said Wittgenstein. 'You can,' I answered; 'I'll bring you the book.' 'I'll come round to yours,' he said. He did soon after, and went to the point at once: 'Where's that anthology? Read me his best poem.' The book was handy; opening it, I said, with 'Legal Fictions' before my eyes: 'I don't know whether this is his best poem, but it will do.' When I had read it, Wittgenstein said, 'Explain it!' So I began to do so, taking the first line first. 'Oh! I understand that,' he interrupted, and, looking over my arm at the text, 'But what does this mean?' He pointed two or three lines on. At the third or fourth interruption of the same kind I shut the book, and said,

'I'm not playing.' 'It's perfectly plain that you don't understand the poem in the least,' he said. 'Give me the book.' I complied, and sure enough, without any difficulty, he went through the poem, explaining the analogical structure that I should have explained myself, if he had allowed me.

EUGENIO MONTALE

I · EUGENIO MONTALE'S 'XENIA'

Of Montale's work, it is to *Xenia* that I must confine myself, the reason being that, while I am very far from inward enough with Italian to offer myself as a critic of Italian poetry, I have been profoundly impressed by *Xenia,* and have cultivated an intimate acquaintance with it (for it really forms one poem). This special attention I have paid it is perhaps the result of a coincidence of accidents; in any case, I have found Montale's poetry peculiarly congenial. What makes it so congenial I can begin to suggest by recalling the occasion when, a couple of years ago, I had the honour, at Milan, to meet Montale. How it was that someone present came to quote from *Le Cimetière Marin* I can't now remember, but Montale and I found ourselves reciting, in relays, Valéry's poem. How far we got I again can't remember, but it was plain that, between us, we could easily have reproduced the whole poem from memory.

The significance of this anecdote is not that I think Montale at all like Valéry, but the contrary. That we should both be able to recall in that way *Le Cimetière Marin* seems to me, though it is Valéry's most rewarding poem, paradoxical. I have, it happens, been discussing it recently with a group of students at the University of York. Not that French literature is my business: I wanted to make and enforce some critical points in relation, in particular, to T. S. Eliot's poetry, and also to the falsities and inconsistencies of some of his most admired criticism – which his own creative practice, as exemplified compellingly in his major work, contradicts. I am thinking of the hints and formulations that were supposed to warrant his being credited with having expounded and espoused a theory of 'impersonality'.

Now I think that great art is necessarily impersonal, and that the true creative impersonality is what we have in the poignancy, the profound movingness, of *Xenia*. As for my 'paradoxical', it registers the fact, not merely that Montale is very unlike Valéry, but that Eliot's prescription of 'impersonality' goes essentially with his insistently expressed admiration for Valéry's poems – admiration which, as formulated, amounts to making the *kind* of poetry Valéry's work represents the very norm of good poetry: the kind of thing that poetry should aspire to be. In the recent discussions of *Le Cimetière Marin* to which I have referred, we found ourselves agreeing that a limiting judgement was decidedly called for, and that it was best put by saying that this poem was a brilliant demonstration of the poetic art conceived as a game. We had been brought to the conclusion that, for all the sonorous felicity with which the theme of death had been enunciated –

> Ils ont fondu dans une absence épaisse,
> L'argile rouge a bu la blanche espèce,
> Le don de vivre a passé dans les fleurs!

– the seriousness of this poetry was the seriousness of a game taken as the most important thing in life. And I produced a warrant for this formulation in what Eliot himself, quoting Thibaudet on Mallarmé in support, had written in 1924 in an introduction to *Le Serpent* (text and English translation, the poem being that which we know as *Ebauche d'un Serpent*): 'To English amateurs, rather inclined to dismiss poetry which appears reticent, and to peer lasciviously between the lines for biographical confession, such an activity may seem no other than a *jeu de quilles*. But Boileau was a fine poet, and he spoke in seriousness. To reduce one's disorderly and mostly silly personality to the gravity of a *jeu de quilles* would be to do an excellent thing.'

The poetry that established Eliot as a great poet doesn't answer in the least to the suggestion of this kind of sophisticated naivety, the significance of which lies in the personal insecurity it betrays – an insecurity that plays a decisive part in his creative drive. Montale is as different from Eliot as he is from Valéry. There is no insecurity behind *Xenia*, and therefore no need for what Eliot calls 'reticence'. If Montale had been 'reticent' in the sense enjoined by Eliot, *Xenia* could not have been written. The point I could make in my seminar was that Montale illustrates in his poem – illustrates irresistibly –

the only kind of reticence that is a virtue in what offers itself as serious poetry. For him, poetry is not a *jeu de quilles* – nor is it for Eliot, but Eliot, though it is in poetry that he explores in painful earnest the meaning of life, never permits himself to recognise unequivocally the fact, nature and significance of human creativity: he is afraid. Poetry that conceives itself as a *jeu de quilles*, however strenuous, cannot be lived with; before long it becomes boring – as, I confess, for all the brilliance I have so admired, I find *Le Cimetière Marin* and *Ebauche d'un Serpent*.

For a major poet such as Montale is, poetry is one's profoundest response to experience. The theme of *Xenia* is as central, important and moving as any human theme can be, and the reticence it requires of the poet is not a refusal to recognise the full nature of what, intimately for him as sufferer, it in reality portends; but the contrary. It is the use of intelligence (and that involves the discriminations of sensibility – *l'intelligence*, I tell my students, is not the same as 'intelligence') that determines how the actual pondered sense of irrevocable loss can be defined and communicated – two verbs that mean one thing to the poet. 'Life' is a necessary word, but life is concretely 'there' only in individual lives, and Montale's art, so different from Eliot's, as well as from Valéry's, achieves, devoted as it is to rendering with delicacy and precision his intensely personal experience, a profound and moving impersonality in the only way in which such impersonality *can* be achieved.

Professor Singh in the foreword to his edition of *Xenia*, which contains the Italian text along with the admirable English translation he has done, makes a comparative reference to Thomas Hardy's *Veteris vestigia flammae* – the epigraph that stands in my mind for the late group of poems in which the English poet, experiencing as one thing the actual privation and the imagined presence, recalls the much loved and 'much missed' woman he will never see again: 'Hereto I come to view a voiceless ghost ...' And there is point in the comparison: a direct simplicity of personal feeling certainly relates the two poets, who in this essential characteristic differ equally from Eliot. The point, however, is inseparable from the constatation to which it leads – that of the striking unlikeness it brings out. 'Simplicity', like all important words, has a range of values: Montale is immensely more subtle, more supple and more diverse than Hardy. The fact is apparent at once in the texture (hardly a felicitous metaphor – but what better is there?) and the nervous life of their verse. Hardy had to fight an unending battle against Victorian 'poetic diction', and the evidence of it is there in the handful of his major victories – as, for instance, in the line I have quoted above, that which opens what seems to me his greatest poem, 'After a Journey'. Montale, on the other hand, is, as poetic 'practitioner' (to use Eliot's favoured term), clearly a master of living – that is, today's spoken – Italian.

I say this with confidence, though I myself don't, I regret to say, speak Italian, so that my acquaintance with the living language is sadly deficient. But my immediate responsive apprehension led rapidly to my being wholly and inexhaustiblly engaged: I have read and reread *Xenia* almost daily since it arrived and find that I know it by heart; and I cannot doubt what 'intuition' and sensibility tell me. There is an effect of spontaneous naturalness, going with a great range of varying inflection, tone and distance, and this effect is the product of that exquisite and sure tact which is consummate art. Montale's verse, in its sensitive precision, answers to what Blake means when he speaks of 'the wiry bounding line'. I had read *Xenia* through a number of times before I came to the point of telling myself that the rhymes of which I had noted (along with assonances) more at each reading insisted so little on conscious attention because of their rightness (that is, decisive inevitability) in relation to rhythm and structure. What goes with the mastery of spoken expression that makes possible the economy necessary for the essential transitions of tone is the distinctive nature of Montale's theme. Here we have the great difference between him and Hardy. If we ask (as we don't) in regard to Hardy's 'woman much missed' what she was like, we can say that she was beautiful, but we have to recognize that she exists only as posited by the poet's nostalgic intensity. She is the woman with whom he was in love 40 years ago. But Mosca in *Xenia* is the highly individual woman apart from whom daily life was inconceivable until the 'catastrophe' of her loss, and is almost inconceivable now.

The difficulty of conceiving it as possible is marvellously conveyed by the poem, which evokes the relations between husband and wife in representative particularity. So compellingly actual is the evoked day-to-day ordinariness that one is inclined to say: 'This is the art of a great novelist' (which Hardy was not). But economy of this kind is impossible in a novel – we come back to the perfection of

Montale's essentially poetic technique. It is notable that, while he conveys so poignantly the inescapableness of his state of privation –

> il desiderio di riaverti, fosse
> pure in un solo gesto o un'abitudine

> The desire to have you with me again,
> if only through a single gesture or habit

– the focus of preoccupation for him is always Mosca herself. The 'self-pity' he avows in the four lines of VII in *Prima Sequenza* has nothing of indulgence about it:

> Pietà di sè, infinita pena e angoscia
> di chi adora il quaggiù e spera e dispera
> di un altro ... (Chi osa dire un altro mondo?)

> 'Strana pietà ...' (Azucena, atto secondo).

> Self-pity, infinite pain and anguish
> his who worships what's *here below*
> and hopes and despairs of something else ...
> (And who dare say another world?)

> 'Strange pity...' (Azucena, Act Two)

The reality of *il quaggiù* that he adores is still Mosca: that is why she exists so potently for us in the poem, filling it with her unassertive presence. There is nothing assertive about Montale himself:

> Dicono che la mia
> sia una poesia d'inappartenenza.
> Ma s'era tua era di qualcuno:
> era di te non più forma, ma essenza.

> They say that mine
> is a poetry of non-belonging.
> But if it was yours, it was someone's:
> not your form any more but your essence.

His characteristic tone is given in

> Eppure non mi dà riposo
> sapere che in uno o in due noi siamo una sola cosa.

> Yet it gives me no rest to know
> that alone or together
> we are one.

I wanted earlier to say that Montale was much more sophisticated than Hardy, but hesitated because of the ambiguous force of the word in English. But I will now hazard that, in a wholly unpejorative sense, Montale – it is an aspect of his unassertiveness – is as truly sophisticated as a major artist can be. The sophistication is apparent in the wit, irony and humour that intensify the effect of profound seriousness characterising his poetry. It is apparent in the way in which he conveys his sense of the supreme reality of Mosca. His delicate intensity of evocation makes us feel that, in a naive sense of 'real', she is a real presence for us – that she is really 'there'. Actually, the unquestionableness of the reality he evokes as Mosca is conditioned by his sense that there is something at the centre of it which, though he responds to it, can't be confidently grasped (we recall Lawrence's insistence that the other person *is* other). Thus the first poem of *Seconda Sequenza*, which begins *La morte non ti riguardava* ('Death didn't concern you'), closes:

> Una tabula rasa; se non fosse
> che un punto c'era, per me incomprensibile,
> e questo punto *ti riguardava*.

> A tabula rasa – except
> that a point there was, though beyond my grasp,
> and this point *did* concern you.

And in the second poem we have:

> È strano che a comprenderti
> siano riuscite solo persone inverosimili.

> Strange that only
> Improbable persons could understand you.

There is no nuance here of cynicism or doubting hesitance in face of the contemplated reality. In fact, Montale's communicated sense of the reality there is in experience is of an essentially fortifying kind. Two of the constituent parts of the whole poem – XIII of *Prima Sequenza* and III of *Seconda* – might seem to have the implicit function of evoking that recognition. To quote the first, which begins *Tuo fratello morì giovane*:

> Fuori di te nessuno lo ricordava.
> Non ho fatto ricerche: ora è inutile.
> Dopo di te sono rimasto il solo
> per cui egli è esistito. Ma è possibile,
> lo sai, amare un'ombra, ombre noi stessi.

And none remembered him except you.
I asked no questions; and now it's useless.
I'm the only one after you
for whom he ever existed.
But it's possible, you know, to love a shadow,
we ourselves being shadows.

The play on *ombra* and *ombre*, which has the air of insistence, doesn't in fact at all tend to make *ombra* mere nothingness. And the other ends:

Coloro che hanno presunto
di saperne non erano essi stessi esistenti,
né noi per loro. E allora? Eppure resta
che qualcosa è accaduto, forse un niente
che è tutto.

Those

who presumed to know it
were themselves non-existent, as we were
for them. And so what? Yet the fact
remains that something happened, perhaps a trifle
which is everything.

I prefaced the discussion of *Le Cimetière Marin* with my group of students by remarking that it was a poem of a kind that didn't exist in English. I meant that we had no poem answering at all to the description, *jeu de quilles*, which could with any plausibility be critically offered us as major poetry. I have said at various times to them, in my provincial way, that it was easy to think of *Xenia*, though it was in Italian, as an English poem. But I must confess that – as I told them also – we have nothing like it in English.

II · EUGENIO MONTALE:

A TRIBUTE

Apart from the advantages it brings the poet himself, one must welcome the Nobel Committee's formal decision that Montale is a great European poet, for the decision as a critical judgement is well-founded. It rests with us to emphasize this truth and make the most of it – us whose concern is about the cultural implications of Europe remade as an 'Economic Community': Montale really *is* a great poet. It may be thought absurd to suggest that any appeal to higher cultural values *could* retard, or in any way affect, the development by which economic progress – the steady raising of what leader-writers, and the world as known to politicians, call the 'standard of living' – becomes the supreme and virtually self-sufficient solicitude of statesmen and, it seems, some bishops. And what frightening grounds there *are* for concern was apparent on the eve of the referendum, when, apprehensive of defeat, the interests intent on ensuring the outcome they had invested their hopes and calculations in, drew on their immense resources and paid for a full-page advertisement in the papers. The advertisement was just this – nothing more: 'Joining Europe means more jobs in this country.' That was not long ago. In the short time since then it has been made quite plain that human nature, with its essential drives, is not so simple as our Americanising civilisation is committed to assuming. Committed; so that Prime Ministers and leader-writers, disinherited like the electorate, go on talking the same old language and emitting the same clichés. But the Nobel prize carries great prestige, and Montale is a genuine creative power: the principle of life isn't quite forgotten, though modern civilised man can realise only feebly what it portends. I will quote at this point from my own epigraph to my last book:

'My preoccupation is to ensure that the living seed exists and that the life in it has the full pregnancy. Just how it will strike and take and develop, as it *must* if there is to be a human future, one can't foresee. Change is certainly upon us, menacing and certainly drastic; to meet it, there must be opportunism – the opportunism that answers to a profound realization of the need.'

Well, I say there that the clear prospect of drastic change should be seen as opportunity. That demands faith, and the fact of Montale should strengthen the faith of the tiny minority on whom any due use of change must depend. In any case, while one is alive one *is* alive, and goes on fighting – fighting to protect the seed from being crushed. So there is good reason for fostering a real belief that Europe has a great Italian poet whose creativity is *in* and *of* the Italian language, and belongs inseparably to that.

This last consideration is both dismaying (in more than one way) *and* a reason for insisting: poetry simply can't be translated. The reason for insisting is a matter of timeliness. 'Democratic' progress in education threatens to eliminate the teaching of languages in schools. This is the path of advance that brings in sight the American condition in which foreign poetry is in general offered to the *élite* only in translation.

In saying that poetry is untranslatable I am not being rude to Professor Singh, but only illustrating the ambiguity of the verb 'translate'. Montale's poetic involves a natural – that is, ostensibly free, but actually strict – use of living spoken Italian. I have for decades known stretches of Dante and things of Leopardi by heart. But Montale is in every sense a modern poet. He has been, he still is, a practising journalist, and Dante and Leopardi were for me very largely obstacles to my perceiving the nature of Montale's art. The intelligence and delicacy of Professor Singh's translations were necessary to my achieving the full conviction that Montale was – is – unquestionably a poet of the greatest distinction and significance.

Montale's characteristics are not confined to *Xenia*, but actually *Xenia* presented Professor Singh with an incomparable opportunity. The poem is more than a sequence; that is, while many of the short constituent pieces can be read as separate poems, it is only in the context of the total poem that they have their full value. The fact that the one theme is being explored facilitates the reader's appreciating the variety of Montale's art – which isn't just variety, but adequacy to human life. For this necessary perception I am immensely indebted to Professor Singh's presentment of text and translation *en regard*.

The virtue of a good translation is the virtue of an intelligent and sensitive crib, for it is only in the language of the poet that poetry can be read *as* poetry. This must be, for those concerned about the cultural future, a disturbing consideration. It is not merely that educated people have ceased to read Italian (as they once used to do); the effective educated public has now ceased to exist – with lethal consequences.

The very small minority that continues to see how much these consequences matter can't accept them. The prospect is desperately discouraging. One can only explore the possibility that, with the aid of the new techniques of communication, a sufficient minority, however minute, might be created to replace the old educated public and keep the seed alive – even to have some influence in the days of the Arts Council. But this is not an occasion for developing that theme, though it must be deeply involved in one's notion of a proper salute to Montale.

I think it appropriate to make my part in the salute an insistence on *Xenia*, which is so pregnantly representative of Montale's genius. Its being devoted in its highly characteristic way to the memory of his wife exemplifies in a major respect the felicitous modernity of the poet's work as an implicit commentary on the civilisation that gives so high a place to economic criteria and economic motivation. I am thinking of the close relation between the supreme emphasis on economic considerations *and* the religion of equality. The significance is the supersession of the organic and the accompanying mechanisation of life. The human individual is regarded as what he is for statistics – a standard human unit. I ought to have said in the last sentence 'what he or she is for statistics'; we have now had formally decreed the equality of women and men for what are accepted as the most important, the distinctively human, purposes.

It is a frightening development, and one sees that, in our economico-quantitative civilisation, it is not only logical but necessary – necessary if competitive productivity is to be restored and maintained. One insists that, essentially, the issue is not a matter of equality or inequality, but of difference – a difference necessary to life, and not only for the continuance of the species.

Xenia is contemporary poetry devoted to a major poet's enforcement of that truth. It is devoted to the evocation of the so decidedly individual woman whose death has left Montale feeling, irremediably, that he is lost without her. The focus is on the woman, his wife, and the intensity of the evocation is the intensity of the desire, the felt need, for what is now missing in life. The reality, both vivid and elusive, is re-created in the diversity of the evoked particular memories, with the play of shifting and contrasting tones. The total poem is an utterly unconventional and utterly convincing testimony to the central truth of life that the proclaimed 'equality' of man and woman denies.

THE 'GREAT BOOKS' AND

A LIBERAL EDUCATION

D. H. Lawrence's would have been the commentary to have on *The Great Books of the Western World,* and the plan of democratic regeneration through the 'Study of the Great Ideas', a study to be pursued with a life-long application and the aid of the *Syntopicon* (Volume I, *Angel to Love;* Volume II, *Man to World*). It is easy to find in his writings very relevant and suggestive things about Ideas, Idealism (and American Idealism in particular), Freedom, and Equality. Opening *Studies in Classic American Literature* I light at once on this, in the chapter on Benjamin Franklin:

> Oh Benjamin! Oh Binjum! You do NOT suck me in any longer.
> And why, oh why should the snuff-coloured little trap have wanted to take us all in? Why did he do it?
> Out of sheer human cussedness, in the first place. We do all like to get things inside a barbed-wire corral. Especially our fellow-men. We love to round them up inside the barbed-wire enclosure of FREEDOM, and make 'em work. '*Work, you free jewel,* WORK!' shouts the liberator, cracking his whip. Benjamin, I will not work. I do not choose to be a free democrat. I am absolutely a servant of my own Holy Ghost.

Mr Robert M. Hutchins in *The Great Conversation* (which explains the plan) addresses the free democrat, conceived as representatively the worker at the assembly line. Work at the assembly line, Mr Hutchins concedes, tends to be, intellectually and spiritually, neither stimulating nor exalting, but the triumph of industrialization it represents has liberated the free democrat into leisure. Or, rather, it has made it for the first time possible for him to be truly a free democrat. And to be truly a free democrat, Mr Hutchins insists with stern logic, is an affair of sustained and resolute hard labour. If, as he says, 'Work is for the sake of leisure', then leisure, he immediately makes plain, is for the sake of work; for the sake, in fact, of what, for all but a conceivable handful of Leonardo da Vincis (and Members of the Advisory Board, with the Editorial Consultants — among whom I am impressed to see a member of my own university), must be incomparably more exacting and burdensome than what they ordinarily call work.

The logic is inexorable:

If leisure and political power are a reason for liberal education, then everybody in America now has this reason, and everybody where democracy and industrialization penetrate will ultimately have it. If leisure and political power require this education, everybody in America now requires it, and everybody where democracy and industrialization penetrate will ultimately require it. If the people are not capable of acquiring this education, they should be deprived of political power and probably of leisure. Their uneducated political power is dangerous, and their uneducated leisure is degrading and will be dangerous. If the people are incapable of achieving the education that responsible democratic citizenship demands, then democracy is doomed. Aristotle rightly condemned the mass of mankind to natural slavery and the sooner we set about reversing the trend towards democracy the better it will be for the world.

The 'liberal education' that the people must achieve in order to qualify, not only for leisure, but for exemption from slavery, is to be identified with the programme of the Great Books: this assumption, taken as virtually axiomatic, is *of* Mr Hutchins' logic, which I did not lightly call inexorable.* The Great Books include (among many others) the works of Plato and Aristotle; the *Summa Theologica* of St Thomas Aquinas; the works of Hipparchus, Galen, and Archimedes, the *Enneads* of Plotinus; the works of Pascal; Spinoza's *Ethics;* Huyghens' *Treatise on Light,* Newton's *Mathematical Principles of Natural Knowledge* and *Optics; The Wealth of Nations;* Kant's three *Critiques,* together with four other works by him; Hegel's *Philosophy of Right* and *Philosophy of History;* Marx's *Capital;* Faraday's *Experimental Researches into Electricity;* the works of Freud.... Liberal education involves mastering these — and not only these — formidable treatises, together

---

* To be safe against the charge of misrepresentation I must report that Mr Hutchins makes this concession: 'On the other hand, the conclusion that everybody should have that education which will fit him for responsible democratic citizenship ... does not require the immediate adoption in any country of universal liberal education.'

(of course) with Homer, the Greek tragic writers, Lucretius, Vergil, Dante, Shakespeare, *Faust,* and so on; and a 'liberal education is the education that everybody ought to have'.

'We believe,' says Mr Hutchins, 'that it is a gratuitous assumption that anybody can read poetry, but very few can read mathematics.' There is no irony here: this is not, as you might suppose, a defence of poetry against a gratuitous assumption; it means that it ought to be possible to assume that the mathematical and scientific classics are accessible to all, and that we must assume it in laying our plans for universal liberal education. 'This is not to say that any great book is altogether free from difficulty. As Aristotle remarked, learning is accompanied by pain.' So if the free democrat, faced with Pascal's *Correspondence with Fermat on the Theory of Probabilities,* or Newton's *Mathematical Principles,* or Kant's *Critique of Pure Reason,* should feel that, so far as *he* is concerned, the probability of profit is not such as to make his applying himself *here* a good use of his time, the answer is, 'Work, you free jewel, work!' One cannot expect to master a great book at one reading; education is a matter of a lifetime; and here, by the way of encouragement, is a ten years' programme sketched. One is free to make one's own approach and to arrive at one's own understanding, since these works, 'we hold', are intelligible to the ordinary man. 'The great books should speak for themselves, and the reader should decide for himself. Great books contain their own aids to reading; that is one reason why they are great.'

As for the *Syntopicon,* it 'will not interpret any book to the reader; it simply supplies him with suggestions as to how he may conveniently pursue the study of any important topic through the range of Western intellectual history. And reading and understanding great books will give him a standard by which to judge all other books.'

I find it hard to decide which aspect of the whole extravagant and enormous unreality is the more astonishing; the idea that liberal education is, or should be, or ever has been, *this;* or the fanatical illusion that one may hopefully set out to prove that this, or anything like it, could be made, by dint of example and leadership and exhortation, the people's way of using leisure (or life) – or a common way – in America or any country. But it is that illusion which has given the grotesque and solemn escapade of academic idealism its aspect of portentous fact: here are the volumes,

expensively produced; the awe-inspiring catalogue of books is
clearly no mere catalogue; the moral and the practical support have
been abundantly forthcoming. I start, then, by asking myself how an
undertaking so utterly uncountenanced by observation and
experience can have been entertained to such effect, commanding as
it has done the devoted labours of learned minds and the financial
backing of men of the world. And it is plain that the extravagance of
this unreality of democratic faith is a kind of corollary of those
disastrous consequences of 'democracy' in education which are
reported by Mr Hutchins:

> The products of American high schools are illiterate, and a degree from a
> famous college or university is no guarantee that the graduate is in any
> better case. One of the most remarkable features of American society is that
> the difference between the 'uneducated' and the 'educated' is so slight.
> The reason for this phenomenon is, of course, that so little education
> takes place in American educational institutions.

I merely quote Mr Hutchins. The delicacy of an Englishman's
engaging at all in this commentary comes home to me afresh at this
point, and I will only say about the facts in question that, going by a
good deal of relevant reading and by what I have gathered in talk
from American friends and informants, I take Mr Hutchins to be
expressing with extreme severity a dissatisfaction with American
education as it is that (among those who may reasonably be said to
have opinions) is generally shared, and for which there are good
grounds.

In so complex a matter it would be rash for anyone, whether
American or foreign, to offer as an adequate explanation any simple
account of causes. Nevertheless, when one considers what one has
gathered about the problem and the grounds for discouragement
facing the American educationist at the university level, it is
impossible not to see the trouble as, in essential respects at any rate,
an American interpretation of democracy. It is the interpretation
assumed as unquestionable by Mr Hutchins himself. This comes
out strikingly in his way of replying to critics of the scheme he
advocates:

> Many convinced believers in liberal education attack the idea of liberal
> education for all on the ground that if we attempt to give liberal education
> to everybody we shall fail to give it to anybody. They point to the example
> of the United States, where liberal education has virtually disappeared, and

say that this is the inevitable result of taking the dogma of equality of educational opportunity seriously.

The two criticisms I have mentioned come to the same thing: that liberal education is too good for the people. The first group of critics and the second unite in saying that only a few can acquire an education that was best for the best. The difference between the two is in the estimate they place on the importance of the loss of liberal education.

The first group says that, since everybody cannot acquire a liberal education, democracy cannot require that anybody should have it. The second says that, since everybody cannot acquire a liberal education, the attempt to give it to everybody will necessarily result in an inferior education for everybody. The remedy is to separate the few who are capable from the many who are incapable and see to it that the few, at least, receive a liberal education. The rest can be relegated to vocational training and any kind of activity in school that happens to interest them.

The more logical and determined members of this second group of critics will confess that they believe that the great mass of mankind is and of right ought to be condemned to a modern version of natural slavery. Hence there is no use in wasting educational effort upon them.

Mr Hutchins complicates the point a little by so gratuitously identifying liberal education with the Great Books programme. But the unquestioning ease with which he assumes the identity must itself be taken as a mark of the decay in America of the tradition of liberal education. And in that decay it seems plain that the axiom assumed by Mr Hutchins had a major part; the axiom that it is an offence against democracy to advocate for anybody anything that everybody can't have. And now, answering his critics, Mr Hutchins with emphatic deliberateness advocates his Great Books programme as the education for everybody. He has indeed gone further; he has said that, if everybody cannot be proved to be capable of this education, then democracy is doomed.

If Mr Hutchins is right, then we can have no hope for democracy; for nothing is more certain than that very few persons indeed are capable of making even a plausible show of submission to the regime of the Great Books – even with the aid of the *Syntopicon*. The conclusion, however, that I choose to dwell upon is that, until the 'democratic' axiom is dropped, it is a poor lookout for liberal education in America. I won't for the moment argue about the relation of the Great Books and the *Syntopicon* to any intelligent idea of education, but will state my firm belief in this form: it is disastrous to let a country's educational arrangements be determined, or even affected, by the assumption that a high intellectual standard can be attained by more than a small minority. This belief has behind it a very different experience from Mr Hutchins'; for the history of education in England has not been what he reports of America.

Severe as would be in some contexts the criticisms I should pass on education in my own country, it would be misleading here not to say that English schools are good. I should be ungrateful if I said otherwise, seeing the profit that, as a university 'teacher', I get out of working with the undergraduates coming from them. These men, of course, are very highly selected. I will not here try to sketch the system by which the minority of the school-attending population ultimately judged capable of benefiting by university education gets to the university. The essential point I have to make is given in the words 'selected' and 'minority': the attempt to establish a democratic educational system in Great Britain has gone on the assumption that far from everybody has the capacity to justify his or her presence at a university – if 'university' is to mean anything – and that there must consequently be a severe sifting. My own observation and experience (it seems odd to have to say so) assure me that that assumption is well grounded. And I will record my conviction that, for a good long while before the well-known postwar educational reforms associated with the Welfare State, very few in Great Britain capable of justifying their presence at a university had failed to get there.

But I see that I must now, in order to convey the force of what I have to say, supply this informative note: Oxford and Cambridge cream the country; no one who can get into Oxford or Cambridge, and wants to go there, goes anywhere else (at least, this is true of England, and I know that the pull of the ancient English universities on Scotland is very strong). Under the postwar Labour government an attempt was made to 'direct', as of right and policy, those for whom the public funds were making university education possible – to direct, that is, to Manchester, Liverpool, Birmingham, Leeds, Sheffield, Bristol, or whatever other university the authorities judged proper, students whom Oxford and Cambridge were willing to admit; but the attempt met with strong resistance and was generally condemned and has been abandoned. So Oxford and Cambridge, as I said, still cream the country.

My point is that there *is* a cream and that it is a very small proportion of the population of university age. Teachers in the provincial universities bear rueful testimony to the fact. When I compare notes with them I find them as a rule very ready to recognize that, in general, by the standards of Oxford and Cambridge, the work in their departments – the education for the guidance of which they have to assume responsibility – is not really at the university level. They hope to find now and then an especially good man who, when they have done all they can for him, can be sent to an ancient university to qualify for an Oxford or Cambridge degree. The disadvantage under which they work is not a condition they would propose to remedy by diverting the best material from the ancient universities and sharing it out. They know – they have good reason to know – that the supply is strictly limited, and that only by the actual concentration can standards be maintained, and that unless they are maintained somewhere the cause is lost everywhere.

What I am trying to convey is that in a country in which there has been no such collapse, and no such hiatus in tradition, as Mr Hutchins reports of American education, it is impossible to question the clear fact: only a minority is capable of advanced intellectual culture. The situation I have briefly sketched amounts to this: Oxford and Cambridge (which, as I have said, cream the country) could become more 'open' only by lowering standards, for no other discrimination than what is represented by these now regulates their hospitality. And if democratic equality of opportunity requires that standards should be lowered, then I am against democracy.

At this point I have to confess that by Mr Hutchins' standards I am not qualified to speak: I have not read most (I think) of the Great Books, and I shall never read them. I know that it would be a waste of my time and energy to try. And yet I had what Mr Hutchins (to judge by his account of the conditions he is familiar with) would judge a comparatively good education. I left school with a very good start in French and German. I spent a great deal of time as a schoolboy writing Latin proses, some of which were commended by my headmaster, Ezra Pound's correspondent, Dr Rouse. I could in those days (so soon left behind!) explain in Greek, observing quantity, stress, and tonic accent (the precise value of which Dr Rouse knew), that I was late for school because I had a puncture in my back tyre. With my Form I read through semi-dramatically the plays of Shakespeare. I worked enough at history (I remember reading, among other things, Trevelyan's *History of the American Revolution*) to win a university scholarship in that subject. At the university I took the Historical Tripos Part I and the English Tripos, both successfully. Then I was able to spend three years in postgraduate research.

It will be plain that I was not, at the beginning of the last paragraph, subsiding into modesty – though it should be equally plain that I have a strong (it is often a painful) sense of my limitations. My aim in these personal notes has been to give due force to the avowal that I have not read the greater number (I suspect) of the Great Books and, knowing it could never be worth my while to make the attempt at working through any such programme, shall never make it. Nor can I easily believe that Mr Hutchins himself, whatever ideal schemes the optimistic zeal of unbridled academic intellectualism may have proposed to him in abstraction, has actually worked through anything like that programme, or will seriously give himself to the attempt. He has had, and has, other things to do.

I have just used the phrase 'academic intellectualism': that seems to me to describe aptly enough the whole ethos of the Great Books – the Great Books, the Great Ideas, the Great Conversation, and the *Syntopicon*. So extreme a form of academic intellectualism could be found, I think, or could at any rate be taken so seriously, only in America, the favouring conditions being those which I touched on some time ago in these pages* when referring to T. S. Eliot's estimate of Irving Babbitt as against D. H. Lawrence and to the conceptions of Culture, Civilization, and Art represented by Pound's *Cantos* (and his pamphleteering). The conditions are those pointed to by Mr Hutchins himself in his account of the past century of American education. Where the living tradition has been so weakened the higher culture that should be *of* it becomes a thing apart, insulated from the world of actualities, where 'serious' living is done, in a kind of academic other-world. The ideal intellectual culture advocated by the promoters of the Great Books is plainly a monstrous unreality fostered by such conditions. The hypertrophied academic innocence, the utter remoteness from realities, the lack of all sense of how things are and what they *could* be, is proclaimed in the belief that this culture might, and must, be acquired by

* 'The Americanness of American Literature' in *Commentary* for November 1952, reprinted in *Anna Karenina and Other Essays*.

everybody. Let us not be academic and esoteric – let us bring it into full and living relation with actualities! Because the great bulk of mankind has never had the chance to get liberal education, Mr Hutchins tells us, it isn't proved that they cannot get it.

The unintelligently intellectualist nature of the academicism is manifested in the belief that *this* is liberal education, and the astonishing ignorance going with the intellectualism in the belief that *this*, or anything like it, was the education of the educated in any past. There must be scores of scholars in America who can provide Mr. Hutchins with compelling corrective notes about the intellectual cultures, and the lines of the liberal educations, of a number of different pasts in which there were powerful educated classes. Always in these pasts there is the strong positive bent, the selective interest, the relation to specific contemporary needs and conditions and to the set of the current in the contemporary movement of life. The type member of the *élite* didn't cover more than a fraction of the reading enjoined on the free democrat by Mr Hutchins. If he *had* (incredibly) occupied his leisure in the prescribed spirit, that would have meant that, at the 'educated' level, there was no living tradition. And where there is no living tradition there is in no real sense a contemporary higher culture and there can hardly be a liberal education.

Perhaps the case today is not as utterly hopeless – not quite as hopeless – as the Great Books scheme would make it appear, even though such a scheme, fervently advocated with wide and powerful support, suggests that all notion of what a living tradition is like has been lost. But I will, at any rate for the moment, put aside talk about 'tradition' (that tricky concept which needs such delicate and positive handling) and make some points that must have occurred to anyone who, as a 'teacher', is concerned with liberal education at a place where, in a modern community, liberal education is at least a recognized and institutional concern: a university. Thinking of correctives to academic tendencies, one tells oneself that there will be this mark of a student's having spent his time not without profit: he will leave the university knowing to much better effect that there are renowned works he needn't take as seriously as convention affirms, and others that, though they will repay the right reader's study, are not for him. For an instance of the first class, there is Aristotle's *Poetics,* a treatise prescribed among the Great Books. There may be some point in a student's looking up the *Poetics* when he is going into Tragedy under the guidance of Gilbert Murray, Jane Harrison, Cornford, and the other anthropologizing Hellenists. But the man who leaves the university able to suppose that in the *Poetics* he has studied an illuminating treatise on the foundations of literary criticism has not used his time to real educational profit – even if he has won high academic distinction. It is characteristic of the academic conventionality of the Great Books ethos to endorse the conventional academic standing of the *Poetics*.

I am not of course being foolish enough to question the importance and greatness of Aristotle – which brings me to the second head of the proposition I threw out in the last paragraph. Every educated person must know something about the nature of that importance and greatness, but it doesn't follow that he need have made a study of Aristotle's works, or that it would have been good economy for him to attempt it. Every educated person must know something about Plato, and will undoubtedly have read some of the works, but it doesn't follow that he must have read studiously through the *oeuvre* listed among the Great Books. And when it comes to prescribing that he must also have read the works of St Thomas Aquinas and Kant and Hegel (I confine myself to philosophers – to which, of course, the Great Books are not confined) it is plain beyond question that the promoters of the scheme not only have no notion of the limitations of the ordinary man (or the ordinary member of the intellectually given minority); they have no notion of the nature of a trained mind – or (shall I say) of that kind of training of the powers of thought which must be central to any real education. The student has to learn, as a matter of firm personal possession, the difference between real thinking and what ordinarily passes for that. It is a difficult and painful business, and one that is far from always forwarded – or even proposed – by the academic regime and environment. To the would-be self-improver faced with the Great Books programme as something to be seriously attempted, the difference, unless he is a genius or has unusual luck, will never present itself in any challenging form. The difficulty of learning what it is will elude his apprehension in the ardours and endurances, the confident new assaults on Everests of knowledge prescribed for him by Mr Hutchins. The typical product of that liberal enterprise, persisted in (if one can conceive of persistence on a big enough scale for there to be a typical product), will be that large, never-at-a-loss knowledgeableness, that articulate intellectuality, that happy confidence among large ideas, which condemns the possessor to essential ignorance of the nature of real – that is, of creative – thinking. And that is no real higher education which doesn't bring the student some first-hand experience of creative thinking – enough at any rate for him to know what it is, and to know the worthlessness of mere confident articulate intellectuality.

A man will hardly justify time and energy spent in reading the works of Aristotle (to take one instance of the many presented by the Great Books) unless he is committed to an intensity of sustained frequentation, and to a study also of the works of the relevant specialists, that will make him something of a specialist himself. Mr Hutchins and his friends, in fact, have not formulated the problem of liberal education as it presents itself today to anyone who proposes really to grapple with it. We are irretrievably committed to specialization, and no man can master all the specialisms. The problem is that of educating a central kind of mind, one that will give the different specialisms a humane centre, and civilization a centre of consciousness. I will add at once, in order to counteract any false suggestion conveyed by 'a central kind of mind', that the hope must be, for those who see the problem for what it is and feel its urgency, to work out different partial solutions at different places.

I myself have suggested, in *Education and the University,* how the opportunities presenting themselves in England at my own university might be taken advantage of for some such partial solution. I mention my book because, while intent on defining principles as sharply as possible, I aim there immediately at practice, and give my scheme in some detail: it is only so, it seems to me, that principle, and the nature of a proposed solution, can be made clear. But here, by the way of emphasizing that my criticism of the Great Books is no mere negative affair, I can only throw out some brief and general indications of the lines on which, I think, experiment should proceed – except that I add: 'I *have* explained, in terms bearing directly on practice, precisely what I have in mind – and I have given my hostages.'

That liberal education should be centred in the study of creative literature is a proposition that will perhaps meet with general agreement. When I insist that for English-speaking people it must be centred in the literature of the English language I have in mind in the first place the distinctive discipline of intelligence that literary study should be. And here I come to a place where, I know, without a particularity of illustration that is out of the question, I cannot be sure of not being misunderstood. It ought to be possible to insist that there is a real discipline of intelligence proper to the field of literary study without being supposed to be indicating the 'New Criticism'. But I should, I know, be ill advised not to say that what I am thinking of is none of the things commonly associated with that description. The real, disciplined application of intelligence to works of literature is one in which intelligence is not distinguishable from sensibility and essentially involves value judgement. I may indicate the force of my insistence by saying Irving Babbitt, T. S. Eliot's enormously learned mentor who hadn't the beginnings of intelligence about the literature of his own time, does *not* exemplify the mind that a liberal education would point to as proof of its success.

But the intellectualist inadequacy of the Great Conversation – of that conception of tradition and cultural consciousness and essential human history – comes out most strikingly, perhaps, in Mr Hutchins' attitude towards American literature of the past; bringing us to another aspect of the central place of literary study in liberal education:

> We thought it no part of our duty to emphasize national contributions, even those of our own country. I omitted Emerson, Whitman, Thoreau and Mark Twain, all very great writers, because I felt that, important as they were, they did not measure up to the other books in the set. They carried forward the Great Conversation, but not in such a way as to be indispensable to the comprehension of it.

Heaven save us from any large supply of the kind of 'comprehension' threatened here! It would be the end of all hope of any renewal of life. On that list of names one has to comment that, odd as it is as a list of the 'very great' American writers, a study of the writers named, intelligently directed, would provide a better approach in liberal education than any represented by the *Syntopicon*. This is the more so because one of those named is truly a very great writer, and his masterpiece, not unreasonably reputed the greatest American classic, a peculiarly good opening for a study of civilization. Actually *Huckleberry Finn,* though excluded from the first list of the Great Books, was let in later. There is a commentary on it in that series of guidebooks (*Symposia:* five volumes of *A Christian Appraisal*) which appears also to have been an after-thought (and since the commentators are all Roman Catholics, and from other hints, there would seem to be a curious history behind it). The commentator on *Huckleberry Finn* pays as good as no attention to the aspects of the book that make it so peculiarly fitted for the purpose in question. *Huckleberry Finn* exemplifies with great force a kind of relation between 'uneducated' living tradition and intellectual culture that the promoters of the Great Books know (one gathers) nothing of; Mark Twain's art brings the folk culture of the frontier into something that is much more than 'folk' and belongs to sophisticated literature. We have here (I make a second point) an unrivalled opening into a study of crucial importance for Americans: the part of the frontier in the history of European civilization in America (a study that, properly developed, would throw some light on the significance of the enterprise under review). Further, *Huckleberry Finn* illustrates supremely well how creative literature can provide, for the purposes of liberal education, the best kind of opening into ethical inquiry (and sociological); for the main theme of the book, abstractly stated, is the problem presented by the inescapable need for concrete ethical decisions in a society that, like any 'Christian' society, has a complex tradition, and is far from univocal in its ethical imperatives and promptings. That the Great Books expositor should not have noticed this interest (the central one) in a great work of creative literature – presented, that is, in the concrete and presented by a profound student, not of the Great Ideas, but of life – constitutes a piquant comment on the intellectual education advocated (and aptly illustrates the force of the description, 'academic intellectualism').

An intelligent study of *Huckleberry Finn,* of course, would go with a study of Mark Twain and Mark Twain's America. And such a study (there is admirable guidance – I am thinking in particular of the work of Bernard De Voto) offers as good an entry into the study of civilized man, and of the problems of civilized living, as a scheme of liberal education could ask for. It is only when intimately related to living experience that thought and knowledge in general or historical terms can have any vitality – can be anything but merely 'intellectual' and academic.

One has to note finally that, in his preoccupation with the Great Ideas, the idea of *a literature* seems to have escaped Mr Hutchins.

'We thought it no part of our duty to emphasize national contributions, even those of our country.' By 'national contributions' Mr. Hutchins means individual and separate Great Books. But *a literature* is a necessary concept, especially for liberal education; and where a country *has* a literature, and a great one, that literature will, in any real liberal education, be very much emphasized: it will be at the centre. And America *has* a classical literature, and one the central line of which explores with great sublety the meaning of American history and the relation of America to Europe: important enough themes for any Western mind. It is a literature that has the advantage of being, while distinctively American, part of the greatest of all literatures. I cannot conceive of an intelligent attempt to solve the problem of liberal education in America that should not make a great deal of that opportunity. I am thinking in particular, of course, of the line of novelists: Fenimore Cooper, Hawthorne, Melville, and Henry James, the line that (and we may associate Mark Twain) may be said to be the distinctively American way back to (or way on from) Shakespeare – Shakespeare who stands as the great presence in the background.

I shall not, I hope, have been taken to be suggesting that liberal education will be merely a matter of literary studies. But the scheme of liberal education for America that assumes the reading of Shakespeare and the reading of Aeschylus (in translation – and 'Great books contain their own aids to reading') to be the same kind of thing must be judged to betray an ignorance of the nature of literature; and a scheme that hasn't a sound notion of literature at its centre has gone wrong. The syntopical ignorance (we may call it) that knows nothing of the nature of true literary study, or of the idea of *a literature,* goes with the intellectualism of the Great Books scheme. And the intellectualism has as a major aspect the pseudo-democratic optimism that pronounces: *this* is liberal education, and everybody should be capable of it, for it hasn't been proved that he isn't; *this,* or nothing, and the free democrat who doesn't qualify deserves the slavery coming to him. It is pseudo-optimism; offered alternative slaveries, the ordinary man has no real choice, for very few *could* tread that intellectual mill, or make any sustained show of treading it. But actually, of course, it is very far from being *this* or nothing. And of no standard, or higher norm, of liberal education can it be said, it is *this* or nothing. The standard must be maintained somewhere, or everything is lost for the whole community. But if the standard *is* established and maintained, and it is a good and vital one, there will be possibilities of education, and of real participation in the cultural heritage, at many levels. What I have been really saying is that it must be intimately associated with a conception – one related to facts, or one that its servants are validly determined to make so – of higher culture as part of the whole community's tradition of humane life.

'BELIEVING IN'

THE UNIVERSITY

It's not just brains! The mind is an instrument, and the *savant*, the professor, the scientist, has been looked upon since the Ptolemies as a sort of upper servant. And justly. The millionaire has brains too: so does a modern President or Prime Minister. They all belong to the class of upper servants. They serve, forsooth, the public.

> 'Ca, Ca, Caliban!
> Get a new master, be a new man.'

That of course is Lawrence. He is giving his answer to the question, 'What then does natural aristocracy consist in?' Perhaps I didn't at the time think of that passage when, attending the by-election meeting of the Liberal candidate to whose nomination paper I had given my signature and to whose election fund a modest contribution, I heard Mr Thorpe's opening address. His first sentence was: 'The Liberal party is in favour of comprehensive schools.' The sentence was brief, and he said no more about education. It's not for that alone that I resolved, there and then, not to expose myself to being counted in future as a loyal backer of the Liberal party.

I had in fact the strong impression that Mr Thorpe was the only intelligent person on the platform. It was during the following speech, the candidate's, that my wife and I – when it had lasted only a very short time – went out. In attributing intelligence to Mr Thorpe I mean by the word something different from what Lawrence so clearly means by 'brains'. I suspect that the Liberal leader knew well enough that education matters and that the triumph of democratic egalitarianism is disastrous for humanity;

being in politics he was (necessarily) acting in the spirit of the politican's maxim: 'Politics is the art of the possible.' Such a divination, pondered, may – will – express itself in the view that, intrinsically, there is little or nothing to choose between the three parties. That view, however (it's mine), doesn't entail upon those whose response to the maxim is '*We* create possibility' a cynically inert indifference in the face of contemporary politics. I say this lest I should seem to suggest that things are simpler than they are. Even those who are bound to applaud the following Laurentian utterance may without inconsistency decide that it is incumbent on them to place their considered and responsible vote in a given election:

> In a great issue like the war there was nothing to be 'done', in Murry's sense. There is still nothing to be 'done' ...
>
> It is no use trying merely to modify present forms. The whole great form of our era will have to go. And nothing really will send it down but the new shoots of life springing up and slowly bursting the foundation.

I open in this way in order to make it possible to deal briefly with the animadversions that Ian Robinson brings against my thought. I should say at once that I have in front of me unpublished paragraphs, sent to me by him, of a draft-review he had written of *Nor Shall My Sword*. He sent them to me with the suggestion that I should use them as incitements to my explaining, for publication, just why I object to being described as 'believing in the university' (I had mentioned in a letter my surprise at having that 'belief' imputed to me for implicit dissent).

In them Robinson tells me some things that I know (he might in fact have found them in what I myself had written), and imputes to me beliefs and positions that are decidedly not mine. And he quotes, with an intention that strikes me as very odd, a passage of mine he approves of, or seems to, for he quotes it in order (as far as I can see) to make plain convictions of his own – convictions he brings with military intent against the misconceptions imputed to me.

The issues involved seem to me as momentous as any could be, and of great urgency. Renewed and reinforced emphases and clarifying restatements are hardly, then, supererogatory, and I am grateful to Robinson for giving me the opportunity to correct misapprehensions which, very clearly, can occur at a level where the offer at correction is certainly worth making.

The unpublished criticism brings together different facets of what it might seem fair to describe as a resistance to comprehending unequivocally – for Robinson sees and doesn't see, and accuses me of the blindness and the inconsistency. In the opening paragraph of what he has sent me, the first sentence of which is 'The flaws are apparent in the new Introduction to *Nor Shall My Sword*', he goes on:

This cannot be a simple judgement, for Leavis is extremely good at seeing what is wrong with Blake's belief in the possibility of an actual earthly paradise. He knows as well as Eliot that it is the pursuit, the genuine trying, that is as near as we can come to Jerusalem, and that restored Eden is a chimera.

The second of these two sentences makes me feel, ungraciously, that even the intended flattering judgement conveyed by way of introduction immediately before can hardly be thought to justify any lift in me, any mild stir, of self-esteem: the sentence can't be described even as a parody of the position I have been bent on defining, or the thought I have worked so hard to express. In using the word 'trying' (with 'genuine' in front of it) in that fashion Robinson is assimilating two unassimilable opposites – with the result that 'pursuit' is a worse than unhelpful word – it doesn't serve thought, it frustrates it. If we ask how he can have failed to see that, the answer is given us in the next sentence: 'Leavis yet wants to say there is something of a "basic nullifying contradiction" in the *Four Quartets*.'

I not only want to say it, I do say it unequivocally, and develop the judgement and substantiate it in a long and careful analytic commentary* on *Four Quartets*, Eliot's major work, which is of the first importance for people of Robinson's kind of concern for the human present and future. It has two characteristics that together explain Robinson's ability to be so wrong about it and so confident: the great innovating poet is irresistibly manifest in it on practically every page, but as a poem of sustained constructive thought on the profoundest of basic questions – the nature of the Real, and its bearing on the human concern with spiritual values – it is very difficult. Robinson, impressed by the here, here, and here again – the local poetry that seems to testify finally that *this* is a major creation – has failed to realize that one can't determine what the poet's position, the nature of his 'answer', is without a very exacting

---

* Forming the third and last part of *The Living Principle*.

sustained attention, often repeated, to the constructive 'music'. Firsthand attention can only be given by oneself. Robinson has had other things to do (there are too many in any case), and the assumptions, the alien ideas, that get in the way haven't, as the years have passed, become less obstructive.

'Trying', I divine with something like certitude, was picked up by him from the close of *The Dry Salvages*:

> Where action were otherwise movement
> Of that which is only moved
> And has in it no source of movement –
> Driven by daemonic, chthonic
> Powers. And right action is freedom
> From past and future also.
> For most of us, this is the aim
> Never here to be realized;
> Who are only undefeated
> Because we have gone on trying.

If Robinson examines the earlier part of the movement he will find indications that Eliot uses 'try' in a special paradoxical sense, and a study of the whole complex poem will confirm the apprehension. To try, in the Eliotic sense, is to train oneself to know, to practise knowing and realizing, that one is without the qualifications for trying. The saint doesn't need to try; he has achieved absolute humility and pure receptivity. To apprehend

> is an occupation for the saint –
> No occupation either, but something given
> And taken, in a lifetime's death in love,
> Ardour and selflessness and self-surrender.

It goes with Eliot's profound conviction of the utter abjectness and worthlessness of humanity. He represents it as knowing ('us' – the small minority who 'try'), or needing to know, that trying can achieve nothing, though it's our ideal aim to have gone on trying to the end. He implicitly denies human creativity.

And there we have the 'basic nullifying contradiction': it's, inevitably, as a poet, with his creative mastery of the English language (itself a product and proof of human creativity) that he undertakes to define for thought, and vindicate, this sense of the Real and humanity's relation to it, together with the nature of 'spiritual values'. If Robinson asks whether it is plausible to suggest that Eliot could have harboured so basic a contradiction and not see how nullifying it was, I can in reply suggest that he might inquire into how, in the face of his years of intellectual experience, he came to write this sentence, which in the text he sent me comes next: 'He [myself] also believes, flying in the face of a long lifetime's experience, that his Jerusalem, the idea of a university, might actually be embodied at institutions with postal addresses.'

If this, as the closing phrase suggests, is to be called a parody (I postpone my comment on the monstrous infelicity of 'his Jerusalem'), it is the kind of parody that, as parodies often do (e.g. Max Beerbohm's), grossly and inexcusably falsifies. It seems to be a discharge of malice, though I don't suspect Robinson of that – I conjecture that it may be animus given off by a Department of Philosophy (I make the suggestion out of experience). In any case, if I deserve to be associated with the belief that he imputes to me, he is, in terms of the same kind of logical cogency, as much open to the imputation himself as I am. *The Human World* has a postal address, and the address is at Swansea, where there is a university. What I am pointing out is that the co-presence is not accidental and non-significant: except from a university, it wouldn't have been possible to launch *The Human World* and keep it alive for four years, just as except from Cambridge it wouldn't, forty years ago, have been possible to launch and establish *Scrutiny*. *The Human World* implies 'belief in the university' not less than *Scrutiny* and my would-be high-level preaching do.

This doesn't mean (I testify out of unforgettable experience) that we had any temptation to dream that our efforts enjoyed, in the way of reception, or were likely to enjoy, anything but hostility or indifferent blankness from the institutional university and those to whom it gave power. Robinson, for one who thought it worthwhile launching *The Human World* and, at the cost of immense unpaid labour, keeping it alive, seems to me astonishingly unrealistic. Such an enterprise calls for ease and closeness of appropriate collaboration at the centre: where could the conditions for that be found except at a university? It entails, if it is to continue, the forming of a public; where are the promoters to find the access and the propagation-centres for this if not at universities?

In my lifetime there have been great changes. I wrote – or finished writing – *Education and the University* in the early days of the second war, and the total change since then has been so great that we may fairly speak of ourselves as living in a different civilization.

But at no time since I began to write, even at the least distant from the Victorian age, was the aim or the hope represented by my 'prescribing' for 'the university' that of getting any 'idea' of the perfect and perfectly functioning institution (university) embodied. I never supposed that contriving to get out of any university we might come to be blessed with anything like a performance of what I call 'the essential university-function' wouldn't involve a great deal of battle (and faith – and well-trained opportunism); but I did then think that conditions could be made very much more encouraging for the minority of both students and teachers who were bent on making the most of the opportunities they should find or contrive.

I indicate here what I mean when, in a paragraph of mine that Robinson quotes, I speak of the 'university as I contend for it' and the 'creating of the university'; this is my way of 'trying' to insist with some effect – 'in face of' the prevailing Robbins' mentality and its consequences – on 'the essential university-function' as being, in our time, to play a major part in restoring to society, and maintaining, an educated public.

My sense of the vital urgency of this human need is more intense now than ever before. In my new book, on the page I normally keep for epigraphs, I have put, after 'Give up literary criticism!' – the stern admonition with which Wittgenstein once characteristically greeted me (and he was never flippant), which is my attempt to recapture some prelusive remarks I made before giving a part of the book as lectures at York in the Michaelmas term:

There's no redeeming the democratic mass university. The civilization it represents has, almost overnight, ceased to believe in its own assumptions, and recoils nihilistically from itself. If you believe in humanity at all you will know that nothing today is more important than to keep alive the idea of the university-function – the essential university-function and what goes with it: the idea of an educated public.

This – it's the first half of the paragraph of which I'll reproduce the rest later – isn't what Robinson quotes, but, had it been possible, it might as well have been; it's as relevant to the commentary for the sake of which he prints the quotation from me he actually does (by way of justifying and enforcing his critical animadversions). With what strikes me as astonishing inconsequence, he quotes it immediately after the point at which I last took off from his text. It runs:

I express my sense of this [indebtedness] when I choose my Blakean title, though not committed – and telling myself so – to anything in the nature of building Jerusalem. My focal preoccupation is with the creating of the university – a very different matter. The university as I contend for it is not an ultimate human goal; it is the answer to a present extremely urgent need of civilization. The need is to find a way of saving cultural continuity, that continuous collaborative renewal which keeps the 'heritage' of perception, judgement, responsibility and spiritual awareness alive, responsive to change, and authoritative for guidance.

He comments on this: 'To put it pessimistically; unless the university *is* Jerusalem, a final human goal and never capable of invulnerable attainment, our situation is desperate indeed, for where is this other sort of university that is going to save our civilization?'

This seems to me – it is tenderness towards Robinson, I hope he will see, that makes me put it in these terms – perverse and *voulu*. I myself insist that our situation is desperate in the extreme, and I should say that I am more pessimistic than he appears to be if my reaction to the menace that faces mankind (but which is faced so little) didn't belong to a level that makes it unnatural to talk of either pessimism or optimism: one is alive, and there is an apprehension in one that puts it beyond all question that one fights in a positive spirit, with all one's perception and all one's powers, on behalf of life – one fights in the strength of something that asks to be called 'faith' rather than 'duty'.

To the irony of the question with which the sentence I have quoted ends I can only reply: 'But I don't want to save our civilization – on the contrary; I want to save humanity and life from it and its accelerating developments as it completes its conquest of our lives.' I shouldn't have replied in this blunt way if the irony hadn't been so gratuitous, and hadn't had behind it the extraordinary pertinacity with which he works the Jerusalem-tactic, so that one suspects him of insinuating that a concern for 'our civilization' is another of the inadvertent Jerusalems that stultify my thought. As for my censured 'belief in the university', what I have said already should have sufficed to exonerate that. But I see reason for insisting that it is important to keep alive the idea of what, for us, should be the essential university-function, which, in my recent formulation, I define by adding 'and the idea of what goes with it: the idea of an educated public'.

And this is the moment to avow with the appropriate force that I don't see how I could have set about making plain what I mean by 'educated class' – I can't conceive how one could proceed to define the 'idea' – in any other way than by intimating with some particularity what might be done at the university. This implies, of course, that genuine concern for the effective existence of an educated class can't be separated from concern for the university. Whether Robinson thinks so or not I am not sure, for I don't know how to take what he says next: 'As long as the genuine search goes on and the belief in the university ... is firmly held, one may survive as a university teacher even after the catastrophic and unmitigated defeats of the post-Robbins era ...'

Knowing Robinson, and having pondered it in its context, I assume it to be an affirmation of a kind of faith: the implicit reference ('as long as the genuine search goes on') to the 'trying' in which he so misguidedly assimilates Eliot and me seems to confirm the assumption. There may be some point then in my telling him that if he gets his thought clear – thought about the relations between fundamentals, possibilities, menaces and urgencies – he will see that it is not good enough to pooh-pooh serious attempts at clear thinking about the kind of intrinsic profit derivable from universities as (with a concern for something better) we know them, or, on the other hand, to justify the profound vital drive, the certitude, the faith that makes one desire to 'survive as a university teacher' by talk about its being the genuine pursuit, the going on trying, that is the relevant, intellectually respectable and realistically conceived 'higher reality'.

He says actually, of course: 'that is as near as we shall come to Jerusalem'. If he asked himself (and it would be fair of one to press the challenge ruthlessly), 'Pursuit of what?' and 'What are the criteria of genuineness?', he would realize that his Jerusalem-play (or ploy) is evasion, and find himself tackling the urgent problem (one we should be tackling collaboratively) in terms that, not being at odds with those I myself deal in, may be said to justify in that sense my own offers.

The problem is beset with difficulties and delicacies; I mean the problem of determining and saying what, in face of the apparently irresistible menace that nevertheless has to be fought, can be profitably done now. One knows, and Robinson knows, that it would be foolish to think of fighting in isolation and that there are a good many others who share, on the same positive grounds, one's horror and one's intransigence. This crucial (I firmly believe) minority can be strengthened by being made conscious, or more conscious, that it forms a community, with an articulate awareness of what it stands for, of the need for active resolution, and of what it aims at – which is neither a foreseen static goal nor a dream-evasion. I have already said that I can't conceive how this could be done unless by thought and exposition in terms of 'the essential university-function' – a phrase and a purposive conception that, with the new, the *unprecedented*, human crisis in view, I suppose myself to have originated.

So when Robinson pronounces that, whatever I have imagined myself to be doing in writing about the crisis, I have really been positing an ideal university that 'is going to save our civilization' and asks 'Where is it?' – ironically, as a way of justifying his representation of myself as prone to fall into the 'Blakean trap', the posited university being Jerusalem, it is, I confess, discouraging.

But Robinson sees me 'fallen into the Blake trap' too often, and detects Jerusalem in my thought always with the same grotesque gratuitousness, the same violence of infelicity. It is some automatism that intervenes in *his* thought and works havoc, and he should look to it; the aetiology should be discoverable. I first came on the trait in *The Survival of English*. 'Survival' seems to me to imply continuity, and the English language exemplifies with peculiar force the importance of continuity as *I* use the word. I make this point because, glancing a little ahead from the irony about my Jerusalem-university, my eye picked up this: 'When Leavis writes of "saving" cultural continuity he has fallen into the Blake trap and also into the trap of despair, for in that sense cultural continuity has not been and will not be saved.'

What 'in that sense' means I don't know, and I think Robinson doesn't either, his impression to the contrary depending on the vague potency in his mind of the Jerusalem-addiction. I'll not here discuss this further (the nature of standards seems to be involved), but return to the instance of the given trait in his book! He says (page 238): 'And yet Leavis himself ... can't resist, in a minor way, the attempt to get things neatly and finally tied up, by an enthusiastic endorsement of the campaign of Professor Marjorie Grene.' By way of making plain what kind of charge he is bringing, he goes on to pronounce:

The effort to see her group as having successfully initiated a philosophic revolution is not only unconvincing in itself, it is falling into the Blakean trap of thinking that revolutions in philosophy *can* be directed and managed in the service of a *telos* – which could only be a modern variant of a finished Jerusalem.

But there was no temptation to be resisted, and I couldn't endorse a campaign I hadn't heard of. When I discovered Marjorie Grene's *The Knower and the Known* (as I did for myself, never having heard of *her*), I had, it is true, been searching for a long while, but not, I concede – or insist, as a professional philosopher with the proper academic equipment of knowledge, purpose and criteria. I couldn't have made any effort to see her group as this or that in philosophic history when I didn't know of any group. But what concerns me immediately is not to vindicate the right (though I stand by it) of academically 'unqualified' persons to come to some important kinds of judgement about philosophers, but the clear instance of the automatism coming into play, asserting itself incontinently, and incapacitating the thinker for thought. Surely it is absurd to suggest as Robinson seems to do (he isn't lucid) that what is to be condemned is the purposive – the telic – in general.

He gets the word 'telos' from *Nor Shall My Sword* – from the introductory chapter ('Life *is* a necessary word') in which I distinguish between what in Blake should be found a source of inspiration and strength, and what I dismiss as at odds with that Blake – the Blake of genius and insight. The *telos* I dismiss is the *terminus ad quem*, the ultimate goal: Jerusalem, the reversal of the Fall and the end of developmental process, is offered us as final in that sense.

It is surely indefensible paradox to make the spirit of my concern for the university a desire, unrecognized perhaps by myself, to establish a final 'Jerusalem'. The concern is certainly purposive, but the *telos* is no more a finality than 'the human world' or 'the third realm' (Robinson chose, after considering both, the title for his quarterly from these two formulations of mine) is conceived as that. The 'essential university-function' as I conceive it is to foster the collaborative heuristico-creative interplay for participation in which – involving participation in the forming or strengthening of an 'educated public' (certainly the organ was committed to attracting a public) – *The Human World* was launched. Both – my university and Robinson's review – are telic, but the *telos* in each case is an implicit denial of finality.

I must record by the way, but with relevance, that I owe 'telic' to Marjorie Grene. I arrived at 'the human world' and my account of the nature of standards in my own way, a literary critic's; but I send my pupils to chapter 6, 'Facts and Values', of *The Knower and the Known* in order that they may study confirmatory analysis and constatation arrived at by a quite different approach. I interpolate this because Robinson has been so energetic and productive in his own field that he can't, I feel (exposing perhaps my own limitations), have had time and energy enough to acquire that inwardness with the philosophy-drill needed for firm resistance to pressures brought to bear by congenial representatives of departmental philosophy, and I can't help thinking that the odd gratuitousness with which he dismisses my use of *The Knower and the Known*, together with the intellectual confusion that stultifies his confident way with 'Jerusalem' and *telos*, is to be explained by influence emanating from the department of philosophy – which, experience suggests to me, is likely to resent any pretensions to a capacity for disciplined, but distinctively non-philosophic (at least by departmental criteria) thinking centred, avowedly, in literary criticism.

'Life is a travelling to the edge of knowledge, then a leap taken. We cannot know beforehand... It is a leap taken, into the beyond...'

That is D. H. Lawrence; it is one of many quotable utterances of his from which I might at any time have chosen my epigraph.

If I 'believe in' the university, the belief has never been the naïvety that has been imputed to me: I have never been naïve enough to suppose that a pattern devised by me would – could – be embodied by revolutionary reformers. Of course there has been change. Three and a half decades ago, when I wrote *Education and the University*, I could hope that I was helping to promote intelligent opportunism, and improving conditions and 'possibility' here and there for brave and enterprising 'believers'. But I didn't think of that as the main aim on which the justification of my efforts depended, though it would be a condition of any success to be hoped for and a sign that I had employed the only possible method of argument to some effect. My attitude, my profound belief, was and is what Lawrence has formulated in a paragraph from which I have already quoted: 'It is no use trying merely to modify present forms. The whole great form of our life will have to go. And nothing will really send it down but the new shoots of life springing up and slowly bursting the foundations.'

But even in this part of the total passage Lawrence doesn't imply that the springing of 'new shoots of life' absolves him (and us) from all responsibility. Himself he is life – and very potently, and he assumes in everything he wrote that the reader who finds him readable (as those who run all the risks of earning the favour of the *TLS* or the Arts Council by classing him with 'thugs' or 'morons' for the most part don't) is life too. He goes on and completes the paragraph with this: 'And one can do nothing, but fight tooth and nail to defend the new shoots of life from being crushed out, and let them grow. We can't make life. We can but fight for the life that is in us.'

Defending the new shoots of life when we feel the life growing in us is a positive business, and entails positive insight, apprehension and belief – with the corresponding effort. If you believe (as I do) that a new conception of 'the essential university-function' is necessary, the only way of explaining what you mean is the way that Robinson offers to discredit. He doesn't just condemn me (I must shift into the first person) for an incompetent advocate; he represents my advocacy as having for aim what it decidedly hasn't, and my 'believing in the university' as amounting to a kind of belief that it most certainly doesn't.

My way of explaining what I mean wouldn't have been possible if I hadn't been engaged in a practical way at a university. And for the last ten years I have enjoyed an experimental freedom for which I am grateful indeed. There has been no question of any attempt, or desire, on my part to prove that a present-day university could be 'reformed' in accordance with any conception of mine. My work has been opportunist and extra-curricular; it wouldn't have been possible but for the actual university, but it didn't fit into any formal academic scheme. It was done for the most part in small seminars, the membership of which was sieved informally with pragmatic implicitness (those who were bored dropped out) so that after a few sessions it deserved to be called an élite. The members were of mixed standing – mainly, I think (for often I didn't know), graduates – postgraduate students, teachers (perhaps) from other departments, together with some undergraduates.

Why did I think this worth while? For essentially the same reason as it seemed to Robinson and his associates worth while to run *The Human World* – which, I say again, could not have been established and kept going except from a university. In fact, to the criticism implied by the remark. 'I can't see how you find it possible to believe in the university', I can reply: 'My "believing in the university" justifies imputing belief to me just as much, or as little, as *The Human World* and *The Survival of English* justify the same imputation directed at Robinson'. For it is indefensible paradox in him to feel he is in a position – one of faith, in spite of the menace which he rubs realistically in – to tell me that I, as a result of my intellectual confusion, am 'trapped in despair', and yet leave it to be understood that in his view the 'going on trying' he supposes he believes in can go on without there being any access to an 'educated public', or any performance of 'the essential university-function'.

I produced this last formulation in the prelusive paragraph of which I have quoted the first half – the paragraph to be printed on the page facing the opening of the introductory chapter of my new book: *The Living Principle: 'English' as a Discipline of Thought*. It is in place now to quote the final half:

My preoccupation is to ensure that the living seed exists and that the life in it has the full pregnancy. Just how it will strike and take and develop, as it *must* if there is to be a human future, one can't foresee. Change is certainly upon us, menacing and certainly drastic; to meet it, there must be opportunism – the opportunism that answers to a profound realization of the need.

I was prompted to this sharpened monitory explicitness, both by the intensifying in the last few years of the menace, and by the undeniable state of crisis that has developed with apparent suddenness – frightening because of the imminence of breakdown it makes present to us, but at the same time, in the failure of the world's confidence in the rightness of its basic assumptions, opening a prospect of new possibilities for the kind of opportunities I have in mind.

It is a commonplace now that the pursuit of the 'democratic' ideal has led to a disastrous loss of standards. I have made it plain in the book that 'the essential university-function' as I discuss it doesn't involve intentions relating to the 'democratic' actuality, or even to a reasonable widely-spread 'Higher Education', except in so far as an adequate performance of the function is needed for the making possible a maintenance of appropriate standards at all levels. I say this in order that I may emphasize that I am *not*, under 'opportunism', thinking of a general reform of the university. The important thing is that the seed shall be sown, allowed to strike deep and root itself strongly, so that the idea is robustly alive – living and potent as an influence.

There are various ways in which this might be achieved, and, at some university, it is not extravagant to imagine, authority itself might favour an intelligent formal provision – one that enabled the university to attract, for a postgraduate course, an élite such I have the profit of working with. There is more than one way in which the university would profit, and the profit to the world at large would be disproportionate. I will repeat what I have said of the 'seed' in relation to which we have a responsibility: 'Just how it will strike and take and develop, as it *must* if there is to be a human future, one can't foresee.'

But those concerned in the founding and running of *The Human World* are strangely blind if they can't see that the hopes, beliefs and impulses it represents will rapidly prove to have been vain if the living seed is extinguished – as it will be without something in the nature of the essential university-function to protect and foster its growth. It would become Robinson to see that he is inconsistently enforcing this truth when he finds himself reporting:

Graduates in Dr Leavis's subject are no longer required at any British university to be able to write grammatical sentences; the science departments are explicitly abandoning first degrees as of any more significance than to provide a kind of academic helotry in order to support the statistics which will keep research in the manner of life to which it is accustomed; and two shaky 'A' levels (which mean nothing) are adjudged to be 'qualifications' for university entrance . . .

No political party will come out against this lethal development – because of the nature of politics. A politician's dominant aim must be to win elections, and in our civilization the quantitative concept has conquered. There can be few people who are not, in some way, aware of the price paid for 'equality'. A good many people – teachers and parents – feel that education matters; but the politician knows that with the majority of the electorate the appeal to jealousy will prevail (disguised and made morally respectable by the clichés of enlightenment). What most obviously bears out Lawrence's conclusion that 'The whole great form of our era will have to go' is the way in which the public has been educated to accept 'standard of living', meaning money and what money will buy, as the ultimate criterion of life. Politicians of all parties share the unquestioning acceptance, and not merely politicians; to talk with the loose generality that doesn't mislead, everyone shares it. Religious leaders more and more betray, speaking out of their modern enlightenment, that *that* is what they too really believe. Yet Lawrence didn't act on his own conclusion: 'There is nothing to be done.' He himself was a force of life, and his adverse commentary on civilised man served the positive insight and impulsion that the life in him inspired. The life is in us too, and makes it impossible for us to wait inertly for the overt disaster – which is now imminent. It is difficult to distinguish between the life in us and the 'shoots of life' it compels us to defend – 'We can but fight for the life that grows in us.' And 'fighting' is encouraging the life that grows, or might grow, in others, who are many – if not by the standards of the quantitative civilization.

But the urgency is extreme; disaster that threatens to be final *is* imminent. It will very soon be obviously not worth while even to attempt to launch a successor to *The Human World*.

MUTUALLY NECESSARY

The editor of *The New Universities Quarterly* suggested that I write a commentary on the contributions devoted to me in the December issue. Recoiling from the impossibility of the task proposed, I at first replied to that effect. On maturer consideration I decided that, in taking the opportunities that Michael Tanner provided for trying to explain further the intention of a difficult and imperfectly lucid book,* I should leave very few of the points made by any of the contributors unrecognized, if not satisfactorily dealt with. I am very grateful to Dr Tanner for giving me the stimulus to fresh thought, and enabling me to clarify at least some things – at least for myself.

Dr Michael Tanner has struck me as having been very forbearing, and more than that: surprisingly generous – generous, that is in a way that takes me by surprise (though I won't pretend to have derived no pleasure from the flattering imputation). I myself have known at close range two persons to whom I confidently imputed genius, and I judge that that word is not attachable to me. One of the two was Wittgenstein. And actually I haven't been so outrageously arrogant in my references to him as my prose style, together with the improvised mode of argument that went with it, allowed Tanner to suppose.

Ian Robinson, in a review he wrote of *The Living Principle* for *The Spectator*, anticipated, so implicitly endorsing, Tanner's

* Dr Tanner's article 'Literature and Philosophy' was one of a group of articles which made up the bulk of the December 1975 issue of *The New Universities Quarterly*. The majority of contributors concentrated particularly on Dr Leavis's recently published book *The Living Principle*.

strictures on my references to Wittgenstein. But I am surprised that Tanner should have been able to suppose that I anywhere recommend that *Fontana* brochure, or express the intention of using it. What I contended was that this is what non-philosophy students, finding that Wittgenstein's text itself beat them, would fall back on. In fact, I couldn't believe that even Mr Rush Rhees could make spareable time spent on Wittgenstein profitable to students of literature – even to most of a set of much above-average 'English' students. So far from being inclined to recommend that *Fontana* production, I insist – this is the explicit point of my referring to it – on its patent worthlessness to those seeking access to Wittgenstein's thought. It's possible that my scepticism about seminars on Wittgenstein's linguistic philosophy for 'English' students exposes my own limitations; but my fated situation has always been to be too pressingly beset, so that the choice between this and that extension of my equipment hasn't been really choice, but has been determined inevitably.

In fact, I don't think that Tanner fully realizes the problem facing the literary student who is both intelligent and serious. One difficulty is that there is too much literature demanding attention. Another main difficulty is raised, or pointed to, by the question: what *is* literary history? It is not possible to draw a firm and finally excluding line round the field of the study of English literature, though where its centre is should be plain. The literary student, among other things, must aim at being intelligent about the large changes in the philosophical climate as they have affected cultivated sensibility in the last four centuries. I have known very intelligent and devoted members of my seminars – research students and university lecturers among them – who, recognizing that, had set themselves to working through Russell's *History of Western Philosophy*. I have told them that they were wasting time and effort they could ill spare; for it was plain to me that that tone expressed the judgement confirmed by Tanner when he dismisses the book as a pot-boiler. Really intelligent men, venturing into a field of discipline which is not theirs, can waste a great deal of energy and incur depression before they arrive at such a judgement for themselves, unprompted. But what does one do when asked for a positive recommendation?

Here I come to one of Tanner's severest reprehensions; one which, as he formulates it, does me what I see as a major injustice. It may be that he is right to censure me for recommending Marjorie Grene's *The Knower and the Known* in any way for use by literary students. He is, however, certainly in error when he assumes that my attitude to the book means that I have the presumptuous self-sufficiency to offer it, against the judgement of qualified philosophers, as a classic of original philosophical thought, and that the affirmation of mine quoted against me means that no argued pronouncement by qualified philosophers will avail to shift me. To have meant that would indeed have been arrogant presumption – but I didn't. What I was actually contending will perhaps please philosophers not so very much better, but at present I find it, not merely defensible, but a necessary expression of my sense of responsibility. It is that it would be useless expecting philosophers themselves, Russell's *History* having been eliminated, to advise helpfully on the problem of what to advise instead. I think that even Tanner betrays that he hasn't sufficiently considered the problem, and it seems to me that what he offers as his positive suggestion when he tells me that I ought to have read and digested the *Blue Book* is really negative, for it amounts to deciding that the problem is insoluble.

I must narrow down to the immediate situation that I am honoured by being (having asked for it) made to face. No one else having shown signs of intending what could strike me as a real offer, I, in desperation, took on the responsibility. Responsibility assumed in such a spirit (in what other could it in any case be?) entails risks – risks not, I think, of doing any serious damage, except to one's own reputation and *amour propre*. Confirmed, then, in my sense that I had to rely on my own unprofessional judgement, I maintained an anxious look-out for something that could really help intelligent 'English' students. That account of how I had happened on Marjorie Grene's book in the Petty Cury bookshop I gave as a reply to Ian Robinson, who, reading a reference of mine to my use of the book, assumed that I must know of the part it had played in a would-be revolutionary philosophic movement – which he dismissed contemptuously. But I hadn't known.

While I am not a philosopher, I don't dispute that the philosophic is one of the necessary intellectual disciplines. I have postulated more than once, and emphatically, that all the major disciplines should be co-present in a university, this requirement being entailed in my conception of the university-function. I am aware that my concern for the function incurs dismissive irony. Nevertheless it is essential to my attempt to convey the conception of thought which I should very much like to get understood by at least some philosophers. How inevitably the concern 'enters in', it is necessary, I see, to make plainer than I have as yet succeeded in making it.

I will start by attending to Tanner's intimation of a lack that disturbs him in my criticism, and challenges me to make good. In his first paragraph, after referring to what he calls – a pleasant surprise to me – my 'famous' encounter with René Wellek and expressing some approval, he goes on:

> But it would still, even after reading Leavis's account of the growth of taste, be open to a philosopher to reply: 'Yes, that's an excellent account of how tastes are formed, become more or less firm, and so forth, but now I would like a *justification* of the taste that has been formed.' And there is nothing in Leavis's answer which explicitly copes with that challenge. So it looks as if, ironically, he may have fallen into the very common mistake of the British Empiricist Tradition – ironic, because he has such a low view of that tradition – of substituting biographical-psychological descriptions for philosophical analyses.

I have included in the passage I quote that last sentence because in it Tanner's assumption that value-judgements in literary criticism are to be justified by philosophical analysis is explicit. Tanner, I think, never escapes from that assumption (in common, I suspect, with most philosophers – that is why I call myself an 'anti-philosopher'); never escapes from the spectral presence and potency even where it isn't explicit or conscious. So he is closed against my essential contention from the outset, and doesn't fully realize what it is even when he seems most open to it. Three pages further on he writes:

> The criteria in terms of which Leavis judges literature are such that his work is bound to come into contact with philosophy at several points, and I shall only have space for discussion of the ones that strike me as being most urgent and problematic. The first, and the most difficult, is the question of the probative force of literature.

Tanner won't object, I think, to my re-phrasing the question as that of the probative process by which, in literary criticism, you establish the soundness or otherwise of value-judgements. That enables me to reply with suitable brevity that there *isn't* one.

His challenge makes one see point in emphasizing that the word 'value' as we have it in 'value-judgement' brings together in a treacherous confusingness two very different things. The sense that everyone takes seriously is the sense the word has when we talk of the value of an article in terms of money. Familiarity (which we all have) with this use entails that the sense in which we know that the value of x is (say) 200 takes no adjusting to. There are grounds for the common-sense assumption that there is a continuity between scientific verification and the process of verifying the necessary valuations that are factually involved in the practical day-to-day business of living. But the assumption commonly made that the continuity extends far enough to justify the challenge implicit in Tanner's 'probative' is fallacious; it doesn't. 'Verifiable', as I have said somewhere in print, must have, if used of literary-critical judgement, an utterly different meaning ('value') from that which it has in natural science – and at the mathematico-logical end of discourse from which the thinking of philosophers seems in general to begin, and continues to treat as the inevitable basic mode.

Probative? – I have had a habit of telling pupils that you can't *prove* a value-judgement. But I go on to say that you can always (no doubt I ought to say 'generally') get beyond the mere assertion of personal conviction. The process of 'getting beyond' is tactical, and its nature is most clearly brought out in the 'practical criticism' of short poems. But what is brought out in this way is the essential critical process. Putting a finger on this and that in the text, and moving tactically from point to point, you make at each a critical observation that hardly anyone in whom the power of critical perception exists, or is at least strongly potential, wouldn't endorse ('This is so, isn't it?'). The ideal is (not usually for the critic, in important cases, a remote one) that when this tactical process has reached its final stage, there is no need for assertion; this 'placing' judgement is left as established.

But I must go on with my effort at explaining the distinctive sense of the word 'verification' that justifies positively my dismissal of Tanner's concern for the 'probative' – his desire that I should explain how the thought for which I take my stand could provide for the need to prove the justice of the 'values' arrived at in the way that I describe. The answer is that there is no such need: Tanner's interpolation of the word 'taste' is merely the philosopher's ingrained habit taking over, and obscuring a reality which is basic for valid thought with a misconception.

In a valid account of the way in which a poem that we meet in is established there is no equivalent of the word 'taste'. If a term were needed it would be 'sensibility', which is so hard to pin down to one value that I avoided it in this note, and said instead that in the participants in a critical argument on collaboration ('creative quarrelling') the 'power of perception' must exist, or be strongly potential. 'Perception' stresses the outward focus, which is on the printed words. But the inward concern is with what the words do in their complex organic interaction, and that concern is a challenge to each critic to be more than ordinarily inward; it involves a self-searching and self-testing – for a profoundly considered and wholly sincere response.

My ancient reply to Wellek in itself can't satisfy Tanner, for Tanner's question as he puts it regards 'the probative force of literature'. In answering Wellek I necessarily held forth on the process of judging a poem, but a poem, or a clutch of poems, is not a literature; for a literature entails a literary tradition, and a tradition entails continuity and what we have to refer to as 'standards' (which, as one of the crucially important words, can't have its meaning fixed by dictionary definition). In virtually repeating my reply to Wellek I describe the nature of criticism in the only way open to me. Original critics are rare; whether rarer than great creative writers (who are certainly rare) I won't discuss (it would be pointless in any case). But this emphasis on rarity doesn't, in relation to my theme and argument, say all.

When a literary tradition is robust, as the English tradition was till quite recently (at any rate, till within my lifetime), the readers who, though not themselves describable as being among the few original critics, are – with the help of these – intelligent about significant creative writing, form, small minority as they are, a nevertheless decisively influential body – a body which is the core of an 'educated public'. Even today when Kingsley Amis is a second-to-none member of the ruling connection which controls all the prestige-generating machinery and the tradition is too decayed for influential people of any kind to be affected by it, or even aware of it, I find myself wondering whether the more or less isolated critically informed and intelligent persons I so often come on mightn't be formed into a new kind of minority public.

The relevantly important words immediately are 'continuity' and 'standards'. Standards relate to criteria, and are always changing. They are changed for subsequent creative writers and for critics by every great writer; this is true of the vital changes – the changes in which vitality manifests itself. But continuity has meant that the surest insight into human nature, human potentiality and the human situation is that accessible in the great creative writers. They establish what human centrality is. They differ in timbre, but they all have genius, and their genius is capacity for experience and for profound and complete sincerity (which goes in them with self-knowledge). The rare real critic too has a more than average capacity for experience, and a passion at once for sincerity and complete conviction. He knows that, in the nature of things, he can't attain to the completeness that is finality, and that some of his certitudes may be insufficiently grounded. But though words used in ordinary ways are felt as merely words, and can't give the quality *an sich* that makes the immediate experience irresistibly real, the nearest the perceptively thinking individual gets to the certainty that he is grasping in direct possession significance itself, unmediated, is in the certitude that he has taken possession of the basic major perceptions, intuitions and realizations communicated with consummate delicacy to the reader in the mastering of the creative work of a great writer.

Such certitude of possession is an ultimate; what could a proof, if proof were possible, add to it? The 'proof' that Tanner is asking for would, it seems to me, be philosophical; and the pages he devotes to me in *The New Universities Quarterly*, flattering as they are in sum, abound in evidence of the difficulty that one habituated to the philosophical discipline finds in realizing the nature of the discipline of thought I am contending for –a discipline developed out of literary criticism. He thinks highly of my treatment of language, meaning and the 'third realm', and regards it as philosophical. No doubt that use of the adjective can be justified. But the account, direct and implicit, I give leads in a central way into concerns that seem to me most decidedly *not* philosophical. The views I express make it plain that I judge it to be of supreme importance that contemporary great creative writers and the literary tradition should be influential. The continuance of the literary tradition in a vigorous state depends on a tiny minority of persons of keen and articulate critical sensibility, and its being influential depends on a much larger reading public that respects and responds intelligently to the judgement of the élite minority. Where the educated reading public has been destroyed, with the serious standards and the prestige they enjoyed (even among those who couldn't apply them intelligently), the tradition is dead or dying, and even, in a country with as rich a literature as the English there will be no more great writers. I describe here, in this (to me) frightening sentence, the world we live in, adding now this: unless – almost incredibly in the conditions which produced the Arts Council – we succeed in rallying the remnants of an educated public, and give them a strong sense of how a new one might be created.

The thought that threw off the phrase, the 'third realm', with the meaning focused in it, entails inevitably such continuing thought – thought which is prompting. The spirit is practical and desperate: while one is alive one fights for intelligence, and the possibility of a fully vital humanitas. I speak for myself in the first place: my preoccupation, issuing out of my thought about meaning and the 'third realm', commits me to thinking (inseparable here from practical effort) about the 'difficult and problematic' business of creating a new educated public. That, I am moved to insist, is the distinctive university-function; an insistence that involves the conception of the English School as a liaison-centre.

The criteria that govern my thinking are not a philosopher's. Because of his insufficient grasp of this truth, major criticisms that Tanner brings against me are invalid because misconceived. I know that my book must be 'disfigured' by ignorance and limited capacity, but he himself in his commentary supplies a reason for any hesitating on my part to 'ask the advice of professionals'. He virtually assumes that literary students, if guided by the right philosophers, might become (in specific 'areas', and guided, at any rate) philosophers themselves. That is, philosophical issues being in question, he can't imagine, in giving advice, any justification for not adhering strictly to professional criteria. The problem is a difficult one, scarcely soluble as things are – as I implicitly admit when I say that in a university all the essential major disciplines should be co-present and the philosophical is one of them.

I imply, indeed say, in postulating co-presence between two of what should be major humane disciplines, that both would profit by it. I should like to think that in my work's becoming the subject of discussion by philosophers (for Tanner's lively critical commentary on *The Living Principle* isn't the only intellectual contact I have had with representatives of philosophy) I might in a modest way have promoted the development in a few universities of relations between the two disciplines – for informal relations at senior-level in the university personnel are the important ones.

This isn't mere public politeness, for my 'suspicion' isn't of the kind Tanner imputes. He generalizes the imputation when, speaking as a philosopher, he misinterprets my attitude towards psychologists and the various kinds of specialist thought coming under the head of Social Science. His defence of Lord Robbins seems to me misleading in its gratuitousness. I remember Robbins as an economist, but he will go down in history as the Robbins of the Report that was so decisive in regard to the essential changes that accompanied the vast extension of 'Higher Education'. I have actually referred in print to an avowedly personal presentment of his views. They don't occupy themselves at all with discussing the problems that form my great concern. One deduces that the main academic business of the university is to promote scientific education, advance natural science, and serve industry. Robbins does, of course, recognize that some other kind of provision should be made, such as might be thought of as doing something to balance the emphasis on natural science: humanity itself should get some attention. He makes it plain that he relies for this complementary function on the social sciences and psychology. The recognition given to the Arts is without disguise perfunctory: they represent amenity, and belong essentially to the margin. Tanner does me an injustice when he says: 'it's clear that Leavis is referring not to Lord Robbins' faith in those subjects as currently practised, but to the very idea that they could ever provide us with helpful information about ourselves.' This is not a necessary conclusion, and I am sorry that Tanner has formed the impression of me that enables him to pronounce so unjustly with such confidence.

I am aware that 'the social sciences' covers a diversity of specialist departments of thought; but psychology is named and specified. It is in relation to a sustained essay, centrally Laurentian, which starts from a disagreement with Freud, that I remark on Lawrence's indebtedness to the specialist books he had read, and read critically, and make the obvious enough point that the extraordinary power Lawrence had of assimilating the abstruse books of distinguished professionals in various specialist fields was an essential aspect of his genius. I say this in a book the sub-title of which is 'Art and Thought in Lawrence', and the typescript of which has been with my publishers since October.* I was at pains to have it brought out on the heels of *The Living Principle* (it is announced for next July) because I hoped that it would make clearer the thought to which that last book is devoted – for I found the misconception-proof conveying of it extremely difficult. It is apparent to me now that I have not achieved complete success.

In expounding Lawrence I express my own thoughts, for I judge him, who was so original, to have been humanly central, and, in his perceptions and main conclusions, ungainsayable. Not that there is complete coincidence: after all, he died in 1930, and though the developments since have borne him out, not even Lawrence could foresee what reactions would be compelled by new concrete situations. I have discussed in the forthcoming book the sense of paradox – the sense of frightening complexities (so different from the Eliotic paradox) – that even before the Armistice of 1918 he conveyed in his use of the rainbow-symbol. But Tanner is wildly out in imputing to me an obstinate reluctance to admit that valuable results are to be expected from specialist labour in specialist fields. Such reluctance would be peculiarly (and stupidly) ungenerous in me; for, though I am very far from having the genius that made Lawrence so unlimited in his range, I owe immeasurably to such reading as I have been able to do of the products of specialist knowledge and thought.

Tanner's mis-divination is to be explained by my failure to make clear what I was attempting in that first part of my book. I found the problem very difficult, and I realized that the difficulties were of a kind that made a faultless performance impossible. I knew that it was incumbent on me to take risks and incur certain adverse criticism. I knew, for instance, that I should expose myself to the charge of ignorance (I *am* ignorant) and be accused of *outrecuidance*. I don't, however, feel that I owe Lord Robbins any apology. His philistinism provided a sanction for one of the worst abuses that flourish in the new universities. It's not merely that 'English' is regarded as a soft option; if you ask who those 'students' are who appear to be playing croquet most of the day, you get the answer: 'Oh, they're social scientists – they're doing social science.' Perhaps this discrimination is unfair. But the social science so immensely 'taken' and 'done' in the democratic mass-university Tanner himself would dismiss as uneducational –

* *Thought, Words and Creativity*, 1976.

and it's largely worse than that.

The signs are that he finds it hard to be just to Andreski, and I'm afraid that I must bear a good deal of the blame! As I have intimated, he has a strong tendency to assume – slips again and again into overtly assuming – that an argument of the kind I offer is inevitably philosophical and challenges the criteria natural to a reader of philosophical training and habit. But what I offer Tanner is not consistently even an equivalent in my 'anti-philosophical' mode of thought. My distinctive preoccupation with the nature of thought and language isn't separable from my preoccupation with the problem of creating a new educated public; hence the part played in my argument by the university and the English School. I say early on in *The Living Principle* that it is not in the spirit of my plan and purpose to draw up anything in the nature of the syllabus. I found it, however, impossible to make plain and convincing the notion of 'English' as a liaison-centre without the illustrative reference to actual specified texts. I kept the number of these to the barest minimum, thinking that this was the way to bring home to the reader the plurality and the complexity of my purpose in the argument of the first part of the book.

The only one of the illustrative texts that represents what Tanner so generously estimates as philosophically important in my work is Conrad's tale, *The Secret Sharer*. Anchored in the argument of the part – that was my intention – it was to point unmistakably on to 'Judgement and Analysis', and prompt the reader to take in full consciousness the vital relation between the two parts.

I've registered my insistence that 'serendipity' or 'fantastic' *outrecuidance* in me is *not* the explanation of my attitude in the matter of the book by Marjorie Grene. Tanner's observation that I don't, when facing the problem of saving non-philosophy students from wasting their time on Russell's *History of Western Philosophy* or the *Fontana* brochure on Wittgenstein, trust professional advice, clearly carries the implication that I ought. But how should I when, in what he relevantly says, he shows that professional advice is likely to be professional and, so, blind to the problem – and to the truth behind it that I, in the desperate conviction that it matters, am trying to get taken seriously? (I wage the canniest battle I know how to fight.)

I don't mean that that truth involves a mere opposition between philosophical thought, or thought that philosophers can treat as rationally discussable, and thought for the clear recognition of which *as* thought I contend – thought that we have at its most potent in the works of the great creative writers. I meant it when I said that I hoped that discussions such as those certainly (I should like to believe) occasioned by the notes on *The Living Principle* in *The New Universities Quarterly* might advance the development of fruitful relations between philosophy and 'English'. Fruitful relations would be informal and at senior-level (I don't believe in 'mixed courses'); but the climate they would generate would have educational consequences at student-level.

I don't imagine that there is a much larger proportion of lively and disinterested minds in the teaching personnel of most philosophy departments than in most English. Tanner is clearly of the élite by the criteria that I have inevitably to see as mine, and I can think at once of collaborative help that, consulted, he is qualified to have given and of an authoritative sally he might have directed at a betraying silliness in a notice of my book by a reviewer qualified by intelligence to have done much better. But what I must do is to formulate some general considerations that justify my belief that there is point in favouring closer relations at the university between philosophy and 'English' – my belief that the logical thinking trained in philosophy is far from irrelevant to the thought of creative writers, or to the profiting by the study of such thought.

I have commented on the implications of Tanner's 'probative' – of his desire that I should add to the account of critical judgement which forms my reply to Wellek an account of how I should proceed to *prove* the rightness of valuations. I point out that the word 'value' changes its value as we move along the spectrum from the coercively verifiable to the 'values' I deal in when I discuss, say, Hardy's 'After a Journey'. I won't go into the justifiableness of my use of the word 'spectrum'. The analogy is convenient; it has some felicities, and I think that everyone will see to it that they aren't bought at too great a price. Most, if not all, philosophers seem, having started from the mathematico-logical end of the spectrum, to be powerless to escape from the limitations implicit in such a start. The discipline itself entails the limitations. They can't get beyond the shift in the force of 'value' that leaves behind the ideas both of the quantitative and of the provable. Tanner, when he asks me to indicate how I should extend the 'verification-principle' – or (what bears a close relation to this) the logical requirement implicit in his 'probative' – to critical valuations, shows that he hasn't escaped.

Nevertheless the limitations of philosophic thought needn't mean that it can never, of its nature, engage helpfully on the products of the creative writer's use of language. I might have hoped, for instance, that Tanner would correct the conventionally slack way in which Ian Robinson, reviewing *The Living Principle* in *The Spectator*, just ignores my analytic refutation of Harding's radically falsifying account of the stretch of unrimed *terza rima* in 'Little Gidding'. Harding (*Experience into Words*, p. 120ff.) turns what the passage conveys into a simple confrontation between the good Christian T. S. Eliot and a reprehensible 'humanist' (in the modern sense of that word). Actually, this account involves a not unwilled (I think) blindness to the astonishing (and characteristic) genius with language that enables Eliot to evoke the logic-baffling *alter-ego* relation that is suggested in this brief extract:

> I was still the same,
> Knowing myself yet being someone other...

I say 'I might have hoped'; but I didn't – there was no reason for it: I don't think Tanner had read Robinson's review. But he does in fact, giving more reasons – bad ones – for his judgement than Robinson gives, take up much the same slackly dismissing attitude to my commentary on *Four Quartets* that Robinson, in his brief review, conveys as his own. What I meant was that there was no disability deriving from a philosopher's habit of thought in the way of Tanner's coming to my defence with a corrective rebuke to Robinson, who in a crucial matter had shown an inert willingness to endorse Harding's falsifying paraphrase.

It is a general truth that I have in mind: the creative writer in his creativity isn't confined to one part of the spectrum; he has the freedom of his native language, freedom along the whole range of the spectrum to use the resources of English, and you can't tell beforehand what liberties will justify themselves. For it is in the common and varied use that creates a language that the resources, the possibilities, have been generated. Those functional qualities which get their strictest development in disciplined special uses to which the philosophical is central bulk, inevitably, large in the unspecialized language of daily use. Action and the practical counting so much, common-sense logic must be a main nerve in any language.

The *terza rima* passage, occupying two and a third pages, is very exceptional in *Four Quartets*, dealing continuously as it does with one imagined situation, which is based on an 'All Clear' recalled from Eliot's experience as an air-raid warden. For the most part it is in a continuous narrative mode, and, in spite of the uncommon-sensical elusiveness of the *alter-ego* relation, the duality that isn't unambiguously double, one should be able to expect a mind trained in the logical discipline of philosophy to see at a reading the gratuitousness of Harding's falsification.

I say this because I take the 'liaison-centre' theme very seriously, and see point in underlining the contention that in the ideal university (which I shall never see) the philosophy department and 'English' would have mutually profitable informal relations. As things are, Tanner's ignorance of the way in which intelligence deals with poetry shocks *me* as much as my brashness in relation to philosophy shocks *him*. I am not thinking of the contradiction exhibited by the reports of our respective sensibilities, about 'St Mawr'. I will leave that aside with (taking the tip from him) the remark that I should like to see how he sets about being probative in relation to his adverse judgement. What I have in mind is all that he says in discussing *Four Quartets*.

I am puzzled by his statement that my elucidation of *Four Quartets* is 'the most sustained piece of criticism that [I have] ever produced of a simple work of poetry or prose'. It is what that pronouncement implies that puzzles me. Surely I have written quite a number of essays on major works of prose fiction that deserve not less to count as sustained pieces of criticism? I suppose that none of these is as long as the study of *Four Quartets* that forms the third part of *The Living Principle*. But isn't my critique of *Little Dorrit* (say) that forms a chapter in the book on Dickens in which my wife and I collaborated as sustained as need be? The greater length of my discussion of *Four Quartets* is due to what made the length necessary: the difficulties with which it confronts the reader – any reader.

It is not only philosophically habituated readers of *Four Quartets* who find themselves at a loss to give a convincing answer when asked what kind of a thing they have in front of them? What order of meaning or interest have they been assuming that they have to make out? Tanner, complaining of a lack of explicitness in me, says: 'he gives no further consideration to the matter of the relationship between poetry and what it is concerned to state, when that is something that can reasonably be called a philosophy.' I note two portents here: Tanner assumes that poetry is concerned to state something, and, further, he assumes that *Four Quartets,* in its bizarre way, is concerned with stating a philosophy. Lest I be charged with being pedantically over-exacting about precision in the use of 'state', I must call attention to the at least (I think) sub-ironic 'gratefully' in the following: 'indeed, in "Burnt Norton" he is using language to "create concepts" – a phrase of D. W. Harding's which Leavis gratefully takes over.' When Harding reviewed 'Burnt Norton' in *Scrutiny* it stood alone, having been published by itself in a fascicule under that bare title. There was no intimation or hint that, out of Eliot's life-experience, the exploratory and constructive 'musical' *procédé* (one made no reference to 'music' then) was to continue, was to be developed towards a goal, in subsequent 'quartets'. It's a shrewd guess that Eliot himself didn't know.

The phrase in Harding's review I was really grateful for was one that preceded 'the creation of concepts'. It was that 'Burnt Norton' 'isn't about anything'. That itself is a statement, but it means that the poem doesn't, in the sense of the verb in which Tanner implicitly demands that it should, state at all. Harding follows up the negative phrase I have just quoted by saying that the poem stands instead of the words 'eternity' and 'regret'. As I point out, discussing in my book the first paragraph of 'Burnt Norton', the poem opens with a succession of what appear at first to be statements; but we soon discover that, in subtly diverse ways, they differ in function from that which the word 'statement' implies. Tanner's excuse for his patent desire to say that *Four Quartets* is the poetic statement of a philosophy that defines what the essence of Pauline Christianity is – 'the relationship between poetry and what it is concerned to state, when that is something that can reasonably be called a philosophy' – Tanner's excuse for this comes near the end of the third 'Quartet', 'The Dry Salvages', where Eliot, as admitting his full personal engagement, at last makes a crucial statement:

The hint half guessed, the gift half understood, is Incarnation.

The notion of literary criticism exemplified in his dismissal of my placing valuation of *Four Quartets* is a philosopher's. His application to me of the Liar Paradox is decidedly – and with peculiar oddity – the philosopher entering the literary field, with his inappropriate dialectical habits, from outside. The critical argument with which, in intention, he lassos me uses 'great' as if it always had the same value. As a matter of fact, though I think that *Four Quartets* is important and repays close study, I'm not in the habit of calling it a 'great poem'. I tell students that we're without hesitation agreed to call Eliot a major poet because he can't be called minor. I save 'great' for more satisfying works and for completer successes. If it doesn't 'state' a philosophy, neither is it the creatively poetic equivalent of a philosophy. It's impossible to say with complete convincingness and due accuracy what it *is* without some account of its relation to Eliot's earlier poetry and to his curiously (and significantly) contradictory record as a literary critic – all of which involves some observations about the kind of man Eliot was.

I will only say at the moment that all the evidence shows him to have suffered from an inner insecurity, and that the poems in the collected volume that we had in the 1920s are by a poet whom we can't call positively religions. The change to the religious phase (which lasted to the end of his creative life, and contains the poetry that interests me most) is preluded by the poem, 'The Hollow Men', that was (and still is) printed immediately after *The Waste Land*. The poem is an expression of utter spiritual bankruptcy, of unbearably conscious emptiness. In its unlikeness to what had gone before, it is unique in Eliot's *oeuvre*. There is no exhibitionism in it, no irony, none of the sense of superiority (related to snobbery) that Eliotic irony conveys (it's directed at other people); nothing but the intense conviction that it's impossible to remain *here* and live.

Of course, there is implicit recognition of the need for what only religious conviction can give in the earlier poems, especially in *The Waste Land*. The need is felt with desperate intensity now, and *Ash-Wednesday* follows! That a traditional impulse lives in his bones (as we say) or (an alternative formulation) that a Christian response to the intensely felt need is active in deep-lying strata of his psyche, that work testifies. But such an intensity of felt privation in such a man after such a history – in a poet whose gift of subtle expression was so clearly served by strongly conflicting impulses (for Eliot was, and remained, a deeply divided man) – produces an anxious, hardly appeasable fear of self-deception. He is suspicious of himself, and suspicious of the medicine contemplated as a cure for the disease. The religious need dominates in the creativity that produced *Ash-Wednesday*, but that work isn't religious in the way assumed by

Anglo-Catholic claimants to the prestige of being able to boast an Anglo-Catholic great poet. Eliot uses his astonishing power of doing 'impossible' things with the English language in order to create a poetry that, while being undeniably Christian in preoccupation, nowhere even implicitly *affirms*. In each of the six poems of which the work is composed there is a contradictory or resistant something to Christian affirmation; none of them affirms, and in the sequence there is no progression. The type-effect is given clearly and simply in the second poem, where the diction is strongly liturgical and biblical and what is most potently evoked in it – the acceptance of death and extinction as final – annuls the Christian belief that the diction implies.

The felt basic difficulty of approach to the possibility of full Christian affirmation is what explains the nature of the first three 'Quartets' – explains what they are, their originality and their strength. The creative drive behind them is intensely and poignantly personal – poignantly in a way implicit in the fatuity of that early doctrine of 'impersonality': 'We are prepared for art when we have ceased to be interested in our personal emotions except as material.'

The poignancy is a matter of the dividedness that entailed in Eliot the refusal to know what he really knew about himself – that self-defensive inability to face the knowledge of what he was which didn't save him from self-contempt.

Tanner's criticism of my dealings with *Four Quartets* is based on a philosopher's assumptions. It is given in brief in these two sentences, which follow directly on from the sentence that refers to the Liar Paradox:

> Eliot tells us in a great poem that the conditions required for the writing of great poetry don't obtain. He, therefore, instead of being a great poet *tout court*, is a great poetic 'case', a subject for diagnosis as well as analysis.

Well, I shouldn't deny that in some contexts it's appropriate to call Eliot a great poet. I do it sometimes myself, but not habitually; my critical bent leads me to refer to him as, in spite of his limitations, a poet of major gifts. I am sparing of the 'great' because, for one thing, greatness seems to me very important, and the word and the idea carry an implication and a valuation that were decidedly incongruous with one's impressions of Eliot.

In another critique of my book (also in sum very flattering) that Tanner wrote for *Books and Bookmen* (December 1975), he says:

It seems to me that Eliot is not strikingly more involved in paradox than any anti-Pelagian Christian artist, though I agree that in him there is a peculiar intensity of revulsion against everything that is 'only living'.

It is desirable first of all for me to say that I recognize Eliot, with the phrase, 'that which is only living can only die,' to be invoking the eternal, and that I too, though I disagree with Eliot so profoundly, think that word indispensable. 'The eternal' and 'eternity' figure in Lawrence's writings, and I can see that they have a necessary function in *his* thought. To me they seem not to conflict in any way with the stress Lawrence lays on human creativity. And if it is the anti-Pelagianism, or the Pauline Christianity, that Tanner assumes to be 'the something that can reasonably be called a philosophy' presented in *Four Quartets,* it wouldn't be a literary-critical or rational defence of the poem or Eliot to say that that 'philosophy' entailed Eliot's doing the best he could (in a creative work) to deny or discredit the creative in man.

Actually it's much more to the point to explain the kind of Christian Eliot became by the kind of man he was and the company he kept – by the incurable inner dividedness that led him to keep such company. He is the critic who, having the acutely personal pressures inside him of impulsion and recoil that from the beginning are manifested in his poetry, laid down in his most exhibitionistic literary style his significantly non-sensical doctrine of impersonality, and who, in one of his critiques of Baudelaire (whom he affected), observed approvingly of that poet that, though he could hardly be called a Christian, he at least believed in damnation. In the same introduction it is (I think) that he quotes, in order to make an unconsciously self-revealing comment on it, this aphorism: *la volupté suprême de l'amour gît dans la certitude de faire le mal.* He valued the distinction of being known as the editor of *The Criterion,* and ran it as he did, letting the Auden-Spender lot of public school fellow-travellers use its review-pages for the purposes they cultivated in *The New Statesman.* A loyal member of the Bloomsbury coterie, he took over the Bloomsbury contempt for Lawrence, adding moral and religious unction of his own in his expression of it ('rotten and rotting others', 'his hymn-singing mother' – for inner insecurity made Eliot a pitiful snob). Pity? – The pity of it is that the distinction, the poetic creativity in him, was real, but was qualified, was limited by his inner dividedness – was conditioned by the paradox. There's no need to see the paradox as being primarily of the kind that Tanner, in his philosophical way, makes it. Of course, in the 'musical' build-up that has in view the theological statement which finally comes just before 'Little Gidding' begins, the phrase, 'that which is only living can only die', evokes the eternal – the timeless, the out-of-time. But Eliot very much wanted to *live* in the ordinary sense of the word, had a profound attachment to being 'eminent' (in spite of line 3 of 'East Coker'), set a high value on the reassuring formalities of 'recognition', and treasured his O.M. In 'Marina' he evokes death as something to be shrunk from in the normal human way as decidedly as he shrinks from the thought of it in 'Gerontion'; and 'Marina' is unique in Eliot's *oeuvre* in that it imagines an escape from the obsession with death and decay that isn't a renunciation of the life that 'only lives'.

But in fact the 'only lives' should, I think, strike the reader of *Four Quartets* as an evasive ambiguity – an evasion on Eliot's part of having to recognize in full consciousness that the supremely, the superhumanly real can't be the completely other-than-life. As Lawrence says, 'we didn't create ourselves', and creativity isn't something that we could *possess*. The creativity apparent on every page of Eliot's strange poem should bring home to every reader capable of seeing what the poem is that the view of humanity as utterly and contemptibly abject is frustratingly fallacious, and derives from some essential lack, some deep-seated wrongness, in the poet himself.

Tanner's way, though his fondness for Eliot's poetry is obviously genuine, of calling *Four Quartets* a 'great poem' and defending its 'paradoxical' qualities, by saying that it expresses an anti-Pelagian attitude, is a philosopher's. The thought I contend for, the thought that develops out of literary criticism, would have summed up its concern with values and significances in the decision to regard the view of life communicated by Eliot's creative work as largely unsound, being incomplete and unbalanced, based on a starved human experience, and off the human centre. Of course, one can't prove the rightness of such judgements; the mode of verification that goes with this order of thought isn't proof, and certainly yields no finality. But it is characteristic of the most important convictions one forms to admit of nothing like proof.

One's 'no' response to a respectable conviction advanced by someone else may have a positive value in one's own economy; it may strengthen one's hold on a 'yes' – on, that is, a relevant positive conviction at which one has arrived. So my 'no' to Tanner's defence of *Four Quartets* in terms of 'anti-Pelagianism', or 'Pauline Christianity', is accompanied by the suggestion that, if he hadn't had a philosopher's habit of thought, he would have abated his claims (implicit in the absolute 'great' of his critical argument) for the damagingly 'paradoxical' T. S. Eliot, and seen that there was an incomparably more satisfying presentment in 'art-speech' of the significance of human experience and human potentiality – found, too, in Eliot's avowed *volte-face* about Lawrence some confirmation of my reading of the lamentable 'paradox'. I refer in 'avowed *volte-face*' to an utterance that, late in Eliot's life, appeared in print. 'Of course I have changed my mind about Lawrence, and what I said forty years ago would have been forgotten but for Dr Leavis's industry.'

Lawrence, Eliot had discovered, was decidedly not a 'humanist' in the modern sense – that is, of the Snow kind; and his 'art-speech' gives no encouragement to spiritual philistinism or human hubris. I enlarge on these statements, which it would be right to think of as speaking for me too, in my next book.

Tanner doesn't endorse Robinson's judgement that my commentary on 'Little Gidding' shows that I paid little attention to that Quartet, but he doesn't – as I hoped that a poetry-reading philosopher would – point out that at least my correction of Harding's fasifying account of the *terza rima* passage is sound. But that would have been a strong reason for reconsidering my rejected, or disparaged, adverse criticism of *Four Quartets*. There are several reasons for the impression I give of having relaxed the intensity of my attention when I come to the uncongenial last of them, which not only concludes the poem, but presents the conclusion to which the sustained 'musical logic' leads up. I don't, in fact, find that there *is* the kind of continuity that the verb 'leads up' implies. The goal of the creative argument, the 'music', is the theological statement. What follows the assured statement, the unambiguous affirmation, is 'Little Gidding', which is of a different order from the preceding three Quartets. There is no longer a need for a phrase-by-phrase elucidation. Helped by Harding, I perceived that the reference to Incarnation was followed up in 'Little Gidding' with more of the theological, but I saw no need to overcome my shyness of bringing theology into my critical argument. The critical point that must, it seemed to me, be made was that in 'Little Gidding' Eliot relaxes; he is in haven at last. The strongest part of the Quartet – in it he is as unmistakably a major poet as in anything his *oeuvre* contains – is significantly that in which he draws on his experience as an air-raid warden. Significantly, because the peculiarities that made him a 'case' limited and starved him in his firsthand living – precluded his having access to that comprehensive human experience without which he was incapacitated for the imagining and producing of a great creative work. Tanner, then, ignores what I point to in my book – the way in which Eliot, towards the end of the passage, comes to the verge of telling himself the nature of his guilt ('the shame of motives late revealed'); and then draws back, the rare moment's courage neatly disposed of in a demonstration of stern and comfortable Christian virtue.

Perhaps both Tanner's and Robinson's conventional impercipience (blindness of the inert *parti pris*) prevailed because, in my embarrassment, I was too unemphatic in making my point. My embarrassed modesty was complex, and there was another factor in it. Although we rarely met and rarely corresponded, Eliot and I knew each other well. The knowledge was a matter of our finding each other so very uncongenial as to generate a great deal of awareness – on my side, certainly diagnostic. I was very surprised to receive a letter from Eliot intimating that he was coming to Cambridge and would like to call on me. The actual call must have taken place either late in 1940 or early in 1941 (it was unique). He stayed a very long while and, when he finally went, left behind a small mound of cigarette-ash on the flat brick hearth in the room where we'd had tea. The pertinacious length of his stay was unmistakably explained by his wanting to feel sure that he had extracted something out of me that, actually, he couldn't get – signs interpretable as an assurance that I shouldn't in future take ill – from *him*, who would continue to think highly of me – his continuing to support the Desmond MacCarthys against me. I deduced later, when 'Little Gidding' was made accessible by being published, that he had been composing that Quartet at the time of his visit to my house. A number of things he said to me appear in that 'All Clear!' passage, and I was (with good reason) a major focus of the guilt-feelings expressed in *The Family Reunion*, the most revealingly personal of his works.

I will add here that I know of several reasons, all different, given by Eliot for his not being among my friends. The first, a quarter of a century ago, was given to a Wykehamist of my acquaintance, who reported it to me. 'I went out of my way to call on him. No good! It must be that I didn't support him enough in the 1930s.' The last was passed on to me by a very intelligent friend of mine who cultivated Eliot, and put the question to him. Eliot answered (it was towards the end of his life): 'I think he hasn't forgiven me about Milton.'

I stand, then, by my account of *Four Quartets*. I stand also by my contention that 'English' should be a liaison-centre, and that, in the 'co-presence' needed to make it that, no discipline of thought is more important than the philosophical to that quite different one, the essence of which I have tried in my book, with inevitable clumsiness, to 'define'. I hoped to get accepted among members of a small philosophical élite that the 'defining' can't be done with philosophical cogency. That, of course, involves some such avowal as the following. I should have been encouraged if Tanner could have been brought to see that it is not mere 'serendipity' in me to insist on recommending 'English' students to read Polanyi's essay, 'The Logic of Tacit Inference'. The essay is short, and that – since it makes so much difference (and for the good) – is a strong recommendation. I confess that I was being consciously provocative in my reference to the epistemological problem. I was imagining the desirable kind of co-presence, and thinking of ways in which both the difference beteen the two disciplines and the profit that might lie in co-presence could be demonstrated.

The ideal co-presence would be informal, but effective informality depends upon a small minority of exceptional individuals. I was imagining, then, one of my most intelligent and experienced seminars having it explained by (say) Tanner in what ways my association of epistemological efficacy with Polanyi must strike a professional as betrayingly ignorant and brash. The students would certainly learn something, but, from my point of view, the most important thing they would learn would be that the absolutely necessary thing they had carried away from Polanyi was not, though Polanyi was a philosopher (a bad one, both Tanner and Robinson think), in any strict sense, philosophical, or to be regarded as a philosophical truth. Nor did it need, in order to be accepted as fundamentally important, to be thought of as a philosophy-accredited truth.

The philosopher's use of language is highly specialized, and it is impossible to turn intelligent literary students into temporary philosophers, and worse than vain to try. But...

Note: I have just, belatedly, read Malcolm's *Memoir* of Wittgenstein, and on p. 39 I find this, quoted from one of the great philosopher's letters:

I then thought: what is the use of studying philosophy if all that it does for you is to enable you to talk with some plausibility about some abstruse questions of logic, etc., and if it does not improve your thinking about the important questions of everyday life, if it does not make you more conscientious than any journalist in the use of the *dangerous* phrases such people use for their own ends? You see, I know that it's difficult to think *well* about 'certainty', 'probability', 'perception', etc. But it is, if possible, still more difficult to think, or *try* to think, really honestly about your life and other people's lives. And the trouble is that thinking about these things is *not thrilling*, but often downright nasty. And when it's nasty then it's *most* important.